The Interpretation Game

The Interpretation Game

How Judges and Lawyers Make the Law

Robert Benson

With a foreword by Ronald K. L. Collins

Carolina Academic Press
Durham, North Carolina

Library of Congress Cataloging-in-Publication Data

Benson, Robert W., 1942-
The interpretation game : how judges and lawyers make the law / by Robert Benson.
p. cm.
Includes bibliographical references and index.
ISBN-13: 978-1-59460-501-7 (alk. paper)
ISBN-10: 1-59460-501-7 (alk. paper)
1. Law--United States--Interpretation and construction. I. Title.

KF425.B46 2008
349.73--dc22

2007045338

Carolina Academic Press
700 Kent Street
Durham, NC 27701
Telephone (919) 489-7486
Fax (919) 493-5668
www.cap-press.com

Printed in the United States of America

For Lesley Ann

And dedicated to the memory of Jorge Luis Borges,
whose crazy stories provided a sane refuge
when I was a law student

Contents

Foreword

Law, like life, is what we make of it.

That maxim is hardly controversial. But it becomes so when that "we" includes judges. The maxim obviously applies to the legislative branches. Moreover, when duly authorized, the executive branches of our federal and state governments also make law. What, then, of the judiciary? Do judges *make* law? Well, yes. Just consider our centuries of common law. Beyond that, however, judges ought not—nay, must not!—make law. Or so the old law story goes.

Contrary to the old story, there is also an old truth crafted in stone. Though few see it, you'll find it on the friezes in the solemn chamber of the United States Supreme Court. As the nine Justices, suited in their symbolic robes, glance up to their left and right, they bear witness to images of the great lawgivers of mankind—from Menes and Hammurabi to Moses and Confucius to Justinian and Charlemagne to King John and Blackstone, among others. The last person in this lineup of great lawgivers is neither a prophet nor a king but a judge—Chief Justice John Marshall.

Make of it what you will, but in 1803 John Marshall *made* law in *Marbury v. Madison*. And for all the trees leveled in the mind-numbing duels over judicial review, the law Marshall made centuries ago remains the supreme law of our land, just as if he had "quilled" it on the parchment of the Constitution of 1787. Could he have ruled otherwise? Yes, of course. But the America we know today—the America of constitutional checks and fundamental freedoms—could not exist without John Marshall's jurisprudential handiwork.

Let me be forthright: Judges do make law. Liberal judges of old like Oliver Wendell Holmes made law. Conservative judges of old like Rufus Peckham did likewise. So, too, with their modern counterparts—liberal textualists like Hugo Black and their conservative counterparts like Clarence Thomas. And the same holds true for the dizzying "jurisprudence" of "balancers" like the circuitous Felix Frankfurter and the confusing Stephen Breyer. For better or worse, much of our law is what they and other judges have made it. Mind you: God did not command them, the Founders did not constrain them, the Constitution's text and history did not confine them, and no judicial oath or code controlled them. Not really. The basic restraint on their power was their conscience, or if you prefer, their will, *and* what the public would tolerate.

At its core, that is the lesson of *The Interpretation Game*. And that lesson goes beyond judges. According to Professor Benson, every bureaucrat, every teacher, every citizen, and every interpreter at some point makes rather than finds law when interpreting legal texts. In the interpretive process, one inevitably breathes his or her life into a text in order to give it this or that "meaning." That's just the way words work. Or more accurately, that is how we make them work.

The Interpretation Game is a sobering lesson grounded in the soil of realism. In that regard, Robert Benson is a sort of modern-day Niccolo Machiavelli, though not in any pejorative sense. To reweave a thread of thought borrowed from the father of modern political science: Others will tell you what the law should be, but I will tell you what it is. Heed those words as you read this slender volume of clear-headed, say-it-as-it-is talk about American statutory law, common law, and constitutional law. (In the Web supplement to his work, Professor Benson applies his straight talk to international law too.)

Beware: What you are about to read flies in the face of what every law student is taught, namely, that *the law* is what some dead souls proclaim/or that *the law* is what a dead-letter text announces/or that *the law* is structure/or that *the law* is neutral/or that *the law* is bound by precedent. If you believe that, believe it like you would a novel by Dickens, Melville, Twain, Stevenson, Lawrence, Cather, or even John Grisham. It all makes for fine fiction.

This debate lingers mainly because law is typically taught from an *appellate judge's perspective*. This judge-centric perspective, of course, deprives students of a variety of other important perspectives. But that is a gripe for another day. For now, it is enough to say that if law schools insist on perpetuating such myopia, they should at least recognize the role of realism in the process. A contemporary example may help to illustrate my point, and one of the key points of *The Interpretation Game* as well.

Two friends of mine—one a respected constitutional law scholar, the other a noted First Amendment lawyer—recently told me how they litigate certain cases before the Roberts Court. There is a class of cases, they observed, in which the only vote that really counts is that of Justice Anthony Kennedy. That is, since four justices almost always line up one way, and four others the opposite way, the key vote is left in the lap of Justice Kennedy. "So I brief my case," one of them said, "in a way that is pitched almost entirely to what I think will win Kennedy's vote." If that takes an originalist or structuralist or minimalist or any other kind of *ist* argument, then that is what will be offered up. That is, he will offer *his* views through *those* lenses. No sensible lawyer, be he in a private firm or she representing the government, would do otherwise. Hence, for the practicing lawyer—the seasoned realist—the quarrel that rages on in the legal academy is of no moment beyond his or her ability to master the various legal arguments and rally them to his or her cause when the case demands. (On that score, may I recommend another book, *Tactics of Legal Reasoning*, by Pierre Schlag and David Skover.)

Now, some would argue that such realism is nihilism, simply. That's bunk! For consider: What great principle is vouchsafed when a texualist judge applies the law blindly to produce a ruinous or ridiculous result? What high value is preserved when an originalist jurist, time and again, selects strands of history to justify a rule so inhumane that even his fellow originalists keep their horrified distance? And how many defenders of "judicial restraint" would honor precedent if it meant saving segregation? If it meant denying the human-rights claims recognized in *Brown v. Board of Education*? No, the nihilist argument cuts the other way—against those who would turn the law into a lifeless abstraction.

Still, as Professor Benson quite aptly points out, the sham of "judicial neutrality" continues during every federal judicial confirmation hearing. As the cinematic C-SPAN lens zooms in on each disingenuous moment, nominee after nominee swears under oath that he or she would never make law but would only "follow" the law in a neutral way. Everyone knows it's a game; all know that the nominees will veer from their representations; and yet, the "neutrality" farce continues. It's rather like the "no gambling" edict in Captain Renault's Casablanca.

By exposing the real workings of the legal profession's trade, Robert Benson (my own professor three-plus decades ago) has done the legal academy and ordinary citizens alike a great service. Read his book, understand it, develop it, grapple with it, and, yes, challenge it. But above all, know this: There is no lie as great as the one we tell ourselves.

Ronald K.L. Collins
Scholar, The First Amendment Center
Washington, D.C.

Preface: The Book in a Nutshell

This is a book for law students, journalists and ordinary citizens who want to know what's really going on when judges and lawyers interpret the laws. It is even for the judges and lawyers, most of whom tell a story about legal interpretation that is simply a scam. I hope to coax them into candor.

The scam is there every time a President or governor nominates someone to wear the black robe of judge and the nominee sanctimoniously swears "to set aside my personal views," or, "not to make law, but to find it." The scam is there whenever courts veil controversial rulings behind incantations of "strict construction," "original intent," "plain meaning," "legislative purpose," and other legal mysticisms. The scam is there whenever a lawyer, bureaucrat or a corporate paper-shuffler tells you, "well, I'm just following the law."

The truth is, there is no such thing as "just following the law." Every judge, every lawyer, every interpreter always makes the law, never finds it, when reading a legal text. And their personal views inescapably play a central role in the making. These facts are of profound importance in a democracy said to be based upon "the rule of law" where lawyers and judges exercise enormous power. Yet public discourse on the topic consists of little more than shallow shibboleths. Most people will grant that it makes a difference whether a liberal or a conservative is appointed to the Supreme Court, but they naively assume that so long as the nominee is deemed "well qualified" by professional peers, and so long as ideological extremists are excluded, we can rest in the assurance that, as John Roberts declared when he was nominated to be Chief Justice of the United States, "judges are like umpires. Judges don't make the rules. They apply them." Pure flapdoodle, but the public, press and politicians fall for it.

This is not a book about who gets appointed to the bench, or whether there are too many liberals, too many conservatives, who is a "strict constructionist," or who is an "activist judge." It is, rather, about the interpretation game that all of these, and all lawyers, play in order to shape the law the way they think it ought to be. I intend to show how this game is played by judges and lawyers of all philosophies—right, left and center. If I were a magician revealing how my colleagues do their tricks, I would be rightly drummed out of the magic profession. But the law is not magic, and lawyers are not magicians, or shouldn't be. The legal profession deserves to have its tricks exposed.

I'm far from the first to attempt it. Oliver Wendell Holmes, Jr. and Benjamin Cardozo, judicial giants of the early 20th century, not to mention many later scholars, tried but failed to get the profession to acknowledge that it makes, and does not find, the law. The profession went right ahead pushing the juggernaut of the Old Story over each new generation of law students. What I call the Old Story is a glorious, clever, complex, but patently false tale describing a neutral set of rules and methods which purport to yield more or less objective answers about the meaning of any legal text. In order to expose the judges' and lawyers' tricks, I will have to get into the Old Story in detail, debunk it, and then go on to describe the actual moves that legal interpreters make in their game.

I write for the serious, sophisticated reader, not for the glib. But what John Kenneth Galbraith said of economics can also be said of the law: "[T]here are no important propositions too complicated to be stated in plain language." I've tried to set out this book's ideas clearly and simply in a main text that stands alone, without legalese. When I can't avoid legalese, I explain it. I put scholarly references in the back of the book to keep them out of sight, like the pots and pans in which the dinner was cooked.

Part One presents the Old Story in detail and tells why it is simply nonsense to contemporary thought. The chapters in this part put legal history within the broader context of general cultural and intellectual history to show that the Old Story is an odd fossil of ancient thought that crumbles in the light of the modern and postmodern thinking that is now common to other institutions and intellectual disciplines. This part goes on to give a new, realistic description of what actually goes on in legal interpretation. Part Two gives practical illustrations of the new view as applied to statutes, constitutions, and case precedents. This part uses several widely known legal texts as paradigm examples: the statutes that once set highway speed at 55 miles per hour, the constitutional case *Brown v. Board of Education*, and the famous common law tort case *Palsgraf v. Long Island Railroad*. An extra chapter on international law, using the Bush Administration's torture memos to illustrate, is published at the book's website, www.theinterpretationgame.info, free for the world to download and read.

Here are the key points of the book, straight away:

- Contrary to the Old Story, interpreters never discover the meaning of a law by finding the "holding" of a case, the "literal words" of a document, the "legislative intent" of a statute, or the "original intent," "structure," or "purpose" of a constitution. These simply aren't things that can be discovered like buried treasures. They are cultural fictions, rather like the Santa Claus myth, useful or not depending upon what the reader and society wish to do with them.
- The interpreters of a law likewise are not really constrained by legal language, precedents, rules, doctrines or principles, because these aren't like the reins of a horse that could control the reader's behavior. They are more like artist's materials which the interpreter uses to create meanings.
- The modern understanding of language and culture shows us that meaning is *not* something that texts possess. It's something that interpreters produce. Laws are no exception. The meaning of a law—whether it's a regulation, statute, case precedent, constitution, contract, will or other legal document—doesn't reside in its text, but in the interpreters who give it meaning. When we say, "What does this law mean?," we are actually saying, "What meaning should we give this law?"
- In creating meanings, interpreters—including judges—have extraordinary license, and are inescapably influenced by their own psychological character, values and personal contexts. In this sense, legal interpretation is subjective. It differs widely with individual personalities.
- Individuals are not free, however, to make up legal meanings willy-nilly. We all view the world, and legal texts, from a certain moment in history and from within our own culture, which enables us to think certain things and not others. Moreover, the desire to persuade others in society to accept our meanings limits idiosyncratic interpretations. In these senses, legal interpretation is constrained by things outside the individual.
- Legal interpretation at bottom, then, is a creative act that ends in an effort to persuade others to accept our meanings. The practices of persuasion differ from time to time and culture to culture, but anthropologists visiting Anglo-American legal culture today would see a ritualistic process in which meaning is constructed in the following way: Interpreters, acting with largely undisclosed political, social and moral values, make claims about what the text of the law is, the importance of its source, and how other interpreters view it. If interpreters with sufficient social power accept or acquiesce in these claims, legal meaning is temporarily established. It is a process that highlights the artifices of ritual while hiding the real values and the social power that

actually determine legal interpretation. The consequences of these observations are large.

The notion that we live under "the rule of law" is, unfortunately, mistaken. We live under the rule of people. It makes a crucial difference who those people are and what values they hold. While "the rule of law" is very important as a political ideal that can influence behavior, it is perilous to let a naïve faith in it blind us to this reality, to believe that words on paper alone protect us. Some who have been so blinded have paid the price in exploitation, and even their lives.

Lawyers and judges claim a special right to rule in the name of law, arguing that their training in objective techniques entitles them to a monopoly on the construction of legal meaning. Their training and techniques, however, are based upon the Old Story about legal interpretation, a story that no longer makes sense. It is a story that conceals the rhetorical moves that are actually made. It masks the political, social and moral struggle for persuasion that actually takes place every time a law is interpreted. It is a story that allows the childish myth to be foisted upon the public that judges are merely umpires, determining what is lawful or unlawful as if they were calling balls and strikes in a baseball game.

We live in modern times. The legal profession should take off the old mask. It should tell the real facts about legal interpretation, even if those facts lead to results that some members of the profession won't welcome, such as these:

- Recognition that legal interpretation is mainly a special form of political and social debate.
- Candid accountability of judges, lawyers, and bureaucrats for the political, social and moral choices that are at stake in every "legal" decision they make.
- Public scrutiny of the personal values of individuals nominated to wear the black robe of judge.
- The spread of informal, inexpensive legal procedures.
- Laws and law-talk in clear English.
- And cutting of massive deadwood from the bramble bush of law school education.

There you have it, in the proverbial nutshell.

Robert Benson
Professor of Law, Emeritus
Loyola Law School, Los Angeles

Acknowledgments

Material from Robert Benson, "The Semiotic Web of the Law," in *Law and Semiotics*, Volume 1 (Kevelson, ed., New York and London: Plenum Press, 1987), and Robert Benson, "How Judges Fool Themselves," in *Law and Semiotics*, Volume 2 (Kevelson, ed., New York and London: Plenum Press, 1988) used with kind permission of Springer Science and Business Media.

Material from Robert Benson, "Semiotics, modernism and the law," *Semiotica* 73-1/2 (1989) used with kind permission of Mouton de Gruyter, Berlin.

Material from Robert Benson, "Peirce and Critical Legal Studies," in *Peirce and Law* (Kevelson, ed., New York: Peter Lang Publishing, 1991) used with kind permission of Peter Lang Publishing.

The Interpretation Game

Part One
The Theory of Legal Interpretation

Chapter 1

The Old Story

[The judges are] the living oracles, who must decide in all cases of doubt, and who are bound by an oath to decide according to the law of the land. [T]he judgment, though pronounced or awarded by the judges, is ... the conclusion that naturally and regularly follows from the premises of law fact ... which judgment or conclusion depends not therefore on the arbitrary caprice of the judge, but on the settled and invariable principles of justice.

—Blackstone[1]

The Old Story—the received wisdom from the past still much in vogue—is rarely told in its full version. Bits and pieces of it pop up in lawyers' briefs and judges' opinions, always on the assumption that the pieces are part of a coherent system. The whole system can be gleaned from model codes and the treatises and articles of scholars who write on interpretation of statutes, constitutions, contracts, and case decisions, all of whom tell a rather similar story, whether they wrote in former times[2] or write in our times.[3] It goes more or less as follows:

The meaning of the law is in the text, put there by the text's authors. There are rules for finding the meaning in statutes, constitutions, contracts, and other texts that attempt to guide future conduct. The rules are:

1. Follow the plain meaning of the words.
2. If the words are ambiguous, apply intrinsic canons (rules) of construction that help clarify the internal workings of the language or the law.
3. If ambiguity persists, look for extrinsic evidence of the purpose the authors intended.
4. Always be certain that your interpretation is reasonable.

There are different rules for finding and applying the meaning in the texts of judicial precedents. They are:

1. Separate the precedent case into its basic elements: facts, procedural history, issue, holding, and reasoning.
2. Focus on the holding (the ratio decidendi, deciding reason, or ground of decision) of the case, and exclude the incidental remarks made by the judge (the obiter dicta).
3. Reasoning by analogy, show how the case at hand is either similar to or distinguishable from the precedent case, and therefore is or is not controlled by its holding.

That, distilled to its essence, is the elixir that has long been found in judges' opinions, treatises, hornbooks, and scholarly articles, which in turn shape public opinion about the rule of law. A fuller dose of the elixir follows.

The Law Is in the Text

Since the law is to be found in texts, the job of the interpreter is to dig out the meanings placed in those texts by their authors. The interpreter—the judge, the lawyer, the citizen—thus finds the law others have written, and does not make it.

The initial step in interpretation, then, is to locate the texts and their authors. Nowadays, the texts and authors are usually easy to find, though it wasn't always so. Texts today are usually officially defined and formally published: statutes, administrative regulations, constitutions, treaties between nations, formal contracts, judicial opinions and so forth. The authors of these texts are, respectively, legislators, administrators, constitutional framers, governments, private parties, and judges.

The reason we can pin the texts and authors down with some certainty is that we share a notion that has prevailed since the 19th century, namely, that the law flows exclusively from the power of the state. This is a key idea of what is called legal positivism: only those laws laid down—that is, posited—by the state are true law. So all we have to do to know which texts and which authors are authoritative is to look for the official rules recognizing which texts count as law and which do not, who has the right to declare the law and who does not.

Things were not quite so easy during the previous 4,000 or so years, though the task of looking for texts and their authors was the same. In the centuries that stretch from the 18th century back to the earliest legal records known to us, those left by the Sumerians in the third millennium before Christ, the dominant belief was that law was part of nature, and the natural law tradition held that there were other texts of law higher than those authorized by the state. It was believed that these natural law texts trumped any mere human positive law that conflicted with them. Although that idea has lost most of its force in secular circles today, it is still very much around and is invoked when people claim that "God's law" or "natural justice" have been violated even though the published laws of their countries seem to say otherwise.

The transcendent texts of the natural law tradition tended not to be written, at least not in the usual way. They were intangible: the will of the gods, God's divine plan, nature, human nature, or pure ideas like "reason," "justice," "equity," or "the good," which, ever since Plato, were believed to really exist as things in nature even if you couldn't wrap them up in a package and touch them.

Yet, to believers, these abstractions worked just like written texts. Both Augustine and Aquinas, for instance, liked to refer to natural law as law "written in the hearts of men."[4] If natural law texts and their authors were difficult to ascertain, then priestly leaders could help out by communicating directly with the source themselves and delivering a written text of the author's intention. Recall that Moses ascended Mount Sinai, spoke with God, and came down with the Ten Commandments chiseled in stone tablets. In later centuries, philosophers, scholars and judges played a similar role when they contemplated other texts of natural law, such as human nature or reason, speculated about the author's (nature, God, a Prime Mover) intentions, and wrote down their findings in treatises or judicial opinions.

Although there is a fundamental disagreement, then, between natural law and positivism about what counts as the text of the law and who its authors are, there is no dispute that the task for the interpreter is to discover the meaning placed in the text by the author. Not surprisingly, both schools of thought share certain common techniques developed over the centuries for doing just that. The techniques don't always provide clear answers or produce identical results in the hands of different interpreters. But they are reliable enough to breed confidence, and objective enough to prevent interpreters from running away with the text and imposing on it just any meaning they wish. (Remember, I'm still telling the Old Story here.) Different techniques have evolved for interpreting legislative texts, contracts and their relatives on the one hand, and judicial texts on the other.

There Are Rules for Finding the Meaning in Statutes, Constitutions, Contracts, and Other Texts that Attempt to Guide Future Conduct

I'll focus on statutes, constitutions and contracts, but these rules generally apply, with slight changes, to administrative regulations, treaties, and similar texts.

1. Follow the plain meaning of the words.

Preeminent among techniques for interpreting these texts is to stick to the literal meaning of the words and don't look at anything outside of them. Do this, the story goes, and you haven't even interpreted the text, you've merely declared the meaning that is plainly there.

There are two basic rationales for the rule. The first is that the words themselves are the surest, safest evidence of the author's actual subjective intentions. After all, people usually do try to say what they mean, and often succeed, so it's prudent to take their words at face value. Unlike the concreteness of the black letters they have bothered to put on white paper, other evidence of what they mean—like their behavior, or things they've said elsewhere, or how others understood them, and so on—can be so fragmentary, cloudy and corruptible that it's best to stay away from it altogether. The second rationale is that the law has to be objectively knowable so that people can rely upon it in planning their affairs. For certainty, it's best to follow the meaning that is objective—in the sense that it's plain to all reasonable people—even when that meaning doesn't jibe with the author's intention. The author may have made a mistake or been careless in using words, and may have meant something else, but law would be too chancy if we had to take such things into account. So the meaning that matters, according to the objective theory, is the one the author actually did put into the text rather than one that may have been intended but failed to make it into print. The first and second rationales sometimes conflict, but their instructions to the interpreter are always the same: stick doggedly to the words.

The Plain Meaning Rule for Statutes

The Plain Meaning Rule has particularly hardy roots in statutory interpretation, extending back at least to the statement of an English judge in 1340 that "we cannot take the statute further than the words of it say,"[5] and surfacing in a famous declaration of the U.S. Supreme Court in 1916 that "where the language [of the statute] is plain and admits of no more than one meaning the duty of interpretation does not arise."[6] Typical of the routine reiteration of it in our day is a remark of the Supreme Court of Ohio: "Courts do not have the authority to ignore the plain and unambiguous language in a statute in the guise of statutory interpretation."[7] Thus, like the Parole Evidence Rule in contract law which excludes evidence of preliminary negotiations, the Plain Meaning Rule for statutes excludes evidence of their legislative history, of legislators' motives and purpose, of others' understanding of the statute, and all other extrinsic evidence of meaning.

The rationale the courts offer for this approach to statutes is nearly always the first one mentioned above, that the words are the safest and surest guide to the actual intention of the legislature. Courts are supposed to be bound by that intention. To go beyond it when interpreting statutes would be, Justice Frankfurter once warned, "to usurp a power which our democracy has lodged in its elected legislature."[8] Occasionally, a court has justified the plain meaning approach on the objective theory instead, intoning that, "The courts shall declare that the legislature meant what it said," or, "We do not inquire what the legislature meant; we ask only what the statute means."[9] But this objective theory is rarely made so explicit. Rather, the courts usually prefer to couch their use of the Plain Meaning Rule in terms of judicial deference to the actual legislative intent.

The Plain Meaning Rule for the Constitution

In constitutional interpretation, too, the ideal for some is to find the answer in the words themselves. This is frequently an elusive quest in the U.S. Constitution, whose majestic generalities like "equal protection, "due process," "freedom of speech," "commerce" and so on defy any one meaning that is plain.[10] But the words are the starting place. Besides, there are many provisions whose meanings do announce themselves literally, such as the one that no person is eligible to be President "who shall not have attained to the age of thirty-five years." A prominent federal judge has said that "[n]o one would seriously argue or expect, for instance, that the Supreme Court could or would twist the Presidential minimum-age provision into a call for 'sufficient maturity,' so as to forbid the seating of a 36-year-old."[11]

The rationale for the plain meaning approach to the Constitution is, once again, that the literal words are the best guide to the authors' original intent—in this case authors whose intent is extraordinarily important because they are the revered 18th century framers of the founding charter of our entire nation.

There is also a contrary tradition in constitutional interpretation that has the flavor of the objective rationale: the tradition that says the text must be read to fit not original meaning but the understanding of successive generations. Judges are usually careful, however, to link even this notion back to original intent, arguing that the framers themselves intended the Constitution to be an evolving instrument of government, not a straightjacket. Whichever rationale is chosen, when the words signaling original or current meaning are plain the courts should not look beyond them.

The Plain Meaning Rule for Contracts

According to an up-to-date contracts hornbook, "the number of cases decided under the Plain Meaning Rule is simply staggering."[12] This is owed, no doubt, to the convenience of the rule for both theories of contract which vie for dominance. The two theories parallel the subjective and objective rationales of statutory and constitutional interpretation, and the Plain Meaning Rule works for them in similar ways.

Under the theory that a contract is a subjective meeting of the minds, the contractual words the parties used may simply be the best evidence of the content of those minds, as even critics of the Plain Meaning Rule admit.[13] Under the contrasting theory that the law has to set objectively knowable standards in order to promote certainty, a contract must be given the meaning a reasonable person would give it under the circumstances, which is to say, its usual meaning—even if, in Judge Learned Hand's phrase, "twenty bishops" testify that "either party, when he used the words, intended something else...."[14]

Moreover, the Plain Meaning Rule dominates contract cases because it helps the courts handle the texts of contracts, which can be such messy affairs. Unlike statutes or constitutions which must have a formal shape, contracts can be cobbled together from oral exchanges, scraps of paper, conduct, and other evidence of agreement. Parties have been known to misunderstand, to change their minds, and yes, even to stretch the truth about such things when their deals turn sour. The law needs to impose a bit of order on this evidence to grapple with it at all. That's why in remote days we required parties to seal their contracts with hot wax and a ring, and it's why we have the Statute of Frauds requiring important contracts to be in writing, as well as the Parole Evidence Rule excluding tentative agreements in favor of the final expression of the parties' deal. All of these are efforts to shape a definitive text from a potlatch of evidence. The Plain Meaning Rule backs them up by insisting upon sticking to that text, so long as its meaning is clear.

2. If the words are ambiguous, apply intrinsic canons (rules) of construction that help clarify the internal workings of the language or the law.

When the words are ambiguous or vague rather than plain, then the interpreter may employ certain interpretive aids or canons of construction that are intrinsic to legal texts. Though many of these canons have been codified in general statutes on how legal documents are to be construed, there is really no official list of them; they emerge from the nature of language and from the case law and scholarship of the centuries. But there is a consensus that the following, which (unless noted otherwise) apply to statutes, constitutions, contracts, wills and similar texts, are among the most important:[15]

- *Grammar and punctuation are assumed to follow approved usage.*
- *Common words are given their ordinary, popular meanings and technical words their technical meanings.* Guided by this canon, the U.S. Supreme Court once decided that a tomato is a "vegetable" because it is ordinarily called a vegetable on the American dinner table even if it is classified a fruit in the botanist's lab.[16]
- *Every word must be given effect.*
- *A specific provision controls a general one.*
- *An interpretation that makes the text valid is preferred to one that makes it void.*
- *The text must be construed as a whole, all of its parts integrated into a harmonious scheme with a coherent purpose.*
- *In pari materia.* On the same subject. Statutes on the same subject are to be construed together as a harmonious legislative scheme.
- *Expressio unius est exclusio alterius.* The expression of one is the exclusion of others. For example, a contract to supply "stewing chickens" automatically excludes "broilers and fryers." A city with express statutory authority to "approve or disapprove" zoning changes has been held to have no authority to "reconsider" them.
- *Ejusdem generis.* Of the same genre or class. When a general category follows a list of specific items of a certain kind, the general category is limited to items of the same class. A contract for sale of a farm together with its "cows, pigs, sheep and all other animals" would not include the seller's pet cockatoo.

- *Noscitur a sociis.* Known by their associates. Words are known by the textual company they keep. A tax exemption for income from "exploration, discovery, or prospecting," for example, has been held to apply to discovery of oil, gas, and minerals, and not to discovery of new drugs, because drugs aren't something for which you explore or prospect.
- *Contracts are construed against those who draft them.* To protect against word tricksters, when more than one interpretation is possible the one will be chosen that is less favorable to the party who wrote the language.
- *Statutes contrary to common law are to be narrowly construed.* Overturned by statute in most jurisdictions, this canon nevertheless influences judicial attitudes toward legislative intervention in traditional common law areas like property, tort, and contract.
- *Penal statutes are to be narrowly construed in favor of the accused's rights.* The canon has been affected by the Constitutional law of criminal procedure, but is still a significant influence in its own right.
- *Social welfare statutes are to be liberally construed to accomplish their intended reforms.*
- *Legal texts should be construed to avoid constitutional questions.* When more than one interpretation is possible, the one that raises no constitutional doubts will be chosen, since it's unlikely that any authors would have intended to write a text that violates the Constitution and it's best to shake the Constitutional foundations of government as little as possible.

3. If ambiguity persists, look for extrinsic evidence of the purpose the authors intended.

If the intrinsic aids have failed to clear up the ambiguity or vagueness, then the interpreter may resort to evidence outside of the text itself. Whether dealing with statutes, the Constitution, contracts or similar documents, extrinsic evidence usually falls into three, roughly chronological, groups: social context of the document, writing of the document, and implementation.

Social context of the document

In 1584, *Heydon's Case* laid down the famous "mischief rule" for statutory interpretation, holding that judges always had to ask themselves, "what was the mischief and defect for which the common law did not provide," "what remedy" the Parliament had devised by statute to cure the mischief and what the "true reason" or purpose of that remedy was. "And then the office of all the Judges is always to make such construction as shall suppress the mischief, and advance the remedy...."[17] In *Heydon's Case* itself the court delved into details of the political struggle between Henry VIII and the Church in order to understand the purpose of a statute that voided church leases. So it is in our day, with courts taking judicial notice or accepting evidence of the historical, social, economic, political, and wider legal context of statutes in order to understand their purposes when their texts are unclear.

In constitutional cases, the practice is unavoidable. The vague abstractions and high purposes of many of the Constitution's clauses force the Supreme Court to produce opinions that sometimes read like short courses in American history and political science. Opinions on freedom of the press or religion often look back to newspapers, churches and politics in colonial times in order to understand the purposes of the First Amendment. Opinions on the 13th, 14th and 15th amendments sometimes disinter the Civil War and Reconstruction, often citing dozens of historical works on the period in a single opinion.

And in the more mundane world of every day contracts, extrinsic evidence of context is brought in under the name of "customary" and "trade" usages, the latter defined by the Uniform Commercial Code as "any practice or method of dealing having such regularity of observance in a place, vocation or trade as to justify an expectation that it will be observed with respect to the transaction in question."[18] Evidence of trade usage has clarified, among other surprising things, that "a thousand rabbits" in the rabbit-raising trade really meant "twelve-hundred rabbits,"[19] and that a contract between a congregation and an orthodox Jewish rabbi silently incorporated the ancient custom of separate seating for men and women.[20]

Writing of the document

What the parties said and did about the text while they were writing it is strong evidence of what the text in fact means. It is to be treated cautiously, of course, and not at all if the plain words themselves and the canons of construction have already yielded a clear answer.

The legislative history of statutes is a particularly rich body of such evidence. Although British courts, thinking it unreliable and time-consuming, typically refuse to examine legislative history, contemporary American courts increase their citations of it every year, the Supreme Court alone now making several hundred references each term.[21] All of the following are relevant and are weighted approximately in the order given:

- Language of the bill as introduced and amended.

- Reports of legislative committees.
- Statements by authors or sponsors.
- Debate on the floor of legislature.
- Messages from the executive branch.
- Testimony at legislative hearings.

When the legislation in question was enacted at the polls by direct vote, the key legislative history documents are the ballot arguments and campaign materials submitted to the voters.

The drafting of the Constitution and its various amendments has left, of course, layers of evidence of the framers' intent, and these have been recovered by historians, legal scholars, and the courts with all the vigor of archeologists working at an ancient dig.[22] Among other evidence, we have James Madison's notes of the Convention of 1787, the Federalist Papers written by Madison, Alexander Hamilton and John Jay as well as tracts written by opponents during the campaign for ratification, papers from state ratifying conventions, correspondence to and from many of the key framers, and Congressional and state ratification debates on the Bill of Rights and later amendments. The courts sift this evidence extensively when searching for the meaning of the Constitution's vague phrases.

The Parole Evidence Rule for contracts excludes some extrinsic evidence of the parties' preliminary negotiations. But the Rule applies only when there is a final written contract, and even then it does not bar extrinsic evidence if the final contract doesn't fully integrate all the terms, or if the contract was based on a sham, contingency, fraud, mistake, or an illegality. In addition, although different scholars draw different fine lines around certain types of subjective and objective extrinsic evidence, the Rule largely allows extrinsic evidence to show the meaning of ambiguous terms in the final contract.[23] One particularly useful extrinsic source is the parties' "course of dealing" during which their conduct evidences a common understanding of terms later put into a contract. In the end, despite the Parole Evidence Rule, extrinsic evidence of the parties' intentions during the writing of the text is as significant for contracts as it is for statutes and the Constitution.

Implementation of the document

The meaning other people gave to the text in practice right after it was written and over the years is said to mirror the text's true meaning. The underlying notion here is three-fold. It's thought that those contemporaries who were present at the birth of the text must have had a better grasp of it than do we who view it through the haze of time. In addition, it's thought that those who have had to put the text into action know how its purpose gets expressed in a practical and changing world. Finally, when people have relied upon a settled meaning in practice, giving special weight to that practical construction promotes the stability that the objective theory of law cherishes. For contracts, all this is captured simply by giving weight to the parties' behavior during the "course of performance" of the agreement, just as weight was given to their earlier "course of dealing."[24] For statutes, the Constitution, administrative regulations and treaties, we look to what has been called "contemporaneous and practical interpretations."[25]

And who provides these contemporaneous and practical interpretations? They are typically provided by executive branch agencies, governors, attorneys general, prosecutors, the police, and other public officials charged with implementing the text. These are people experienced in enforcing a particular law. Often they have even originated and drafted it. The legislature in many instances has delegated broad discretion to them to fill in the details of the legislative policy according to practical needs. Their interpretations are therefore entitled to great deference. And the longer and more consistent the interpretations have been, the more deference is owed. Though not absolutely controlling, a long-standing official interpretation can be a mountain to move, as a taxpayer once found out who attempted to overthrow an interpretation of a federal agency that had been followed for 34 years by the agency, the courts, and other taxpayers.[26]

The courts, the public, and legislatures also produce contemporaneous and practical interpretations that are given deference. Court decisions interpreting legal texts are of course followed within the judicial hierarchy of their jurisdictions, but decisions from outside jurisdictions construing merely analogous texts are also looked to as significant practical constructions. Even the public's behavior can sometimes evidence a law's meaning. If the blind walk with guide dogs and the public rides bicycles through the local park, despite a posted ordinance reading "Dogs and Vehicles Prohibited," it is likely that a judge will understand, as the public does, that the ordinance just wasn't meant to apply to guide dogs and bicycles.

The most important practical constructions of statutes, however, may come from legislators themselves. After a statute is born, legislators monitor its lifespan by holding hearings, issuing committee reports, making statements in floor debate, and enacting related legislation. All these constitute practical interpretation of the statute by its own author. Of course, the views of a handful of legislators can't be taken as an interpretation by the body, so views of individual legislators expressed outside of the legislature in, say, speeches, books, or affidavits, are entitled to little or no weight. The greatest weight must be reserved for instances when the whole legislature, aware of the interpretation given its statute in practice by others, re-enacts the statute as is or refuses to amend it, which can be taken as acquiescence to the existing interpretation. Legislative inaction might be thought of as the "Hound of the Baskervilles" rule: A federal appellate court once wrote, "What we find most significant in the legislative history in the Senate is the same thing that Sherlock Holmes found to be crucial in solving the case of the Hound of the Baskervilles—the failure of the dog to bark. The ... bill was discussed endlessly.... Yet we have not found in the Senate debates, and appellees have not called to our attention, one single suggestion [that the bill would change the law on the crucial issue]."[27]

4. Always be certain that your interpretation is reasonable.

The final rule is you should take care that the previous three rules have not led you off the path of reason. Reasonableness has always been an overriding requirement for the law under any of the classical jurisprudential theories. In natural law theory, law flows from and therefore must be in accord with God's will, the nature of the universe, or human nature, all of which are assumed to be governed by an ultimately harmonious, rational scheme for human existence. In positivist theory, law is by definition a rational order capable of description by the tools of logic and empirical science, so any decision that upholds an irrationality as law must have fallen into some methodological error.[28]

The law, in short, always beats with the pulse of reason, which can be felt in every interpretation. The judges and lawyers constantly appeal to "consistency," "logic," "practicality," and the other manifestations of reasonableness. To talk law is, for them, to talk reason. Indeed, it could be said that the distinguishing mark of legal discourse over political, literary, artistic and other discourses is that it is above all a discourse of reason. The legal profession also knows, as an English judge once put it, that it is always "an advantage to make clear ... that the law is in accordance with sound common sense."[29] But beyond this sort of permeating habit of reason, what it comes to in the actual practice of reading legal texts is this: First, the interpreter has to keep the various rules of interpretation reconciled in an internally coherent order. Second, the interpreter must be alert to the external effects of every interpretation; irrational consequences are a sign that the interpretation is wrong, because the law is not irrational. And these demands for both internal and external reasonableness get expressed quite specifically in our doctrines on interpretation of statutes, constitutions and contracts.

Here are some of the doctrinal mechanisms by which internal rationality of interpretation is assured:

- The previous steps are followed in order (first plain meaning, then intrinsic aids, then extrinsic evidence).
- Many of the canons of construction force internal coherence.
- The various legislative history and extrinsic evidence documents are used according to a rank order of their weight.
- The coherent overall purpose or structure of a legal text, especially of the Constitution, is kept in mind.

Similarly, there are doctrines for keeping the external consequences of interpretations within bounds of reason.

In statutory interpretation it is said to be "the golden rule" that when the literal words of a statute yield "ridiculous, "absurd," or "manifestly unjust" results, you must depart from the words so far as necessary to avoid those results, since the legislature cannot possibly have intended them.[30] Blackstone stated the rule, illustrating with a classic example debated at the famous law school in twelfth century Bologna: "As to the effects and consequence, the rule is, that where words bear either none, or a very absurd signification if literally understood, we must a little deviate from the received sense of them. Therefore the Bolognian law, mentioned in Puffendorf, which enacted 'that whoever drew blood in the streets should be punished with the utmost severity,' was held after long debate not to extend to the surgeon, who opened the vein of a person that fell down in the street with a fit."[31]

In federal Constitutional law, reasonableness is imported through the Due Process clause requirement that laws must have a "rational basis" and that official action must not be "arbitrary" or "capricious."

And in contract law, though it is often said that "the court may not, under the guise of interpretation, make a new contract for the parties"[32] or "contradict the clearly expressed language of the contract," it is equally true that people contract for practical rather than irrational ends and their contracts must be so understood. As the Restatement of Contracts underscores, the parties will be taken to have had reasonable intentions, and language will be given the meaning that a reasonable person could attach to it.[33] And if people contract for purposes so unreasonable as to be socially unconscionable, the courts will impose reason upon them, either under the Uniform Commercial Code which explicitly forbids unconscionable contracts, or under the courts' own notions of reasonable public policy.[34]

Those are the rules for interpreting legislative and other texts that attempt to guide future conduct. For interpreting judicial texts, the Old Story tells of different rules.

There Are Rules for Finding the Meaning in the Texts of Judicial Precedents

It is, of course, the hallmark of the Anglo-American common law system that much of the law is found in the decisions issued by judges in individual cases. Appellate judges explain their decisions in written opinions that are formally published in print, then disseminated in electronic databases and in law libraries throughout the country. There, other judges, lawyers, and their clerks find the decisions that are similar to the case they are working on at the moment. If the case at hand resembles previously decided cases, they can be fairly confident that it will be decided the same way since the doctrine of stare decisis ("let the decision stand") obliges judges to follow the precedent decisions of the higher courts which have authority over them. The highest court in a jurisdiction technically isn't forced to adhere to its own precedents, but it is a rare day when it fails to do so. And, except in special instances, no court is bound by the precedents of courts in other jurisdictions, but every court frequently finds such outside precedents to be useful guides to its own decisions.

This power of precedent lies close to the heart of what has well been called the genius of the common law, according to the Old Story. Case by case, the judges weave the seamless web of the law from the thread of previous cases. The basic structure, the fundamental principles, remain the same. Each new case merely adds connective tissue between principles. When changed social conditions require the principles to be extended, or to be allowed to fall into disuse, the web is extended or curtailed one loop—one case—at a time, changing subtly at the margins while leaving the structure of the law itself intact.

Working case by case over many centuries, judges discovered bedrock principles of justice, the rights and duties required of humans living together in a complex society, and wove upon them the great webs of the common law of property, torts, contracts, crimes and other areas. In early days, this was almost wholly a system of law found in cases, the accomplishment of the judges alone in which the legislative and executive branches played little part. With the rise of the legislative and administrative state in the 19th and 20th centuries, and the opening of new areas of law unheard of in simpler times, the starting point for most of the law is now in statutes and administrative regulations rather than cases. But the ending point is still in the cases: the statutes and regulations need to be applied to specific people in specific situations; people argue about these applications; their arguments go to court, where judges interpret the statutes and regulations in accordance with the rules discussed earlier; but their decisions are recorded, and the same respect for stare decisis that built the original common law now weaves an interpretive gloss case by case over statutes and regulations.

It's impossible to imagine an Anglo-American legal system without this doctrine of stare decisis, so firmly is it rooted in our history and practice. And if it weren't so rooted, we would have to invent it, for only when judges follow precedent can we be assured:

- That the law encourages social stability and is predictable enough to rely upon in planning our affairs.
- That like cases are treated alike, which is an essential part of justice.
- That judges adhere to the objective rule of law rather than to their own personal and philosophical preferences.
- And that the legal system avoids the inefficiency of deciding old questions over again every time they arise.

What, then, are the rules for correct application of stare decisis? How can we be certain in this contentious field that we and other interpreters are accurately "following precedent" and not distorting the precedents according to our own biases? These are the rules:[35]

1. Separate the precedent case into its basic elements: Facts, Procedural History, Issue, Holding, and Reasoning.

This is basic drill for the first year of law studies, as every law student knows only too well. Mastery of the technique of parsing case texts into these distinct elements, or some close variation of them, opens the door to "thinking like a lawyer."

Facts

What we want here are the raw facts of who did what, when, where, how, and so forth. Include only those facts that are legally relevant, that is, that bear directly on some issue in the law suit. If, for example, a woman sues a railroad for injuring her while she waited for a train, relevant facts will include exactly where she was standing and exactly how she was injured, but not that she was poor, the railroad rich, the day hot, and she was taking her daughters to the beach.

Procedural History

Who sued whom, when and where, the type of legal claim made ("negligence," "breach of contract," "violation of constitutional right to equal protection," etc.), and the actions of the various courts that heard the claim.

Issue

The precise legal issue that the court had to resolve to dispose of the case.

Holding

The court's ruling on that legal issue.

Reasoning

The rationale given by the court for its holding.

2. Focus on the holding (the ratio decidendi, deciding reason, or ground of decision) of the case, and exclude the incidental remarks (obiter dicta) made by the judge.

Under the traditional theory, and in general British practice, the ratio is the principle of law put forth by the court as the basis of its decision. Under the somewhat narrower "material facts" theory more often heard in the United States, the ratio is the court's holding limited to the facts that it has found to be material. It would be a mistake to exaggerate the differences between the two theories, for what they have in common is more important: an agreement that it is possible to combine the essential facts and legal reasons into some statement of the one key basis for the decision. This is the ratio, or in more common parlance, the holding of the case, and you will have already identified it in step one, if you have done your job properly, when you were forced to separate the holding from the facts, issue, and reasons. The dicta in the case are everything else the court said that is not necessary to the holding. Dicta may be interesting, but are no part of the precedent to be followed under the doctrine of stare decisis.

3. Reasoning by analogy, show how the case at hand is either similar to or distinguishable from the precedent case, and therefore either is or is not controlled by its holding.

You need to show the similarities, or dissimilarities, between the case at hand and the parts of the precedent case that were essential to its holding. This is a subtle and disputatious craft. It is sometimes made easier and sometimes more difficult by having not just one but a long line of precedents with which analogies must be drawn; the long line may help reveal the principles underlying each case's holding, or it could muddy the waters with too many factors to consider. Through years of experience, however, lawyers come to master this skill. Judges master this skill and more: surveying the landscape of precedents and analogies from a position above the disputing parties, the judges are able to discern the overall pattern of principles that constitute the structure of the common law, and to render their decisions accordingly.

•••

Those, then, are the traditional rules of legal interpretation, rules which reassure us that we live under the rule of law and make it still sensible today to heed Blackstone's admonition of two centuries ago:

> [H]ow difficult and hazardous a thing it is, even in matters of public utility, to depart from the rules of the common law; which are so nicely constructed and … connected together, that the least breach in any one of them disorders for a time the texture of the whole.[36]

Or so the Old Story claims.

Chapter 2

The Modern Story

The life of the law has not been logic: it has been experience. The felt necessities of the time, the prevalent moral and political theories, intuitions of public policy, avowed or unconscious, even the prejudices which judges share with their fellow men, have a good deal more to do than the syllogism in determining the rules by which men should be governed.

—Oliver Wendell Holmes, Jr.[1]

The Old Story about legal interpretation is still told today, yet it survives like some odd species that has survived the disappearance of its habitat, an iguana in the shopping mall, a doctor with bleeding-kit in a little black bag standing in a hospital full of electronic imaging equipment, a man in top-hat driving a one-horse shay down the freeway. The world in which the Old Story made sense, if it ever did, no longer exists. It's not just that new ideas about law have come along to challenge the old. They have: the new theory sees the old abstractions of legal logic and rigid rules of reasoning as a fairy tale, and replaces them with much more realistic observations of how we use law and how we actually reason about it. But you would be wrong to conclude that what's going on here is merely a battle between a new and an old theory of law. These new legal ideas are just a small, and far from the most significant, reflection of the new world that we've inhabited since around the turn of the 20th century. It's this whole new world in which the Old Story about law is so egregiously out of place.

It's worth bringing that world into our gaze for a moment. Any discussion of the new legal ideas which omits that context will be hollow and miss the point.

The Modernist Revolution[2]

The gulf that separates our era from the past is as profound as the gulf between the Middle Ages and the Renaissance, or between ancient Babylonia and classical Greece. It is the gulf between the candle and the light bulb, the horse and the automobile, the iron cannon and "Star Wars" weaponry. It divides the thinking of Newton's mechanics from Einstein's relativity, Galileo's telescope from Heisenberg's indeterminacy principle, Comte's rigid positivism from Freud's analyses of dreams. It separates Wagner's musical dramas from Schoenberg's twelve-tone scale, jazz, rock 'n' roll, and Cage's compositions of silence. Eliot's Middlemarch from Joyce's Ulysses. The architecture of the Beaux Art from the designs of the Bauhaus. Whistler's Mother from Picasso's Les Demoiselles d'Avignon. On the one side are Victorian manners, slavery, and woman as property; on the other are the sexual revolution, the struggle for racial equality, and woman as person. Noting the sharp break with the past and trying to fix a moment, Virginia Woolf once deadpanned, "On or about December, 1910 human nature changed."[3]

Any plausible list of the changes that caused that chasm to open between the 19th and 20th centuries, and to widen precipitously into the 21st, would have to include the immense but maldistributed economic growth; the huge increases in food and population; the move from country to city; the new communication devices of telephone, radio, television, automobile, airplane, satellite, and computer; the increase in speed, power and precision of machines that both create and destroy; medical advances; and the invention of recording and the motion picture.

What these and other material and technological changes did was at once to disrupt our lives and to empower us. More people than at anytime in the past suddenly had the power to change their lives, or saw at least that their lives were changed by human forces. Economic growth empowered us to buy change directly in many forms. Communication technology empowered us to conquer time and space. Machines empowered us to extend human strength and skills to proportions previously reserved for the gods. Film technology empowered us to create new versions of reality different from our traditional creations by oral and printed word. Medical technology even empowered us to make new human body parts and at times, to cheat death. No one can ignore these changes, save those who have isolated themselves heroically in horse-and-buggy religious communities, and those in less developed countries which modernism has not fully touched. This is simply the environment in which citizens are born and must survive in our times.

The new environment inevitably brought a change in attitudes about how to make sense of the world, about how life was to be lived. It dawned on us that in a significant way we make our own lives. Even before the beginning of the century people in large numbers began to turn their backs on a past in which life was thought to be controlled by mysterious or mechanical forces and humans didn't matter much in the big scheme of things.

In terms of an old metaphor, for the first several thousand years of recorded history humans had acted as if they were on a stage in a drama written and directed by God, Nature, or other mysterious forces. After the scientific and philosophical revolution of the 17th century, that is, after Galileo, Newton and Descartes, the metaphor had changed but human fate had not: the drama of the world came to be seen as a giant machine of matter and motion, with humans as mere cogs in the mechanism. With the arrival of 20th century modernism and its vast increase and redistribution of power, the metaphor changes again. This time humans are at center stage and see themselves as writing, directing and acting the drama, even building the stage itself. In the new view, to worry about God's existence, or humans as cogs in the universe's machine, is to lose sight of the key reality of life as it's actually lived: we, individually and together, control our own fate, are largely responsible for making our world in all its glories and horrors.

The horrors, to be sure, are all the more horrible for being of our own making, and this realization produced an undercurrent of angst and, ironically, a sense of powerlessness, particularly among artists. But at least we had no more excuses for our evil, and this was galvanizing for many. In 1933, John Dewey and a group of 33 intellectuals released the Humanist Manifesto, setting out the principles for a new secular philosophy of humanism, and ending: "Though we consider the religious forms and ideas of our fathers no longer adequate, the quest for the good life is still the central task for mankind. Man is at last becoming aware that he alone is responsible for the realization of the world of his dreams, that he has within himself the power for its achievement. He must set intelligence and will to the task."[4] If the new attitude could be summed up in two words, the words would be subjective and pragmatic.[5] People who feel responsible for their own fate look inward to see who they are and where they're going. The world that matters is the subjective world of their own minds. The very outside "real world" becomes less real, less objective once we realize that our mental experience of it is our primary reality. The important question of life is how we're going to shape that experience, individually and collectively.

You can watch this new view appear on the canvases of artists between 1900 and 1920 as old-fashioned "realistic" representations of the outside world are first fragmented then fade completely into mental abstractions. (Compare, for samples, Picassos of the 1890s with Picassos of 1910, look at Kandinskys of 1915, Maleviches of 1920.) You see the new view in the notion of Freud's theories and Joyce's and others' novels that sub-consciousness is the primary reality. In 1914 Kafka enters in his diary: "What will be my fate as a writer is very simple. My talent for portraying my dreamlike inner life has thrust all other matters into the background...."[6]

Nor is this subjectivism just a thing for artists with sensitive souls. It goes to the roots of theoretical science. About the time Picasso and the cubists were showing objects from multiple perspectives of time and space on a single canvas, Einstein was working out the similar notion that time and space are relative to the position of the viewer. Scientists used to look at the universe and see "lumps of matter moving about in accordance with certain laws," both the lumps and the laws existing independently of our minds. But in the words of one historian of ideas: "After the full impact of relativity had been felt, however, little was left of this ingenuous belief in the scientific image of objective reality, as faithfully registered by the senses. It began to be recognized that the familiar picture, far from being a genuine photographic reproduction of an independent reality 'out there,' was rather more on the order of a painting: a subjective creation of the mind.... [T]he formulations of Einstein made clear that 'even space and time are forms of intuition, which can no more be divorced from consciousness than can our concepts of color, shape or size. Space has no objective reality except as an order or arrangement of the objects we perceive in it, and time has no independent existence apart from the order of events by which we measure it.'"[7] Less than a generation later, the physicist Heisenberg laid down his famous indeterminacy principle, according to which "we cannot observe the course of nature without disturbing it" since our own attempts to observe are invariably part of the observation. Heisenberg: "[W]e can no longer consider 'in themselves' those building stones of matter which we originally held to be the last objective reality. This is so because they defy all forms of objective location in space and time, and since basically it is always our knowledge of these particles alone which we can make the object of science.... Thus even in science the object of research is no longer nature itself, but man's investigation of nature. Here, again, man confronts himself alone."[8]

It was dawning upon others, too, that the nature of the objects they study depends upon the observer's point of view. Take language. Or, take everyday "real world" objects for practical use. Near the turn of the century the philosopher Peirce, the linguist Saussure, and later the philosopher Wittgenstein and others observed that words have no inherent meanings, contrary to millennia-old assumptions that words were reference labels for external things or for thoughts. Words, instead, are arbitrary markers in language games and take on different meanings according to the game we're playing. They get their meaning from the way we use them. The artist Duchamp had made a similar point before 1920 by putting "readymade" objects (an upended bicycle wheel, a bottle rack, a urinal) into art exhibitions, radically changing their meanings by changing their context for the viewer. In American philosophy, Peirce, James and Dewey's various versions of pragmatism stated the new subjectivity in terms of a general, humanist social philosophy. "Experience is our only teacher," wrote Peirce, while James told an overflow audience in New York in 1906 that what we really mean when we say our beliefs are "true" is that they work for us, they are "advantageous to our happiness."[9]

At bottom, though, modernism is not primarily an intellectual pastime. Masses of ordinary, untheoretical people who have never heard of Einstein's relativity or of William James, and who think Picasso cockeyed, are living the subjective and pragmatic modernist life. Eagerly and without theory, empowered popular culture has been rushing to write new scripts for every human drama, even the basic ones of sex, life and death. The rush is even faster today than it was in 1934 when Cole Porter wrote the theme song to his stage musical "Anything Goes!" "The world has gone mad today, And good's bad today, And black's white today, And day's night today.... Anything goes!" The people, in short, are dazed by the changes of our era, but they're dancing.

Thought Window

Is Moral Relativism Something to Worry about?

This subjective, modernist pragmatism is a down-to-earth, human-centered way of understanding the world. Opinion about it seems to divide into two camps. In one camp are the optimists who find it liberating: common-sense individualists, practical skeptics who are suspicious of hawkers of eternal truths, and social reformers who feel that since we alone are responsible for our destiny we'd better get organized. Their buoyant spirit is reflected in the lives of such early modernists as the anthropologist Margaret Mead, and the historian and city planner Lewis Mumford.[10]

In the other camp are the pessimists who see in it only despair: those who feel that life is bleak and absurd without life-saving net of eternal religious or scientific truths, and those who fear that if everyone's beliefs are respected as "true for them" we'll sink into an "anything goes" hedonistic moral relativism which gives us no ground to condemn the horrors committed by Nazis and other fanatics.

The optimists respond. First, they point out, life isn't bleak for anyone who hangs on to the spontaneous joy that children possess before they're taught that there is supposed to be something more. Nor is it absurd for anyone who knows the inner satisfaction that comes to creative artists—and every life is a creative work of art. Second, this need for some outside absolute value to validate one's views is itself culturally relative. Not all cultures suffer from it. Third, it's well worth remembering that it is the absolutists who have often produced our history of horrors.[11] From Torquemada to the Nazis, and before and after them, the horrors have rarely been committed under the banner of moral relativism, but usually under banners of eternal truths. They wage war with "God on their side," Bob Dylan warned. If anything, pragmatic relativism is a civilizing influence. It promotes tolerance of the other's point of view. It renders stale some of the old clashes of "truths" for which people used to kill one another. It gets people looking for common ground of mutual survival on a small planet.

Perhaps most important, you may understand another's point of view without endorsing it, and without weakening commitment to your own. The desire to persuade others to share your point of view needs no justification other than your concern for them, mutual interest, or your creative zest for a better future. And your condemnation of horrors from Aztec cannibalism to Nazi genocide and South African apartheid needs no justification beyond your own self-defense, concern for others, mutual interest, and the realization that the "truths" on which such ideologies rest have turned out to be qualities that their own advocates claimed to repudiate: usually, fraudulent mystification, bogus science, naked greed, or just plain self-deception.

While this philosophical debate is worth following because it does play a role in political and legal rhetoric, it probably affects the intellectual angst of a relatively small number of people more than it affects society at large. No one in the debate talks about reversing, or even slowing, the underlying economic and technological changes. And it's these changes, not philosophy, that drive modernism, causing us to think differently than our ancestors did about how to live life.

Legal Modernism

Oliver Wendell Holmes, Jr., a confidant of Peirce, James and Dewey, is generally credited with being first to open the windows of the law to modernism. In essays before the turn of the century, he elaborated his maxim—which sounds like a line from Peirce or James—that "the life of the law has not been logic: it has been experience." The law, he asserted, "cannot be dealt with as if it contained only the axioms and corollaries of a book of mathematics."[12]

In 1907, the year of Picasso's Les Demoiselles d'Avignon and two years after Einstein's special theory of relativity appeared, the legal philosopher Roscoe Pound called for a revolt against traditional legal education in favor of training in the social, economic and political context of law. "[L]egal monks who pass their lives in an atmosphere of pure law," he wrote, "from which every worldly and human element is excluded, cannot shape practical principles to be applied to a restless world of flesh and blood."[13]

Movements for the sociological study of law followed. The "Brandeis brief" began to fashion a new style of legal argument filled with sociological data. By the 1920s and 30s a yeasty generation of legal scholars calling themselves "Legal Realists" expressly noted the new "realistic," "pragmatic," "functional" approach that was transforming science, philosophy, architecture, the arts and other fields, and announced they would explore its implications for law.[14] The Realist impact spawned specialties in law within sociology, political science, anthropology, psychology, economics, and other fields. It broadened traditional legal scholarship. It is the tap root of the late 20th century scholarly movement in Critical Legal Studies. From Holmes to Critical Legal Studies and beyond, all these are threads of modernism, all part of the 20th century phenomenon of people assuming for the first time that human problems and their solutions originate within, not beyond, humans themselves. In law, as in other fields, that assumption upsets the old stories inherited from the past. Specifically, it leads to a series of new conclusions.

The Law Is Not in the Text, But in Experience

In dethroning logic and putting experience in its place, Holmes invited lawyers simply to notice the anthropological fact that law actually arises from human behavior and values rather than words or abstract rules. As Holmes put it in "The Path of the Law":

> [J]udicial dissent often is blamed, as if it meant simply that one side or the other were not doing their sums right, and, if they would take more trouble, agreement inevitably would come. This mode of thinking is entirely natural. The training of lawyers is a training in logic.... The language of judicial decision is mainly the language of logic.... But ... [b]ehind the logical form lies a judgment as to the

> relative worth and importance of competing legislative grounds, often an inarticulate and unconscious judgment, it is true, and yet the very root and nerve of the whole proceeding.... I cannot but believe that if the training of lawyers led them habitually to consider more definitely and explicitly the social advantage on which the rule they lay down must be justified, they sometimes would hesitate where now they are confident, and see that really they were taking sides upon debatable and often burning questions.[15]

The Old Story got it wrong. By defining law only as something in authoritative texts, it put social blinders on lawyers and judges. It restricted them to techniques of logic and sentence-parsing. Social context, the very stuff of which law is made, was kept back stage while the stiff, formalistic drama of legal reasoning was performed out front. And, lest the authority of the actors be doubted, it became dogma that one should never peek behind the curtain. Justice Fortescue in 1458:

> Sir, the law is as I say it is, and so it has been laid down ever since the law began; and we have several set forms which are held as law, and so held and used for good reason, though we cannot at present remember that reason.[16]

Retorted Holmes: "It is revolting to have no better reason for a rule of law than that so it was laid down in the time of Henry IV."[17]

Roscoe Pound, denouncing the Old Story as one of an implausible "mechanical jurisprudence," put it crisply: we have to decide what the law really is for us, law in books, or law in action, and the decision is clear for anyone with a concern for human problems as they are actually lived.[18] Moreover, focusing on law in action leads to a realistic appraisal of the subjectivity of legal actors, a point on which Judge (later Justice) Cardozo drew a bead in his famed Yale lectures of 1921:

> We are reminded by William James in a telling page of his lectures on Pragmatism that every one of us has in truth an underlying philosophy of life, even those of us to whom the names and the notions of philosophy are unknown or anathema. There is in each of us a stream of tendency, whether you choose to call it philosophy or not, which gives coherence and direction to thought and action. Judges cannot escape that current any more than other mortals. All their lives, forces which they do not recognize and cannot name, have been tugging at them—inherited instincts, traditional beliefs, acquired convictions; and the resultant is an outlook on life, a concep-

> tion of social needs, a sense in James' phrase of "the total push and pressure of the cosmos," which, when reasons are nicely balanced, must determine where choice shall fall. In this mental background every problem finds its setting. We may try to see things as objectively as we please. None the less, we can never see them with any eyes except our own. To that test they are all brought—a form of pleading or an act of parliament, the wrongs of paupers or the rights of princes, a village ordinance or a nation's charter.[19]

Legal texts are cultural artifacts, products of their time and their makers like any other human-made object, like novels, or clay pots, or maps. Law itself is not a thing but an activity, like writing, or trade, or travel—an important one by which we are continually trying to govern our behavior with one another. No one would define travel as something in an authoritative map. And no one would confuse reading a map with travel in the territory. Yet that's what happened with the law. The textual reflection of it became confused for the activity itself. To know the text was to know the law.

Of course, it's not at all silly or absurd that this happened. It's perfectly understandable, once you look at the historical context. The earliest laws were issued by patriarchal strongmen, kings, and priest-shamans, backed by destructive force and by invocation of mystical sources. They were first transmitted as oral chants and prayers, then with the emergence of writing in the third millennium B.C. they were carved in clay or chiseled in stone and erected on huge monuments at the temple or city gates. Unveiled as the word of the gods in order to secure obedience, the texts themselves became holy icons. Now that those particular gods have faded in the distance of time, it's easy for us to see that the texts issued in their names were a pretext. Ruling castes—above all, men subjugating women, foreigners, and the classes below them—who had the exclusive knowledge of writing and interpretation used them to control others.[20] "The code establishes the social power of a priestly group of interpreters of the law," says a scholar of legal linguistics, " ... the power of the code is time and again located in the hidden and ambiguous character of its source and the correlatively priestly status of its interpreters."[21]

Keeping the source of law ambiguous and the language specialized, the priestly interpreters maintained their position throughout history even as faith in the divine origin of law faded. Another scholar notes:

> Secularization of the law has consisted not in doing away with the "incomprehensible nature of authority" but in censoring any mention of this. When formerly it was divine in its origins authority "re-

> sounded," and its voice was heard like Biblical thunder, unassailable, irrefutable and unintelligible. Today, in its secularized form, authority still derives its effectiveness from being incomprehensible, with the centralized state installed on the Papal throne.[22]

The interpreters simply became secular priests, their power continuing to reside in their claim that the commands of the law emanated not from them but from authoritative sources which happened to communicate in a language only they could understand.

It is a fine question just when the high-water mark of this priestly legal caste was reached.[23] Law was largely transmitted orally for thousands of years, even after the invention of writing, through ceremony, ritual and recitation, mechanisims that relied upon priestly castes who knew how to perform them. The written-law tradition empowered the interpreting castes even more. Some say it was the Roman jurists who set the record. They not only produced a labyrinthine web of casuistic texts (tackling such questions as the liability of a ball thrower whose ball hit the hand of a barber whose razor then slit the neck of a slave he was shaving),[24] but later also built a systematic body of artificial rules, the rational and harmonious architecture of which rivaled the Coliseum itself. The rules recounted in Chapter 1 on plain meaning, intrinsic aids (including virtually every canon of construction), extrinsic evidence of purpose, and reasonableness, can all be traced to the Romans. Others would give first prize for priestly interpretation to the Church and to academic scholars at the law school in Bologna in the 11th and 12th centuries who revived Roman law. Their techniques influence European law to this day. Still others insist that the so-called Pandectists of the 19th century were the best, refining law to a finely tuned mechanical system in the name of "German legal science." And, of course, the English common-law judges are not to be overlooked. From the 12th century on they developed their own labyrinth of rules and case law texts, accessible only through them, and successfully obscured their source in the mists of time and custom. "[T]he law will presume [the ancient rules] to be well founded," Blackstone declared in the 18th century, "not that the particular reason of every rule in the law can at this distance of time be always precisely assigned...."[25]

It would be absurd to posit a conspiracy of lawyer-priests stretching over several thousand years to explain this persistence of specialists who claim that the law is hidden in texts that only they can decode. The explanation is simpler than conspiracy. Rulers rule, in part, through words. Words can instill fear, cause obedience, inspire action, communicate, and do many other things rulers find useful. A professional class of wordsmiths—priests, scholars, lawyers—arises to help rulers to do these useful things with words. Their importance, indeed their jobs, depend upon making the words powerful, and controlling their use. Empowerment is accomplished by enshrining the text as the central, unquestionable object, placing its origins in divine will, nature, reason, positivist science, or time immemorial. Control is accomplished by developing a language of interpretation known only to the group. It's as simple as that. Nor need we posit that these professional wordsmiths have all been disingenuous charlatans, though their ranks have notoriously been filled with more than a few cunning schemers. It is quite plausible that many deceived themselves, easily contented to find that self-interest in maintaining their own status happened to coincide with the religious, philosophical, or scientific thinking of their day.

There Are No Categorical Rules for Finding Meaning in Statutes, Constitutions, Contracts, and Other Texts that Attempt to Guide Future Conduct

The Old Story insists that its doctrines provide fairly firm rules which constrain the interpreter of these texts, indeed, that the rules even form a systematic "science of law." The modern story shows that, far from being a science, these doctrines aren't even rules, for they provide no meaningful constraint upon the subjectivity of interpreters. In fact, they invite a kind of sophisticated scam.

1. There can be no rule that plain meaning must be followed, because words have no plain meanings.

The problem here is not merely with those terms that everyone admits are vague. The law finds those fuzzy phrases indispensable—"reasonable person," "due process," "equal protection," and so on—and they alone keep much of the language of the law from having any plain meaning. The problem, however, is rooted more deeply in the nature of all language, none of which ever has any inherently plain meaning. It's true that we communicate every day with words that are instantly understood, and from that experience it is an effortless conclusion that the words themselves possess clear meanings. Effortless, but erroneous. To believe that words are containers or labels for meanings—or, in a modest version of the same idea, that words have a core of settled meaning surrounded by a penumbra of vagueness—is to subscribe to a theory of language that modern linguists, philosophers, anthropologists and many others have rejected as naive.[26]

Label theories of language come in different forms. The oldest holds that words actually refer to things, either concrete or intangible things but in any event things we can identify well enough to know when we've found their correct labels. Another theory, John Locke's in the 17th century, was that words are labels for ideas in the mind, used when people want to make their hidden thoughts visible to others in order to communicate. Much later, behaviorists came up with the theory that words are the labels for the human behavior they stimulate. That idea was modernist in its focus on behavior, but it still missed the mark. The common error of all the theories was to assume that a word is an equivalent name for something else—things, thoughts, or behavior—that a word, in effect, works like an equation: "word = ______." On this assumption, the job of interpreters is merely to fill in the blank side of the equation. They do it either from their own knowledge of the language, or else by turning to a dictionary, which is a list of words and their equivalences, sort of a mechanical decoding device.

Modernists have shown these theories to be untenable. The main problem is that the number of ways in which the blank side of the equation may be filled in is, in fact, infinite. The same word is capable of changing its meaning each time it's used in a new context. "A word is not a crystal, transparent and unchanged, it is the skin of a living thought and may vary greatly in color and content according to the circumstances and the time in which it is used," as the ever-quotable Holmes put it in one of his opinions for the United States Supreme Court.[27]

The point is not esoteric. You can verify it by paying careful attention to the way you and others around you use the same word to mean different things in different contexts. Moreover, there can never be a dictionary of all words in all contexts because contexts are as infinite as culture itself and culture is constantly inventing new meanings for words by using them in new contexts. Schoolchildren always rejuvenate language this way in order to set themselves apart from the older generation: "hot," "cool," 'bad," "tough," "radical" and other seemingly simple words with ancient etymologies suddenly give new expression to the lively hormones of the young. Advertisers use words in new contexts to call attention to their products: an automobile is sold as a "Cherokee," a cigarette as "True." Professionals do it to develop nuances in their specialization, as well as to keep a monopoly on insiders' knowledge: "Boot up" your computer and "download" the data. Lawyers do it in a (usually vain) attempt to mold language precisely to their intentions: "Hereinafter, 'received' shall mean 'postmarked." Artists do it to expand our imaginations.

It is misleading, then, to think of words as labels for anything. It seems more accurate to think of them as tools we use for our many activities, or markers (like chess pieces or checkers) we use in various language games we play. Their meaning depends entirely upon the activity, or the game, in which we use them. We use a hammer to drive a nail, then to prop open a door; its meaning differs for us with each use. We use a chess king to play chess, then to decorate a sand castle at the beach; it has different meanings to us in each case. We use the word "chicken" to sell someone an edible fowl, then to ridicule someone as a coward; we've given the word different meanings in each context. The tool, the game markers, the words don't have meanings themselves. As the philosopher Wittgenstein concluded, meaning is use. (Nor does the original, ancient use of words enjoy any special privilege as real meaning. Original use rightly fascinates etymologists, but if we were bound by it a "tort lawyer" would be nothing but a "crooked advocate," a proposition with which at least some today would disagree.)

In short, the plain meaning rule which pretends to decode meaning from words alone is impossible to credit as a serious attempt to understand legal texts. Among many other scholars, the late Professor Corbin, mid-20th-century sage of American contract law, struggled over a long career to make the legal profession see this, with meager results. To fail to challenge the plain meaning rule would be "incompetent, and even intellectually and morally dishonest," he wrote.

> It is sometimes said, in a case in which the written words seem plain and clear and unambiguous, that the words are not subject to interpretation or construction. One who makes this statement has of necessity already given the words an interpretation—the one that is to him plain and clear.... I shall continue to do my best to ... demonstrate that no man can determine the meaning of written words by merely gluing his eyes within the four corners of a square paper; to convince that it is men who give meanings to words and that words in themselves have no meaning; and to demonstrate that, when a judge refuses to consider relevant extrinsic evidence on the ground that the meaning of written words is to *him* plain and clear, his decision is formed by and wholly based upon the completely extrinsic evidence of his own personal education and experience.[28]

Corbin died in 1967. The plain meaning rule lives on. The mystery of how such an implausible method of reading texts could maintain such a hold on the legal profession is explained largely by history. Naturally, there is also the functional answer offered by the Old Story: that law is a quest for certainty and precision, for known rules that one, or one's neighbor, cannot escape at whim by changing the rules to suit self-interest, so we'd best stick closely to the exact words as understood by most people. But that practical need could not alone have misled the legal profession into anything as impossible as the plain meaning method of interpretation. It is the historical grip of successive castes of priestly interpreters that explains the survival of the plain meaning rule. In the beginning, when law was mixed with magic and religion and culture was transmitted orally, it was vital to stick to the exact words, according to an historian of primitive law:

> These ancient laws were invariable texts. To change a letter of them, to displace a word, to alter the rhythm, was to destroy the law itself, by destroying the sacred form under which it was revealed to man. The law was like prayer, which was agreeable to the divinity only on condition that it was recited correctly.... In primitive law, the exterior, the letter, is everything; there is no need of seeking the sense or spirit of it. The value of the law is not in the moral principle that it contains, but in the words that make up the formula. Its force is in the sacred words that compose it.[29]

The invention of writing only exacerbated the exaltation of form over substance. Now even the option of memorizing oral formulas was closed as the law was increasingly expressed in esoteric marks (glyphs) accessible only through a small circle of literate priests (hieros). The insistence upon the precision of the hieroglyphs continued to be a principal technique by which professional interpreters controlled the law, down through the Roman jurists, the medieval scholars at Bologna, and the English common law judges. Eventually the technique became unquestioned custom. By the 16th century, Shakespeare could resort to the plain meaning rule to get Antonio out of trouble in *The Merchant of Venice*, knowing that he drew on a tradition rooted in millennia of legal practice: Antonio defaults on his loan to Shylock, by the written terms of which he shall therefore forfeit "a pound of flesh nearest his heart." In a quick double dose of irony, the court awards judgment to Shylock according to the literal words of the document, but then uses the same words to prevent his satisfaction:

> The words expressly are 'a pound of flesh.'
> Take thy bond, take thou thy pound of flesh;
> But, in the cutting it ... shed thou no blood,
> nor cut thou less nor more
> But just a pound of flesh; if thou tak'st more
> Or less than a just pound—be it but so much

As makes it light or heavy in the substance,
Or the division of the twentieth part
Of one poor scruple; nay, if the scale do turn
But in the estimation of a hair—
Thou diest, and all thy goods are confiscate.[30]

While he's ridiculing the plain meaning rule here, Shakespeare is also reporting its tenacity in the law. It would come as no surprise to him to learn that there are judges sitting today who still exact their pound of flesh through the plain meaning rule.

2. The intrinsic canons of construction are too contradictory and enigmatic to be called rules, and are ignored as often as they are used.

They have been compared to proverbs and aphorisms: there seems to be wise advice in them for every situation, but nothing you can really pin down, and nothing you have to pay attention to if you don't want to.

In a sort of battle-by-Chinese-fortune-cookie, for every canon that is pulled out, its opposite can be produced.[31] (All quotations are from actual cases or statutes.)

On the One Hand	On the Other Hand
Grammar and punctuation are assumed to follow approved usage.	"Courts are not bound by grammatical rules." [C]ourts ... will disregard the punctuation or will repunctuate...."[32]
Common words are given their ordinary popular meanings, and technical words their technical meanings.	If "context or other considerations show a contrary intent," then common words may have technical meanings and vice versa."[33]
Every word must be given effect.	Words in a contract which are wholly inconsistent with its nature or with the main intention of the parties are to be rejected."[34] "Words having no meaning or [not] in harmony with the legislative intent ... may be treated as surplusage."[35] "Superfluity does not vitiate."[36]

On the One Hand	On the Other Hand
A specific provision controls a general one.	"[T]his rule does not apply except when there is some repugnance ... between the specific and general...."[37] Moreover, "particular clauses of a contract are subordinate to its general intent."[38] And , "it is a cardinal rule ... that the courts look at the language of the whole act ... and if ... they can collect from the broader expressions ... the real intention of the legislature it is their duty to give effect to the broader [over the more specific ones]."[39]
An interpretation that makes the text valid is preferred to one that makes it void.	But only "if it can be done without violating the intention of the parties,"[40] or "if the [statutory] language will reasonably permit...."[41]
The text must be construed as a whole, all of its parts integrated into a harmonious scheme with a coherent purpose.	This rule "has no application where the words of the statute are so plain as to require no judicial interpretation and, in doubtful cases ... will not be applied counter to the evident intent of the legislature."[42]
Statutes *in pari materia* (on the same subject) are to be construed together as a harmonious	"[I]t is only when one statute is unclear that another should be called in aid to explain it."[43]
Expressio unius est exclusio alterius. The expression of one is the exclusion of others.	The *expressio* maxim "is increasingly considered unreliable ... for it stands on the faulty premise that all alternative[s] ... were necessarily considered and rejected...."[44]
Ejusdem generis. When a general category follows a list of specifics, the category is limited to things of the same class as the specifics.	*Ejusdem generis* "rests on a mere presumption, easily rebutted by anything that shows the larger subject was in fact in the [author's] view."[45]

On the One Hand	On the Other Hand
Noscitur a sociis. Words are known by the textual company they keep.	"That a word may be known by the company it keeps is, however, not an invariable rule, for the word may have a character of its own not to be submerged by association."[46]
Contracts are construed against those who draft them.	"[T]he rule that uncertain provisions are to be interpreted against the party who caused them is but one of the standards for decision, and it must be balanced against others...."[47]
Statutes contrary to common law are to be narrowly construed.	"We do not consider ourselves at liberty to apply any rule of 'strict construction' to this or any other statute simply because it happens to be in derogation of the common law."[48]
Penal statutes are to be narrowly construed in favor of the accused's rights.	"Penal laws are not enacted for the encouragement of crime and the protection of criminals, but for the sole and express purpose of punishing and suppressing crime and thereby protecting society, and it is the paramount duty of courts to so construe them...."[49]
Social welfare statutes are to be liberally construed to accomplish their intended reforms.	"The remedial nature of legislation does not justify a construction which gives to statutory language an application and meaning not intended by lawmakers."[50]
Legal texts should be construed to avoid constitutional questions.	Courts "cannot press statutory construction to the point of disingenuous evasion' even to avoid a constitutional question."[51]

Even if you ignore the tit-for-tat nature of the canons and latch onto one of them that seems to make sense for the text at hand, you will find it's so enigmatic that you can apply it to justify pretty much any result you'd like to reach. This is because virtually every canon has a vague cloud at its core which can fog over a multitude of situations: phrases like "approved usage," "ordinary and technical," "given effect," "specific and general," "narrowly construed," "liberally construed," and so on.

The cloud can become downright mystifying for anyone honestly seeking guidance. Under the canon of ejusdem generis, when a general category follows a list of specific items the general is limited to things of the same genre or class. But what is the class? The canon doesn't help you identify it. You're limited only by your imagination, and by what you can persuade others is reasonable. A contract for sale of a farm together with its "cows, pigs, sheep and all other animals," does not include the seller's pet cockatoo if the class of animals is identified as economically productive farm animals, or quadrapeds; but does include the cockatoo if the class is identified as economically valuable animals, or domesticated ones. Likewise, it is said that a text is to be "construed as a whole, all of its parts integrated into a harmonious scheme with a coherent purpose," and that "statutes in pari materia are to be construed together as a harmonious scheme." But there are as many coherence schemes in legal texts as there are patterns in Rorschach ink blots.

A major federal statute, for instance, prohibits racial discrimination in housing, allows exemptions, and sets up an enforcement agency to prosecute violators. The prohibition, exemption, and enforcement provisions could well conflict, but can be integrated into the harmonious scheme of your choice depending upon whether you impose the coherent purpose of "ending racial discrimination," the coherent purpose of "balancing racial discrimination with freedom of association," or the coherent purpose of "allowing the prosecutor discretion to root out the worst forms of racial discrimination."

Or take the coherent purpose of the Constitution: is it to set up a government of limited powers, or separated powers, or dispersed powers, or to promote political representation and protect minorities, or to promote commerce, or something quite different yet? Different coherence schemes lead to different results. Or take a typical array of local government ordinances: one requiring environmental protection, one regulating planning and zoning, one subsidizing housing, one controlling sewers and roads. What is the coherent subject of which they are each a part? Environmental protection? Housing? Promotion of the economy? Orderly urbanization? Pursuit of the general welfare? Pick your subject, get your result. The pieces can be made to fit many patterns. All such efforts to harmonize legal texts work just like The Wizard of Oz. Imagine that text as a childhood coming-of-age dream: The Yellow Brick Road may be the path to fortune, the Cowardly Lion is probably false courage, and fear of the Wizard represents needless fear of the unknown. Now imagine it as a political allegory for 1890s Populism: The Yellow Brick Road becomes the gold standard, the Lion is William Jennings Bryan, the Wizard is the President of the United States. And so on, according to the templates of your imagination.

Forgetting the canons

In the final analysis, none of this jousting by maxim really makes a difference anyway because the canons may be ignored with impunity. The courts feel perfectly free to treat them as a sideshow and simply to turn their backs on them. "These rules are not the masters of the courts," the Minnesota Supreme Court once said, "but merely their servants...."[52] The remark was directed to specific canons, but has been retargeted by subsequent courts against them all. Justice Frankfurter remarked on another occasion that the canons "are not in any true sense rules of law. So far as valid, they are what Mr. Justice Holmes called them, axioms of experience."[53] Another federal judge denies that they are even valid as axioms, asserting that as expressions of experience they "are just plain wrong."[54] And the scholarly authors of a current classroom text on legislation surely call their shots correctly when they observe that "almost everybody thinks the canons are bunk."[55]

3. Extrinsic evidence of intended purpose cannot constrain interpreters because the evidence is limitless, manipulable, and unordered, and because "intended purpose" is usually a fiction anyway.

The third rule of the Old Story was that if the first two rules failed to clear up ambiguities you could bring in extrinsic evidence of intent. With this, the Old Story nearly lets the mask slip off of its claim to objectivity. We've seen that the first two rules, on plain meaning and intrinsic canons of construction, fail to resolve ambiguities if the interpreter so desires. Now we're told to attack the ambiguities with anything within reach—the entire range of historical, social, and political data of which judges may take judicial notice—in an evidentiary free-for-all. Would we feel constrained if we had been invited to referee a game, the third rule of which is that we may consider any type of ball, token or object as the scoring piece, the play may take place on or off the field and even outside the stadium, anyone on or off the teams may be considered a player, and we may count any move as a scoring point so long as the players and fans permit it?

Now legal modernists are generally enthusiastic about historical, social and political data because it breaches the myopic plain meaning rule and begins to grapple with law as it is actually lived; it moves away from law in books to law in action. So the modernist point is not that these materials should be ignored (though some, like some legislative history materials, should be discarded as fraudulent). It is, rather, that it is impossible to use the materials the way the Old Story claims to use them: as objective instruments to discover an intended purpose put into a text by its author. Here's why:

Limitless evidence

The Old Story doesn't even purport to have any doctrines limiting the scope of evidence that may be considered. Interpreters consider not only government documents and expert witnesses but often take judicial notice of information in newspapers, magazines, private letters, economic and sociological data, scholarly studies, books, television, and elsewhere. Both in its *Dred Scott* decision upholding slavery in 1858, and in its *Brown v. Board of Education* decision in 1954 ordering racial integration of schools, the U.S. Supreme Court considered copious historical evidence of the social context, writing, and implementation of the Constitution. Was it enough, was it indisputable, was it incomplete evidence in either case?

In deciding whether women have a right to abortion under the Constitution, should evidence of social context include theological, moral, philosophical, scientific, medical, sociological, and economic information, or just some of these? Which competing evidence within each category should be used? In interpreting the racial discrimination ban in the federal Fair Housing Act of 1968, are press reports relevant showing that the bill was passed four days after Martin Luther King was assassinated, that there were fires burning in the black ghetto, and that troops were stationed in the Capitol basement?

In deciding whether the federal Racketeer Influenced and Corrupt Organization Act applies to spousal blackmail in a divorce case, is it crucial that Congressional documents reflect a lot of concern about the Mafia and none about divorces at the time the Act was passed?

The Old Story offers no principled way to answer such questions. Its practitioners plunge into the extrinsic evidence, trimming and organizing it in a way that seems best to them, then announcing that "the" extrinsic evidence leads to certain conclusions. But of course they have selected some evidence and suppressed other on the basis of their own appraisals of its value. Modernists know this subjectivity is inescapable, that history and social context can't be constructed any other way. But they ask to see the appraisals openly articulated and defended rather than hidden under the traditional pretense that the extrinsic evidence is coldly and objectively "there."

Manipulable evidence

Much extrinsic evidence is crassly manipulated by others before it gets to lawyers or judges, so what the legal system sees may already be a distorted picture. Sociological, historical, and even "hard" scientific or statistical data are notoriously susceptible to the creative massage. (When, for example, the federal government threatened to cut off highway funds to states in which 50% of the drivers were exceeding the national 55 mile-per-hour speed limit, those states showed a remarkable jump in compliance virtually overnight. Later it was discovered officials had simply moved the electronic measuring equipment to spots where bad road conditions forced slow speeds.) In addition, fictional writing on the one hand and the paper shredder on the other have often provided false accounts of context, intentions, and implementation of legal texts. But these clandestine manipulations are not the most cynical. The prize for cynicism goes to the officially approved, judicially endorsed, fraud in the public records of legislative bodies, particularly of the United States Congress.

While we have no reason to doubt the veracity of prints of Congressional bills or of committee reports which analyze legislation, witnesses' testimony and documents received at public hearings on the other hand are often changed before being published. The Congressional Record, which by statute is supposed to be "substantially a verbatim report of proceedings" on the floor of the House and Senate, is in many ways a journal of lies.[56] That printed record is hard to reconcile with the video version of it recorded by C-SPAN. About 70% of what appears in the Record is never spoken.[57] But the 30% still need not actually be uttered. Members may send "revisions" and "corrections" down to the print shop before the Record appears the next day, revising what they actually said to what they wish they had said. Under the guise of "corrections," positions have been changed 180 degrees, avowals erased and added, and, with the cooperation of another member, whole new dialogs concocted. Disgruntled members of Congress sued, unsuccessfully, in 1984 to try to force the Record to a higher standard of verbatim accuracy.[58] All this is a scandal, but the Record is a scandal for other reasons as well. On a normal day, what it actually records are the words of a few delivered to a half-empty chamber in which only the recorders are listening. Many of those words are "canned colloquies" written in advance to plant some desired interpretive spin on the legislation being enacted. "It is handed to the other actor and the two of them read it like a grade B radio script," according to a former member of Congress who became a federal judge.[59] Yet, like fish leaping for the bait, the courts frequently latch on to fragments from the Congressional Record—sometimes six or eight words will do—as the crux of a statute's meaning. At last count, the federal courts were citing Congressional Record statements in five or six hundred cases a year, and many thousand more references were made in unreported cases, administrative agency decisions, and lawyers' opinion letters.

In state legislatures, verbatim floor debate is rarely recorded and published hearings and committee reports are few, so legislative intent is fabricated from other materials that at least some state courts are willing to accept: internal letters, staff memos, correspondence from lobbyists, and other unpublished documents dug from the files of individual legislators and previously known only to a few in the legislature as a whole. Some courts even credit affidavits or live testimony of former or current legislators who claim to report what was said about a bill in the legislature years earlier.[60] Attorneys litigating the meaning of statutory language have been known to write such affidavits, fly to the capital in search of any legislators who will sign them in exchange for political favors, and return to the courtroom the next day with a triumphant declaration of legislative intent.

Unordered evidence

The Old Story provides no rules to rank the various types of extrinsic evidence. News reports may be given more credit than an historian's treatise, a flare of rhetoric in Senate debate more than sociological data, a scientist's testimony more than business practices, economic statistics more than psychological tests, a private diary more than a President's speech. Or vice versa. Or all may be given equal weight. Or no weight. This is not to say there could not be a definitive rank order for such evidence. It's common sense that different types of evidence will strike us as weighty or not according to the context, our purpose, and our values. We do the weighing, subjectively, ourselves. The Old Story denies this common sense, insisting upon the sham that certain types of evidence are inherently weighter than others and therefore that interpreters are objectively constrained by it. Yet revealingly, the story offers no formal rules for ranking, and anyone who looks at ten or twenty judicial opinions will see that judges assign different weight to extrinsic evidence to suit the needs of the moment.

There is something of a custom in constitutional interpretation, it is true, of giving special weight to celebrated editorialized materials like *The Federal-*

ist Papers and Madison's fragmented notes on the Constitutional convention. But legal doctrine has not assigned that weight. Certain historians, lawyers, and judges have; others are skeptical of its wisdom. (Madison himself adamantly disapproved of the idea of using of his notes or other personal opinions of the framers to interpret the Constitution.)[61] Perhaps equal insights may be gained from the anti-federalist *Letters from the Federal Farmer,* the Articles of Confederation, newspapers and pamphlets of the era, the debates in the state ratifying conventions, letters and diaries of the framers, and the debates of the first Congress in which many of the original framers sat. A fuller understanding may require attention to historical data on colonial property ownership, the debtors' rebellions, commerce, religious conflict, penal practices, land speculation, and the exclusion of women and slaves from contracting and voting. All these materials, among others, have been used from time to time as extrinsic evidence of Constitutional meaning. Their weight is up to the interpreter. Legal doctrine sets them no fixed position in any hierarchy of authority.

Likewise, records of legislative history, far from falling into the neat rank suggested earlier by the Old Story, bob like flotsam and jetsam in the wake of a bill's enactment, awaiting any scavenger who can piece them together into a plausible interpretation. "Unhappily," admitted Justice Frankfurter, "there is no table of logarithms for statutory construction. No item of evidence has a fixed or even average weight. One or another may be decisive in one set of circumstances, while of little value elsewhere. A painstaking, detailed report by a Senate Committee bearing directly on the immediate question may settle the matter. A loose statement even by a chairman of a committee, made impromptu in the heat of debate, less informing in cold type than when heard on the floor, will hardly be accorded the weight of an encyclical."[62] Frankfurter's refreshing realism is undercut only by the dogmatism of his last sentence ascribing little weight to statements made in the heat of Congressional debate. In practice, when it suits their purpose judges frequently accord decisive weight to precisely such statements. Frankfurter himself did the same. The ordered hierarchy is actually a constantly shaken grab bag.

The fiction of intent or purpose

Benjamin Franklin's intent seems clear from these words in his will: "My fine crabtree walking stick with a gold head, curiously wrought in the form of the cap of liberty, I give to my friend, and the friend of mankind, George Washington. If it was a sceptre, he has merited and would become it."[63] Obviously, he intended Washington to have the stick. No one having raised any doubts about that intent, and no other problems having appeared, Washington indeed got it. In such circumstances, practical people and the law are on pretty solid ground in speaking of "the intent" of an author of a legal text. Such circumstances are more often the exception than the rule, however, in litigated cases. The reality of "intent," even of a single author, begins to wobble as soon as problems push on it. When two or more authors' intentions are at work, as in a contract, you can retain the notion of intent only by winking at the artifices necessary to hold it together. When dozens, hundreds, or thousands of persons, as in legislatures, constitutional conventions, or direct ballot initiatives, have "authored" a legal text, intent dissolves into a fairy tale requiring complete suspension of disbelief. The problems with the idea of intent have long been documented by modernist writers.[64]

Levels of intent

Our intentions can be stated concretely or generally on a ladder of abstraction, so it's always difficult for others, or sometimes ourselves, to know which statement is the most meaningful. Each of these is a plausible statement of Franklin's intent: 1) He intended Washington to have his cane. 2) He intended to express his friendship for Washington. 3) He intended to invest Washington with a symbol of sovereignty for the benefit of the country. 4) He intended to honor Washington. Washington cherished the gift and passed it to his brother in his own will, but suppose he had disdained it and used it to clean mud from his boots. Could Franklin's heirs have sued for return of the cane on the ground that his true intention had been defeated? Assuming other legal hurdles could be overcome, the answer would depend in part on whether Franklin's intent is taken at level 1) or levels 3) or 4).

Each of these is a plausible statement of the intention of the authors of the equal protection clause of the 14th Amendment:[65] 1) To say nothing about schools. 2) To overturn the Black Codes. 3) To add constitutional underpinning to the Civil Rights Act of 1866. 4) To assure that state laws operate the same upon blacks as upon whites. 5) To assure racial equality. 6) To assure equality between men. 7) To assure equality between people. As the statements move up the ladder of abstraction they increase their scope and sometimes conflict with a more concrete statement that went before. Legislative intent of statutes is the same.

Each of these is a plausible statement of the intent of Congress in enacting the national 55 mile-per-hour speed limit law in 1973: 1) To slow speeds on the highways. 2) To save fuel. 3) To save lives. 4) To save fuel and lives. 5) To make the burden of fuel saving fall disproportionately on western states with higher driving speeds. 6) To stand up to the Arab oil cartel. 7) To show the public that Congress, unlike the Nixon administration, had an active energy policy. 8) To make America independent of foreign oil. 9) To strengthen national defense. 10) To promote the general welfare. Some of these intentions encompass others, some conflict, and some no longer applied with the passage of time though the law was still on the books for years before being repealed. The result in a particular case may depend upon which intention you discern as dominant, yet the Old Story about interpretation offers no criteria by which to choose one over another.

Unforeseen circumstances

Authors of legal documents frequently fail to foresee circumstances in which their texts eventually land, and naturally leave no evidence of their intentions about them. A mayor of St. Louis left $200,000 in his will in 1851 "for relief to all poor emigrants and travelers coming to St. Louis on their way to settle the west." In 1934, his descendants sought to dissolve the trust, then grown to $1,000,000, on the ground that the west was settled. They lost, and the money is still spent on travelers aid today at the St. Louis bus station, but the court obviously had to guess about the benefactor's intentions regarding a situation that had never crossed his mind.[66]

Did the authors of the equal protection clause of the 14th Amendment to the Constitution intend it to require racial integration of public schools? Segregationists roared "No!" when the question arose in 1953–54, pointing to the widespread practice of segregating schools both before and after 1868 when the Amendment was adopted. But in *Brown v. Board of Education* the Supreme Court observed that mandatory and free public schooling was not yet common in 1868, and seemed to suggest that the real question was what the authors would have intended had they foreseen the vast development of public education and its critical importance as of 1954. On that question there was no evidence, so the Court apparently (it's hard to tell from the opinion) imputed an intent. So it goes whenever changed circumstances surprise an author's original intent: the courts have to "imaginatively reconstruct," that is, guess, what the author probably would have intended, and that means we're really dealing with something other than author's intent.

Irrelevant intentions

Actual intentions may have little to do with the language of the legal document. The point applies to private as well as public texts, but a good description of the problem appears in a dissent by U.S. Supreme Court Justice Scalia regarding legislative intent (which he also dislikes for other, anti-modernist reasons). The constitutionality of a state statute requiring school prayers turned on whether the legislature's purpose in enacting it was secular or religious. Scalia let go a fusillade of realpolitik:

> [A] particular legislator need not have voted for the Act either because he wanted to foster religion or because he wanted to improve education. He may have thought the bill would provide jobs for his district, or may have wanted to make amends with a faction of his party he had alienated on another vote, or he may have been a close friend of the bill's sponsor, or he may have been repaying a favor he owed the Majority Leader, or he may have hoped the Governor would appreciate his vote and make a fundraising appearance for him, or he may have been pressured to vote for a bill he disliked by a wealthy contributor or by a flood of constituent mail, or he may have been seeking favorable publicity, or he may have been reluctant to hurt the feelings of a loyal staff member who worked on the bill, or he may have been settling an old score with a legislator who opposed the bill, or he may have been mad at his wife who opposed the bill, or he may have been intoxicated and utterly unmotivated when the vote was called, or he may have accidentally voted "yes" instead of "no," or, of course, he may have had (and very likely did have) a combination of some of the above and many other motivations.[67]

Access to intentions

We have no access to most of the intentions Scalia lists. So, too, with the real intentions of will makers, contractors, treaty negotiators. They are the private contents of individual minds, unrecorded in any formal way, discoverable often only by the flimsy evidence of which gossip is made, or not at all. The Old Story about interpretation, of course, knows this and partly for that reason makes some effort to exclude flimsy evidence through the plain meaning rule, parole evidence rule, statute of frauds, stiff formalities to make a will, sworn signature requirements, and so forth. In other words, by these doctrines (which, however, ultimately fail to work) the Old Story confesses that access to actual intentions is so poor that it will not pursue them. Instead, it will pursue records of intentions that the legal system, as a practical matter, can find and handle. And for the most part these will be incomplete records that fail to reflect real intentions.

Whose intent counts?

When a document has more than two authors, the law is uncertain who counts as an author. Here are some of the sources to which courts attribute authorial intent from time to time: Corporate contracts—executive officers, the board of directors, and any employees or agents whose conduct during the "course of dealing" or "course of performance" of the contract can be offered as evidence of the corporation's "intent." Administrative regulations—a single agency head, a board of several members in whom legal authority resides, the division and bureau chiefs down the bureaucratic hierarchy, legal counsel, field employees who implement the regulation, officials in the White House or the governor's office who oversee executive branch policy, and legislative committees and staffs who oversee the agency. Statutes—the legislative author of the bill, co-sponsors of the bill, committees that prepared the bill, legislators who voted for it, those who voted against it (taking their reasons for opposing the bill as meaningful understanding of its provisions), all 535 members of the Congress or all members of other legislative bodies, executive branch officials who drafted and pushed the legislation or those who opposed it (taking their opposition as meaningful understanding), the president or governor who took a position on the legislation and who signed it or vetoed it, lobbyists who worked for or against the legislation, the general public, the political, historical, or social circumstances which gave rise to the legislation, and subsequent legislatures and executive administrations that, either through their announcements and actions or their silence and failure to amend, expressed a certain understanding of the legislation. Constitution—James Madison; Madison, Hamilton, and Jay; key framers at the Constitutional Convention; proponents at the Convention; opponents at the Convention; all delegates who attended the Convention; all delegates to the Convention, including those who boycotted; state ratifying bodies; pamphleteers and lobbyists pro and con during ratification process; those who voted for or appointed delegates to the Convention or state ratifying bodies; citizens eligible to vote; early Congresses in which many original framers of the Constitution sat; political, historical and social circumstances which gave rise to the Constitution; and later counterparts to all of these during adoption of amendments to the Constitution.

Adding individual intentions together

This problem is fatal by itself to any notion of an intent held by a group of individuals. The difficulty is that, at least when individual intentions differ, we have no way of adding them together into a single intent. When we speak of "the" intent of a group, we do not employ any method of arithmetic, psychology, sociology, or physiology that combines multiple contents of subjective minds into a single thing. There is no such method. We employ, instead, the method of literature; we speak pure fiction. How, for example could we combine the intentions of a legislator who voted for the 55 mile-per-hour speed statute to do the Majority leader a favor, another who read the bill's language carefully and hoped to save lives, another who had not read it and wished only to please a contributor, another who intended to save fuel but expected actual speeds to slow to about 60 if the limit were set at 55, another who wanted only to put pressure on the Nixon administration to come up with an energy policy, and so on through the 535 members of Congress? The usual way out of this quandary is to ignore it. The next way is to aver that you have abandoned narrow "intent" to seek "legislative purpose" instead. But the move to purpose is merely a move up the familiar ladder of abstraction to a statement that is general enough to cover all legislators' specific intentions. Such statements nearly always either fail to embrace some ("the purpose was to conserve energy" fails to cover the legislator who wished only to please a contributor, and several others) or are vacuous ("to establish an energy policy," or, better yet, the generic "they intended that the words of the bill become law"), unable to guide concrete cases.

At this point, some interpreters begin to supplement their talk of purpose with "presumptions." We must presume the legislature acts for coherent civic ends; we must presume that legislators are reasonable; we must presume that the legislators have delegated their individual intentions to a few key actors and therefore intend to endorse whatever their delegates do; we must presume the legislature responds to the social-political context of the time; we must presume that a legislature has a general spirit or mood; we must presume that statutes are a bargain struck between interest groups to maximize their welfare; we must presume that the Constitution has a coherent structure, or that its purpose is to set up a government of limited powers, or separated powers, or dispersed powers, or to promote political representation and protect minorities, and so on. As philosophies of government, these presumptions may or may not have something to recommend them. One may even argue that it is good government to implement them through a fiction of legislative intent or purpose. But they and the fiction must be defended for their own sake, then, as the interpreter's philosophy of government, and that is quite a different matter from the Old Story's claim that the interpreter is discovering legislative intent.[68]

Discretion to honor, or ignore, intent

The final problem with the notion of intent is that even if we could find it, it is up to us whether we want to honor it or not. It is natural, but wrong, to believe that a text must mean what its author meant it to mean. A text, like any other cultural work, has meaning for us whether we choose to adhere to the author's intent, give it a bit of weight, or to ignore it altogether. And in interpreting laws, our actual practice is to sometimes adhere to, sometimes weigh a bit, and sometimes ignore, what we believe to be the author's original intent. This is especially true of Supreme Court justices who on many occasions have proclaimed their allegiance to the original intent of the Constitution's framers: they have just as frequently dealt the cards of Constitutional meaning with a poker face of absolute silence about original intent. The reverse is also true: justices who have made much of the need to struggle free of original intent in the name of an "evolving" Constitution have never hesitated to invoke the names of the framers when useful to confirm desired results.

Thought Window:[69]

The Wizard of Oz, Michelangelo, Casablanca, and the Constitution: Original Intent Anyone?

Is the meaning the author originally had in mind the true meaning of a work? Rather than turn the question into an intellectual riddle, let's look to see how we actually answer it every day, what our actual cultural practices are.

Often we do take author's intent as the one that really counts, particularly when what we're after is communication of a message. If your kids send you to the store with a note reading "quart of chocolate ice cream," you'd better not come home with a quart of motor oil and a lame excuse that you read the text only as suggesting an analogy. So too, with wills, love letters, and the instructions on how to light our gas furnaces: author's meaning holds a mighty interest for us.

But when we see the text as something other than the author's messenger, sometimes we privilege the author's intent, sometimes we don't. Dylan Thomas told us that his lines on being "green and carefree, famous among the barns/ About the happy yard and singing as the farm was home" recall his childhood at his aunt's farm in Wales, but many of us would say the poem means more to us than just that. Thomas might agree. It was e.e. cummings, I believe, who, when asked if he meant a certain thing by a poem he had written, replied, "I do now that you point it out to me." At times, we don't' even care whether the author would accept our meaning; the work has meaning for us on our own terms. This is particularly true in art museums, where the rule for many is that "beauty is in the eye of the beholder," and in the galleries of modern abstract art where you hear whispered, "I suppose it's one of those that means whatever you want it to mean." At the same time, there is a contrary tradition, rooted in Renaissance individualism and boosted by modernist subjectivism, of valuing artist's intent above all else. When the U.S. Customs Service classified Brancusi's bronze "Bird in Space" as a taxable knickknack it failed to acknowledge this tradition, but a court set the Service straight and reclassified the bronze as a duty-free sculpture, honoring artist's meaning. When Robert Rauschenberg was commissioned to do a portrait of art dealer Iris Clert, he sent a telegram reading: "This is a portrait of Iris Clert if I say so." Many in the art world agreed, because for them artist's intent trumped everything. Here are some other examples of our mixed habits of privileging and ignoring author's intent:

The Wizard of Oz

Generations of Americans now think of this only as an enchanting coming-of-age story, or a classic fairy tale of Everyperson encountering Good and Evil on the road of life. Few know that on one level the author, journalist L. Frank Baum, wrote it in 1900 as a political allegory for the Populist movement. Oz is the abbreviation for ounce, and the Yellow Brick Road is the gold standard. Dorothy wore silver shoes (not ruby red as in the movie) which represent free silver coinage. Dorothy is Everyperson, the Tin Woodman is the industrial worker (who, dehumanized by working in factories, lacks a heart), the Scarecrow is the farmer (who lacks a brain to know what his best political interests are), the Cowardly Lion is William Jennings Bryan, the munchkins are the "little people," the Wicked Witch of the East stands for bankers and capitalists, and the Wizard is the President who rules by trickery and deception. Baum's later statement that his story was meant only as pleasure for children was disingenuous in light of his Populist activism and the story's allegorical sympathy with the Populist call for an alliance of farmers, workers and common folks to expose political fraud and overthrow the power of the industrial capitalists. This is not the story told to children today. Everyone is quite happy that the author's original intent has been forgotten. Yet for millions the story has true meaning.

Michelangelo

When the Vatican began to clean Michelangelo's frescoes in the Sistine Chapel in the 1980s, the familiar soft, rounded, muted figures suddenly emerged as sharp, vividly colored (hot pinks! apple greens!) cartoon-like characters. Howls went up from the international art community: Michelangelo was being destroyed! When the dust of controversy settled, the evidence seemed to suggest that the restoration had not damaged Michelangelo's original work but had brought it back to life. What was removed was nearly 500 years of smoke, air pollution, and previous restorations. They had created the muted, sculptural forms that later generations took to be the genius of the artist. Some continue to dispute the evidence, others accept the "new" fresco style as Michelangelo's original intent and respect it for that reason, others now ignore the artist's intent and cherish the memory of the familiar forms which had become a canon of excellence for so much art criticism. Others speculate that Michelangelo foresaw the deterioration of the works, and deliberately painted them "too sharp, too bright" at the outset so they would tone down gradually over the centuries. Still others recall the various periods when Popes, oblivious to artist's intent, have ordered the genitalia on the frescoes' nudes to be painted over. Some of these positions seek to honor original intent, some to discount it. All are ways that viewers give meaning to the artistic text.

Casablanca

After computer technology made it feasible to add color to black-and-white movies, video producers began buying up the rights to the old first and second generation movies. Casablanca and other classics that had assumed hallowed meanings for film buffs were turned into splashy color versions for home viewing. Many agreed with actor Jimmy Stewart that colorization is "morally and artistically wrong." They urged the government to follow European nations whose laws give artists a continuing "moral right" to prevent any distortion of their works, even against copyright owners. Woody Allen testified to the U.S. Senate that colorization against the director's intent is "sinful.... If the director is not alive and his work has been historically established in black and white, it should remain true to its origin." Frank Capra, then 87, wrote to the U.S. Copyright Office: "I chose to shoot It's a Wonderful Life in black-and-white film. The lighting, the makeup for the actors and actresses, the camera and laboratory work, all were geared for black-and-white film, not color. I beseech you with all my heart and mind not to tamper with a classic in any form of the arts." The protests did not halt colorization. Too much money is involved. Color versions increase sales and rentals of home videos, and bring television stations bigger audiences. More people saw The Maltese Falcon in color in six months than saw the original black-and-white in the previous ten years. "There is a great deal of elitism involved here," said the owner of a colorization company, "the intellectual intent of a few to impose their own views and tastes on millions and millions of Americans." Well, I'll still take my Casablanca and others in black-and-white, thank you, but clearly there are lots of people who get as much meaning from the color versions. Moreover, we anti-color types haven't consistently respected artist's intent either: surely the old filmmakers didn't intend to have their movies reduced to miniature screens, projected in tones of glaring grey TV light, cut off at the edges, and viewed by two people in a living room.

Moral

Original intent is sometimes important to us, sometimes not. We have no consistent cultural practice. The question, then, whether the Constitution means what its framers originally meant (assuming we could discover that), depends upon what cultural practice we wish to adopt, and why. Seeking the Constitution's past has been justified on the grounds that it encourages social stability, protects settled expectations, taps the wisdom of our ancestors, is required by our "social contract," or produces a reverent devotion in the populace for a sacred civil text. Disregarding the past has been justified on the grounds that we don't want our Constitution to be a straightjacket for succeeding generations but a living document capable of fitting changing social needs, nor do we want to honor ignominious chapters in our nation's political history, nor privilege past moralities that we now find cruel or barbaric. Which of these values you and the justices privilege depends upon your and their philosophies of life and government, not a rule of language or law.

4. By making "reasonableness" its ultimate requirement, the Old Story quietly welcomes subjectivity after all. Moreover, the doctrines supposedly promoting rationality are fantasies.

So long as reason was some divine plan (in the days of natural law) or mechanical process (in the days of legal positivism), it seemed sensible to believe that the pulse of reason beating within the law originated in those immutable, outside sources. With modernism, the immutable sources disappear. Holmes could finally proclaim that "the common law is not a brooding omnipresence in the sky,"[70] precisely because reason was no longer a brooding omnipresence in the sky either. The pulse of reason beats within the law only to the rhythm of our own hearts. And one person does not march to the same beat as the next.

The Old Story about interpretation, much in the manner of Victorian sexual morality, quietly enjoyed this reality while piously denying it. Recall that one of the old doctrines—the "golden rule" of statutory interpretation—explicitly calls upon judges to avoid "absurd" or "manifestly unjust" results, a clear invitation to subjective judgments, because what is absurd or unjust to one person may seem reasonable to another.

Moreover, in the practice observable by any lawyer or judge day to day, interpreters do not follow the orderly steps from plain meaning to intrinsic aids to extrinsic evidence of purpose, then test for reasonableness. Rather, they rest their arguments upon one step alone, or any combination of steps, in any order. They are often silent about the other steps. Or else they temporarily rearrange the steps into a new coherent order. This is a particularly tempting move to make with evidence of intended purpose, because the so-called "purpose approach" enjoys such an ancient and honorable reputation that it's just as easy to think of it, and not the plain meaning approach, as the dominant tradition in legal interpretation. It goes back at least to Aristotle who wrote that "it is right, where the legislator's rule is inadequate or erroneous in virtue of its generality, to rectify the defect which the legislator himself, if he were present, and had he known it, would have rectified in legislating.... This is in fact the nature of the equitable."[71] It is embodied in the "mischief rule" of *Heydon's Case* of 1584.[72] It was captured quaintly by Plowden in the 1574 case of *Eyston v Studd*:

> It is not the words of the law, but the internal sense of it which makes the law, and our law, (like all others) consists of two parts, viz. of body and soul, the letter of the law is the body of the law, and the sense and reason of the law is the soul.... And the law may be resembled to a nut, which has a shell and a kernel within, the letter of the law represents the shell, and the sense of it the kernel, and as you will be no better for the nut if you make use only of the shell, so you will receive no benefit by the law, if you rely only upon the letter, and as the fruit and profit of the nut lies in the kernel, and not in the shell, so the fruit and profit of the law consists in the sense more than in the letter.[73]

Right down to our times, the purpose approach echoes through the opinions of the centuries just as loudly as the plain meaning rule. Its legitimacy is established in such famed decisions as *Riggs v. Palmer*[74] (a boy who murdered his grandfather by poison was not permitted to inherit the estate left to him in the grandfather's will, on the ground that the underlying purposes of the statute of wills could not have embraced homicidal heirs), *Holy Trinity Church*[75] (church was permitted to hire a foreign preacher, on the ground that the statute forbidding anyone to "assist ... migration of any alien ... under contract ... to perform labor or service of any kind" was intended to stem the influx of cheap, unskilled labor, not Christian ministers), and legions of other cases. "There is no more likely way to misapprehend the meaning of language—be it in a constitution, a statute, a will or a contract—than to read the words literally, forgetting the object which the document as a whole is meant to secure," wrote Judge Learned Hand in a 1947 opinion.[76] But like others, Hand would take the plain meaning route when the need arose, holding in another case that, "this is not a situation in which it would be proper not to follow the literal meaning of the words."[77] In short, judges and lawyers dip into, or ignore, plain meaning, purpose, and the intrinsic canons, in any order and when convenient.

- The canons of construction do not force internal coherence, as the Old Story has it, but are a set of open-ended contradictions, as shown above.
- Legislative history and other documents of extrinsic evidence are not used according to any rank order of weight, as noted above.
- The coherent overall purpose or structure of a legal text, especially including the Constitution, is in the eye of the beholder, as in Rorshach ink blots and the Wizard of Oz, previously mentioned.

Nor do the old doctrines promoting rationality of external consequences function as announced. Whether it's the golden rule of reasonableness in statutes, the rational basis or other test for constitutionality, or the insistence on reasonable ends for contracts and other private documents, the standard of reason is inevitably subjective: one interpreter's rationality may be another's absurdity. Well-known examples include *TVA v. Hill*,[78] where some justices thought a federal statute protecting endangered species required a $100 million dam to be abandoned to save the three-inch snail darter fish, while other justices found that absurd; and *Korematsu*[79] and related cases where a majority of justices without evidence presumed the existence of a rational basis for the mass internment of Japanese-American citizens during World War II, while the dissenters saw nothing but the rationalization of racism. More mundane examples can be found by the thousands in which the courts purport even to finely tune the degree of reason they require under categories of "strict scrutiny," "rational basis," "arbitrary and capricious," "substantial evidence," and other labels. One need not read many cases before concluding that the labels are inconsistently applied among courts, among judges on the same court in the same case, and even by single judges over time—indeed, that the labels are applied, perhaps subconsciously, after the interpreter has already determined whether the ultimate consequences are desirable.

Thought Window:[80]

Sometimes Plain Meaning, Sometimes Purpose

• At the urging of ranchers whose sheep were involuntarily serving as dinner food for local coyotes, the California Legislature passed "an Act fixing a bounty on coyote scalps" in 1891. Soon, in the capitalist spirit, "coyote farms" sprung up, whose proprietors raised Canis lupus for their valuable scalps and sold them to the state. The state of California felt obliged by the literal words of the statute to pay the bounties until it could repeal the law.

• In the elections of 1982, the governor of Pennsylvania pledged never to repeal the traditional prohibition on local gambling. A strong majority of state legislators was also on record opposing local games of chance. In a 1983 bill to revise the Pennsylvania codes, "for the purpose of deleting obsolete laws and consolidating and renumbering the codes," a clerk or a machine inadvertently included the number of the section prohibiting local gambling in the list of sections to be repealed. The Legislature passed the bill and the governor signed it, ignorant of the mistake. When someone discovered the error, poker games broke out all over the state. The governor and legislative leaders, aghast but believing the state powerless to halt the gambling because of the plain meaning of the repeal, rushed an emergency bill through the Legislature to reinstate the law.

• Congress reformed the immigration laws in 1986, providing amnesty to illegal aliens who applied for legal residence before May 5, 1988. But several federal courts across the nation extended the May 5 deadline for hundreds of thousands of applicants to May 16, August 31, and other dates. The courts reasoned that the Immigration and Naturalization Service had misled and confused applicants about the deadline, so it would have been unfair to hold them to the statute's literal words.

• Five days before Christmas, the *Los Angeles Times* reported: "Parking officers in Los Angeles will no longer write up violations of most posted signs on Christmas and other holidays, it was announced Friday. No parking will be allowed at red curbs, in bus zones or where stopping and parking are banned around the clock. But most other minor violations will be ignored under a new policy of the Department of Transportation.... The policy does not have the force of law, but its provisions are the same as those of a proposed ordinance the city Council is expected to pass, possibly in January." The no-enforcement policy had been requested by merchants whose customers were having a hard time finding legal parking places during the Christmas shopping rush.

There Are No Meaningful Rules for Finding the Meaning in the Texts of Judicial Precedents

The claim that judges are significantly constrained by case law can no longer be taken seriously. If all that is meant by the statement, "judges follow precedent," is that they often choose to adhere to broad policies set by earlier courts (say, permitting capital punishment, prohibiting racial segregation, requiring the jury to be instructed on comparative negligence), the claim is true but trivial. For they also sometimes dodge the policies, which are usually vague enough to permit wide, even conflicting, variations when applied. In any event, it is not primarily the text of a precedent case by which the judges know what the policy is; they know it by knowing the social, political, and judicial cultural context of the policy and its makers. The Old Story's claim about precedent is the much stronger one of stare decisis that the texts of prior cases themselves control judicial behavior. And this claim is naive.

By the 19th century, aided by the spread of inexpensive printing, officially published reports replaced the odd collections of notes by private individuals that had for centuries passed as case law. Judges increasingly moved from oral, to written, to printed opinions. A case report was now an authoritatively authored, officially published, widely available text, in a definitive format. The caste of legal interpreters had managed to upgrade and re-enshrine the judicial text in a form suitable to the conditions of the industrial revolution and the centralized state at the very moment when the industrial revolution and the state threatened to overwhelm judicial texts with a tide of legislative texts less respectful of the customs of the common law and its elites. It remained only for Dean Langdell of Harvard Law School to play "legal theologian," as Holmes called him,[81] and turn case texts into the Holy Grail. In the 1870s, Langdell threw out the traditional textbooks and lectures. He substituted "scientific study" of the "principles" of law by the sole means of reading the concrete cases in which they "develop." Langdell's case method was the unique product that law schools would sell. Other university departments, or self-study, could not compete with it. The case method also assured law practice of increased complexity, prestige, and business. A vast expansion of law schools, and the rise of organized bar associations to exclude those who had not had formal training (which, not accidentally, kept out people of color, women, Jews, Catholics, and the immigrant poor, who were generally not admitted to the schools) quickly followed. The rest is history. The case method of pedagogy gave the law schools and practicing lawyers protected marketplace niches, but at the cost of making American law students, professors, lawyers, and judges Langdell's prisoners.[82] They are its prisoners even today, despite the following devastating objections:

- What goes into a case decision in the first place is, of course, a subjective selection by the judge from the stream of life that has brought the case to court. What gets left out is as interesting as what is included. Too often the economic, political, philosophical, and social contexts are omitted or selectively picked. (Langdell encouraged this to promote law as an independent science. Someone once wrote that "[i]f law is, at all the product of society, then Langdell's science of law was a geology without rocks.")[83] The judge may also often ignore with impunity specific facts, other cases, ideas. So the opinions are frequently most telling by their silences, and subsequent interpreters always have the option of looking back at the original context of the case to gather a fuller picture.

- Then of what is written in the opinion, how are we to analyze it? The case method as a teaching technique requires surgical dissection of precedents into components that the judges themselves in former eras had never insisted upon with any rigor. Facts, procedural history, issue, holding, dicta, and reasoning are law professors' categories, imposed from the podium to organize discussion and instill rigor in mushy student minds. Even today, when these categories can be spotted at all in the cases, it is likely the judge has stated them in a way that law professors consider unsatisfactorily mushy. So there is the problem that categories now considered indispensable to "lawyer-like analysis" of case law do not arise from the practice of judges but from the practice of professional educators.
- There is next the insuperable problem that no one can agree how to identify the content of key categories, particularly facts, holding (ratio decidendi), and dicta. A holding for some is merely an explicit or implicit principle of law appearing anywhere in the opinion, so finding it can resemble the pea-and-thimble game at a carnival. For others it is the court's ruling of law relating to only the material facts. But there is no litmus test for materiality. Even facts the court itself asserted, or denied, were material, may be denied, or asserted, to be material by a subsequent interpreter. A holding for one interpreter has often turned into a dictum for the next, and vice versa. Compounding the problem is the reality that the content of each category may be stated at various levels on a ladder of abstraction (a problem we've run into before). Facts, holding, dicta, and reasoning may all be stated narrowly so as to seem to apply only to a next case that is the precedent's identical twin, or broadly so as to seem to apply to all evils of the world. The problem kills any illusion of an ascertainable set of facts or definitive ratio decidendi. Taking the notorious snail-in-the-ginger-beer case (*Donoghue v. Stevenson*) as his example, a contemporary legal philosopher once made a modest list of facts that might be taken as material, and asked how many alternatives would be generated by stating them at different levels of generality:

> The number of permutations of n objects taken two at a time is n(n–1), taken three at a time is n(n–1) (n–2) ... etc. If, for example, the total number of fact-elements and levels of generality of statement of these in Donoghue v. Stevenson were 6, the number of logically possible alternative rationes would be 720; if the former number were 10 the logically possible alternatives would be 3,628,800.[84]

- There is, in addition, the problem that there is no agreement about which precedental texts deserve most weight. As the occasion demands, some interpreters will rely especially upon majority opinions, some upon dissents, others upon well-reasoned opinions, moving opinions, old opinions, recent opinions, or opinions by renowned judges. Historians even give weight to judges' off-the-bench speeches, letters, diaries, and conversations, and these may ultimately influence subsequent interpreters of the primary text. Finally, when several justices produce individual opinions in a single case, none commanding agreement of a majority, subsequent interpreters will nominate as the holding their favored morsels from various individual opinions.[85]
- Then there is the problem of the *exceptions* to a precedental rule. For example, while we often say that the *Miranda* rule governs the law of constitutional confession, it is more accurate to say that the exceptions to *Miranda* are so numerous as to have denied the 1966 precedent of much of its staying power—so much so that C.J. Rehnquist, the rule's most ardent critic, found no need to overrule the beleaguered precedent when he finally had a choice to do so.
- The sheer number of appellate cases renders stare decisis futile. In the past, when published cases were few, it was easier to reconcile them into groups that appeared somewhat stable. But modern technology has destabilized the case law by expanding it exponentially. First, mass production of the printed word, and later, electronic movement of words, made so much case law available that every lawyer can find fistsfull of precedents in support of or against virtually any proposition. Tens of thousands of decisions of state and federal courts are currently published in America each year (and that's only a small portion of those actually decided). It may not be accidental that the early Legal Realists started questioning the coherence of the case law a generation after Shepards' Citation Service was inaugurated in 1873 allowing lawyers to track every subsequent citation of a precedent and therefore to see the quick changes it undergoes in the hands of later interpreters. The technological basis of the early Shepards'—index cards and cheap paperback printing—was paleolithic, of course, compared to today's computer searches of case law. Computer technology has dispersed power to hundreds of thousands of individual lawyers in the form of instant, infinitely flexible paths of access to hundreds of thousands of precedents and subparts—even single words—of precedents. By permitting access to subparts, the computer fragments the precedents into

> puzzle pieces which lawyers and judges may then reassemble into a precedental reading of their choice.

•••

Isn't this kind of thinking about the instability of judicial precedents terribly dangerous? What happens to the law as a source of stability predictable enough to rely upon in planning our affairs? What happens to the fairness of having to treat like cases alike? To our expectation that judges adhere to the rule of law rather than their own preferences? To the basic efficiency of avoiding treating every new case as if it's the first time the legal system dealt with it? In short, where will we be without stare decisis?

Well, we will be pretty much where we have always been. My objections to the Old Story's version of stare decisis aren't recommendations for reform, they're descriptions of what we've already got. The case law has never been stable. The idea that people rely on it in planning their affairs is, as Cardozo wrote decades ago, "for the most part a figment of excited brains."[86] What stability there is in the law and in people's affairs is brought about by the expense and slowness of using the legal system at all, and by the basic stability of the economy and culture. Are like cases treated alike now? Only when judge or jury see them as alike. There is no objective rule of law in the cases; judges cannot escape the inevitability of making law in part through their own value preferences. And the efficiency of avoiding reconsideration of settled questions exists only so long as no one cares to finance litigation claiming that his or her new case is really different.

Would the world of law fall apart if we were to abandon the pretense of stare decisis? We live mostly without the pretense now in the hundreds of thousands of administrative law decisions that constitute the bulk of case adjudications carried out by the legal system today. We allow 80 percent of our decisions in the federal courts of appeals to go unpublished.[87] Trial court decisions are rarely published at all. So, already most cases neither serve as precedents themselves nor are publicly held to the pretense of consistency with stare decisis. We reject the doctrine outright in alternative methods of dispute resolution like counseling, mediation, negotiation, and arbitration. And of course, the rest of the world gets along without the doctrine quite well. Most other legal systems are built upon European civil law models which (although they do take account of policy trends in judicial decisions) formally reject stare decisis, generally publish very sparse case reports, and sometimes even forbid the judge to mention earlier cases.

Reactions to Modernism

Today, after several generations under modernist influences, the legal profession seems to divide roughly into the following groups:

1. *Anti-modernists*,[88] who think legal modernism is simply wrong as a matter of logical analysis. They take the instability in the law not as a sign of subjectivity, but as a sign—as Holmes teased—that one side must not be "doing its sums right." The view, which differs little from Old Story legal formalism of previous centuries, still dominates the thinking of judges, some law professors, a fair number of attorneys, and much of the public. They do find it hard to deny the evidence showing heavy subjective influences in the law. But they find the subjectivism regrettable and dangerous, rather than inevitable. Most of those in the legal and judicial professions, they admit, may do their sums wrong most of the time, but the anti-modernists, at least, will get it right. They start from an a priori assumption that the law by definition must be a logical, or rational, or coherent, or moral system, and then reason logically, rationally, coherently or morally to one best answer or clear principle in any case. Or, they will exalt "textualism," "originalism" or "strict constructionism" as a path to correct legal answers. In short, the anti-modernists never absorbed the anthropological approach of the Legal Realists, who look for their definition of law at the way people actually use it in society. For anti-modernists, the law still is a brooding omnipresence in the sky.

The tenacity of the anti-modern view can probably be traced to the sociological conditions of its three primary well-springs: first, the judiciary assumes that its continued power and prestige depend upon perpetuating the belief that it is a caste of oracles who find right answers in sacred texts, so judges constantly speak to the public accordingly. Second, the law professoriate is particularly skilled at starting from brooding omnipresences in the sky and organizing cases and materials into idealistic coherence schemes. Professor Grant Gilmore mocked this practice in *The Death of Contract*. Coherence schemes are the key product professors sell that sets them above students, bench, and bar. Many of their schemes hold genuine insights for law reform, but the authors confuse what they think ought to be the law with what the law actually is. They organize classroom casebooks according to the schemes, where students get the idea that the law is a coherent abstraction and learn to lament that so little of law out on the street and in the courtroom conforms to it. Third, it is commonplace political rhetoric, absorbed by the public through high school civics classes and television sound bites, that "ours is a system of laws not of men [sic]," and that this "rule of law" sets us apart from many other nations. Most of the public, even if cynical of corruption, do not participate in the legal or political system so have little occasion to doubt that the "rule of law" ideal could come true if the lawyers and judges would just do their sums right.

2. *Open modernists,* who find legal modernism obvious and accept its practical implications. These lawyers agree that you never find the right answer in the law, only doctrines to be manipulated and arguments to be made. That those who have more resources to play the game have a better chance of winning. That what you need above all to predict the outcome of a judicial decision is to know who the judge is, what his or her values are, and what institutional and social values are at stake.

Included in this group are legions of practicing lawyers who have little or no theory in their heads about legal modernism, but who have arrived at modernist insights through the school of hard knocks as they draw the water and hew the wood of the law day after day. Also included are those law professors who downplay the case method and formalism in favor of empirical, practical, social, economic, political, philosophical and historical materials. Many political scientists are open modernists, publishing compelling statistical studies demonstrating that judicial behavior is driven by the judges' personal values and ideologies.[89] In addition, there are the legal academics who say that since legal doctrine cannot constrain interpreters' discretion, interpreters should self-consciously guide their discretion to facilitate one philosophy or another: most notably, some urge a progressive philosophy to protect those who have been traditionally powerless in law and civic life, while others argue for a conservative program of protecting whatever private parties have agreed to by bargaining in markets or in legislative lobbying.[90] Then there are the reformers in the governmental process, pushing for more accountable, efficient, cheaper, and fairer ways to resolve disputes and set social policy than by formal adjudication and the legalese that goes with it. There are the citizens' and other interest groups who know that appointment of judges is a keenly political event, and must be lobbied accordingly because the judges' personal values will inevitably affect their interests for better or for worse. But alas, there are few courageous, introspective judges, candid about the roots of their decisions, and willing to justify them openly on the basis of the values at stake rather than the mystifying formulas of the Old Story.

3. *Reluctant modernists,* who admit that modernist analysis is largely right but think it best to do nothing about it and to keep it hidden. Many are apolitical legal careerists, comfortable in the thought that the legal profession has great influence in society and desirous that its traditions not be disturbed. Others are an informal network of sophisticated judges and law professors who find the subjective manipulations of the law to be a virtue not a vice. In their

eyes, it is the very genius of the law to be flexible while appearing rigid, changing to meet social needs while seeming to guarantee social stability. It is an amazing trick that ought to be applauded by all who cherish orderly social change, for it's the only system that will work, they say, in a pluralistic democracy where consensus on social policy is in constant ferment. Belief in "the rule of law" encourages the people to put aside policy clashes in favor of loyalty to a process which resolves them peacefully. Judges' talk of "plain meaning," "canons of construction," "stare decisis," etc. is just the traditional yet flexible language which allows them to reach flexible results while maintaining the loyalty of the public at the same time. Like a magic trick, the process will be ruined if attention is focused on the slights-of-hand by which it is accomplished. The public will come to assume a nihilistic, "anything goes," attitude, and lose faith in "the rule of law" in favor of Machiavellian, possibly violent, pursuit of self-interest. One reluctant modernist law professor once wrote that "the myth of linguistic certainty" in the law is culturally important in the same way that "the Santa Claus myth" is, and we should hold on to both.[91] There is another, large group of reluctant modernists who, discomfited by the law's moral relativism, indeterminacy and political nature, seek refuge in the actual practices of bench and bar. These practices, they feel, are mostly morally informed, rational in a way, and apolitical at least on the surface. This is because, they argue, the mechanisms of the legal process itself promote moral purposes, fairness and rationality, or because legal reasoning constitutes a sort of "singing reason," or "practical reason" by which sensible people balance many considerations to arrive at judgments in practical affairs. The ordinary judging of sitting courts works well enough to prove that we have nothing to fear from the radical implications of legal modernism.[92]

In short, the anti-modernists still wear the mask of the Old Story because they believe in the story, while the reluctant modernists wear the mask because they believe in the mask. To an open modernist, the latter's belief in the mask seems undemocratic, based upon a paternalistic, unfounded fear that the people will resort to anarchy if told the truth about the machinations of the legal system. It also seems unduly Pollyannish about the fairness and utility of the judges' "singing" or "practical" reasoning. Explanations of how their reasoning works dwindle off into pleas to trust their intuition. But one wonders if the song of reason would sound different if sung by a group with different sociological characteristics than the establishment elites who now dominate the bench, or by judges who don't feel they must wear a mask to be on the legal stage.

Fortunately, we don't have to trust their intuition or wear their mask. We can get a more precise understanding of how legal interpretation really works—and learn not to fear it—with the insight of postmodernism.

Chapter 3

The Postmodern Insight

Man ... has become [governed] ... by enclosing himself in a set of meaningful forms, webs of signification he himself has spun....

—Anthropologist Clifford Geertz[1]

As the 20th century turned into the 21st century, there was a lot of talk in the air about a new way of seeing things, a feeling that the modernist era had run its course. We have entered, it is said, the postmodern period.[2] It's easy to dismiss this talk as passing fad when you hear "postmodern" applied to clothing fashions and the cuisine in those restaurants where dinner costs a week's wages. The term postmodern itself may soon be yesterday's trendy jargon.

Taking that risk for want of a good substitute, I'll use postmodern to describe the changes that are undeniably simmering beneath a wide range of more enduring cultural phenomena, among them art, music, architecture, literature, literary theory, anthropology, historiography, philosophy, and indeed, hard science. Toilers in each area, who rarely look beyond the fences of their own fields, tend to think that they alone are turning up new ground, and they invent their own tags for what they do. Thus we get "deconstruction" in philosophy and literature, "post-structuralism" in anthropology and the social sciences, "chaos theory" in science, and "postmodernism" elsewhere. But it is the latter term that increasingly seems to be the common tag exchanged as specialists look up from their labors and realize that others are doing something similar.

There is no common technique among postmodernists, nor common politics, nor even a common sensibility, yet there is a common insight. I hazard a working description: The postmodern insight is that the meaning of anything—language, history, science, a painting, a building, a poem, a novel, a law—is assembled by the humans who attempt to understand it, from complex component parts which can always be shattered and reassembled different ways into different meanings, like a collage. Every new assembly is an interpretation of the components, which gives them meaning. And since each of us always views our world from the standpoint of some assembled interpretation in our own heads, there is no external, objective standpoint from which to view any other, no single "true" or "best" collage. You can catch the idea from some of the examples in which it has surfaced in the arts:

Cortazar's 1963 novel *Hopscotch*[3] invited the reader to read it as "many books," including one that ended half-way through and another that was constituted by hopscotching through all the chapters in a chaotic sequence listed in the frontispiece.

Calvino's 1979 *If on a Winter's Night a Traveler*[4] is a novel composed of ten broken shards of incomplete novels wrapped in a meta-novel about the reader's own act of reading those novels and whether that act was a novel.

In Perec's 1980 novel *Life: A User's Manual*,[5] the author takes each of the 32 dwellings in a Paris apartment building and inventories its contents, furnishings, and the lives of dozens of inhabitants, their ancestors, chance encounters, and other details—all in disconnected fragments that may or may not refer to one another. The main character spends 10 years learning to paint and 20 years traveling around the world painting 500 port cities. Eventually, each painting is pasted to plywood and cut into a 750-piece puzzle, then reassembled, taken back to the site where it was originally painted, and washed clean, leaving a blank.

In 1966, Venturi issued his manifesto for a new architecture, which was followed by a revolution in our building styles:

> Architects can no longer afford to be intimidated by the puritanically moral language of orthodox Modern architecture. I like elements which are hybrid rather than pure, compromising rather than clean, distorted rather than "straightforward," ambiguous rather than "articulated," ... redundant rather than simple, vestigial as well as innovating, inconsistent and equivocal rather than direct and clear. I am for messy vitality over obvious unity. I include the non sequitur and proclaim the duality. I am for richness of meaning rather than clarity of meaning.... A valid architecture evokes many levels of meaning and combinations of focus: its space and its elements become readable and workable in several ways at once.[6]

Numerous postmodern architects took up this challenge by reassembling fragments of historical styles into pastiches of pediments, columns, cupolas, and the rest. The architect Gehry has gone beyond that by deconstructing his buildings into component objects (he has even designed a freestanding hallway unconnected to other rooms) or colliding them together, and composing some of them of discordant construction industry materials like chain-link, plywood, asphalt shingles and metal.

This is, of course, provocative stuff. The Florida legislature was so provoked that it considered a bill to outlaw it by statute in 2006, at least as applied to American history: "The history of the United States shall be taught as genuine history and shall not follow the revisionist or postmodern viewpoints of relative truth. American history shall be viewed as factual, not as constructed."[7]

Yet postmodernism is hardly more than a rediscovery of the subjectivism inherent in modernism all along. As we shall see shortly, the philosopher Peirce's reflections on the theory of signs and meaning laid the intellectual basis for it even before 1900. And certainly you see this same shattering and reconstruction of meaning when the Dada artists named their movement in 1916 by thrusting a knife into the French dictionary and coming up with "dada" ("hobbyhorse"), when Porter penned "Anything Goes!" in 1934, when Joyce published the collage of fragments called *Finnegan's Wake* in 1939, when Cage by mid-century was composing music by piling up chance sounds and silences from strange materials, when McLuhan collapsed meaning into its medium, when Jack Kerouac turned fiction into "reality novels" and then back again, and when the existentialist philosophers saw that "man makes himself" from among many possibilities. All this happened before the term postmodern was coined. Sauntering through any major museum of 20th century art, your head swims with materials, objects, perceptions and concepts that have been taken apart, isolated, mixed and reconstructed in constantly changing formations of new meanings. You get that all through the six decades from Duchamp to Rauschenberg, even before coming to any current galleries of postmodern art. As for history, the Florida legislature acted 75 years too late to head off Professor Becker of Cornell, whose 1931 address to the American Historical Association has been called the most famous short piece of writing in the profession. In it, Becker explained the inevitability of subjective interpretation of facts. He titled his address "Every man His Own Historian."[8]

Nevertheless, there does seem to be a new intensity about this attitude, and you see it everywhere, from cuisine to hard science. Why now? The more superficial explanations attribute it to the usual swing of the generational pendulum, or tie it to concrete political events that changed social consciousness on a broad scale: the bomb, the war, the assassination of political leaders, environmental disasters, or even Rock music. But the impact of such things lasts only as long as a generation's social memory and, without denying their role, it's important to notice the deeper forces that seem to be working a more permanent change in the way people make sense of their world. Those deeper forces lie in the same material and economic changes that shook us into modernism and shaped most of the last century. Drastic as they were in 1900 and after, they have now clearly taken off into an ultra-revolutionary phase. The communications revolution and high-consumption capitalism, particularly, are hot engines of postmodernism. The ability to put our eyes, ears, words, or entire selves, virtually anywhere in the world in a matter seconds or hours, to receive images, sounds, and words back from that world, and to reproduce, store, and mix them, shatters our locally ordered existence and offers us an endless smorgasbord of cultural experiences from which to compose our lives. Or should we say, from which our lives are composed for us? For much of this is forced upon us by the technology, especially television, which composes our lives into a hodge-podge of experiences. I call this the TV Scramble Effect.

High-consumption global capitalism, which I dub the Fajita Pita Syndrome, is the other irrepressible force of postmodernism. It has created a "global shopping center," which produces through advertising a "ceaseless transformation in style, a connoisseurship of surface, an emphasis on packaging and reproducibility," in the words of one sociologist. Its consumers are "a new global class of customers linked via borderless mass media with mass culture, omnivorous consumption, and easy travel.... [L]ocal traditions have been swamped by the workings of the market. Anything can be bought, and to speak of intrinsic value is mere sentimentality.... It makes much of brand names (even ironically) because they have become the furnishings of our cultural 'home.'"[9] Thus capitalism teaches that the things we value may be put together from inexpensive, mass produced components, invested with meaning by being given a name or slogan which may have nothing to do with the function or history of the object, then quickly consumed and disposed of in order to start a new cycle with other goods.

Thought Window:[10]

Hot Engines of Postmodernism

The TV Scramble Effect:

By the time they reach adulthood, typical American children have watched 30,000 hours of television, in which the average length of a shot is 3.5 seconds and subject matters—high/low, trivial/profound, disastrous/amusing, commercial/non-commercial—are constantly mixed in a rapid kaleidoscope of images. The effect on human consciousness is momentous. "We have become so accustomed to its discontinuities," says a well-known critic of television, "that we are no longer struck dumb, as any sane person would be, by a newscaster who having just reported that a nuclear war is inevitable goes on to say that he will be right back after this word from Burger King....

One can hardly overestimate the damage that such juxtapositions do to our sense of the world as a serious place." On the other hand, television is also a prime instrument for political and economic change in authoritarian cultures where these TV discontinuities teach inhabitants that their lives could be put together differently.

The Fajita Pita (fah-HEE-ta PEE-ta) Syndrome: Cultural change under capitalism's system of high consumption often shows up first in cuisine, which is even more of a hair-trigger indicator of trendiness than is fashion clothing. In southwestern United States in the 1980s, fajitas (plural) were introduced as a new dish in upscale restaurants. Marinated, cheap cuts of beef carved in thin belt (faja)-like strips and barbecued with onions and peppers, they had long been known along the Texas-Mexican border region as a common folk dish. After their rebirth in upscale restaurants, it spread rapidly downscale to other restaurants, then over to supermarket meat counters. A fajitas boom was on and soon chicken fajitas were added, then shrimp, unheard of in Tex-Mex. At the same time, the pita, a flat, round, unleavened bread that opens like a pocket, had been popular in the United States for many years. Arab and Greek restaurant owners had introduced it from their homelands where it dates to Biblical times, and stuffed it with beef, lamb, garbanzos and other fillings. The coup of combining the two traditions was struck by the Jack-in-the-Box drive-through, fast-food chain, with restaurants all over the west. Wanting to cash in on the fajitas boom, but needing a handy, forkless way for customers to eat it on the run, Jack- in-the-Box didn't hesitate to throw away thousands of years of food history, to merge Tex-Mex, Arab and Greek cultures and languages, and to launch a media blitz advertising campaign: the "fajita-pita" was born, to rave reviews from the customers. The business press reported skyrocketing net earnings for Jack-in-the-Box. Within a couple of years, sales were down and the fajita-pita was fading out. So it goes with the mash-mix-and-consume global customers of mass capitalism. Lyotard, the French philosopher of postmodernism, has also described the scene: "One listens to reggae, watches a Western, eats McDonald's food for lunch and local cuisine for dinner, wears Paris perfume in Tokyo and 'retro' clothes in Hong Kong." This is the way the economy subverts fixed values and the past, and produces the postmodern sensibility.

Postmodern Law

It should come as no surprise that the legal profession, too, reflects these times.[11] Postmodernism surfaces in the law in many ways. The computer revolution, allowing vast storage, retrieval, fragmentation and reconstruction of case law, has already been described. DVD, fax, satellite communication, and air travel have also shattered once local, orderly modes of law practice into rapid bits and pieces that are being combined in new ways. High-consumption capitalism is also at work, showing up in rapid growth of the number of lawyers, fast disintegration, merger, and creation of law firms, non-lawyer ownership and management of law firms, mass marketing of legal services, and development of new products like "check-the-box pleadings," "do-it-yourself, Plain English will forms," "preventive law," counseling, and "rent-a-judge" and other alternative methods of dispute resolution.[12]

In legal scholarship, postmodernist feminists have pulled apart the Old Story about legal interpretation to reveal not just its indeterminacy but its patriarchy: the preferences it gives to aggressive values of male dominators both in substance and in habits of speech and reasoning.[13] These scholars reconstructed legal explanations into narratives that replace traditional legal reasoning with broader, androgynous accounts of being in the world, and that reach different legal outcomes. Critical Race theorists likewise deconstructed law to reveal how it is interwoven with racial assumptions.[14] Of other developments in legal theory, none was so spirited as the movement of scholars known as Critical Legal Studies.[15] CLS breathed new fire and skill into the Legal Realists' project of unmasking the law as subjective and indeterminate, and generally acknowledged its links to that modernist movement. Its writers went beyond Realism by invoking deconstructionist philosophers and others, but they were mainly driven by the postmodern experience of their generation that culture can be taken apart and put back together in countless different ways. In their words, they "trashed" legal texts, rules, doctrines, and practices, showing how they could be reassembled to produce opposite results, and they did it with both gusto and despair. This statement by a leading CLS theorist clearly comes from the same passionate campground as Venturi's statement about architecture:

> [T]he goal is not to convince people by lucidity. It's not to grasp or control their minds by the explicitness and the beauty with which we get at the real structure of reality. But rather to operate in the interspace of artifacts, gestures, speeches and rhetoric, histrionics, drama, all very paradoxical, soap opera, pop culture, all that kind of stuff.[16]

As for the reluctant modernists' "singing reason" and faith in the mask of the law to keep social peace, CLS found them to be poorly supported myths that serve only to hide the ideology of power groups of the status quo, restricting our vision of how we may reconstruct our social and legal reality.

Now defunct as an organized movement of scholars, at least in America, CLS nevertheless deposited a lasting critique of law.

To a considerable extent, all of this reconfirms the modernist point that almost anything goes in legal interpretation. And in the eyes of its anti-modernist and reluctant-modernist adversaries, it goes too far, threatening to throw us into solipsism, nihilism, and anarchy, with everyone free to make personal collages of legal meaning and call that the law. Fears like these have provoked in some an ill-concealed desire to set fire to the postmodernists' shirts and run them out of the legal academy. The dean of one law school fumed that "anyone who believes that the law has no fixed meaning, that its words can mean whatever you want them to mean, has no more business teaching at a law school than an atheist has at a school of theology.... They have a duty to depart the legal academy."[17]

The dean seems to have given in to the old impulse to shoot the messenger of alarming news. He ignores the TV Scramble Effect and the Fajita Pita Syndrome that are really at the bottom of the changes in law that worry him. In any event, his fears don't seem quite so worrisome once you take a look at the assembly side of postmodernism and focus on the way that humans make meanings. It may be that many postmodern legal scholars have been more vocal in the provocative work of deconstruction. But reconstruction is possible, indeed, unavoidable. We are always jointly reconstructing our reality. And in looking anthropologically at how we do it, we come face to face not with solipsism, nihilism, and anarchy, but with the familiar political and social culture within which we live and argue every day. Legal meanings are not, in the end, determinate and stable. But neither is it true that just anything goes in legal interpretation. What goes is the same common stuff and the same slow processes by which we make all meanings in our culture, some noble, many abominable, but all of them ours. We have met the enemy, and it is us.

In the spirit of visiting anthropologists, and with the tool of postmodern semiotics, perhaps we can begin to understand how we do what we do to ourselves. (Don't let words like "semiotics" scare you. They are, after all, only words.)

Postmodern Semiotics

Meanings are cultural artifacts produced in the course of history. To acknowledge that they are not produced according to some transcendent Rule external to society is not to conclude that they are produced by no rule at all. Individuals cannot create wild, personal meanings for law any more than they can coin wild, personal meanings for words. To some small extent, they may create them in their own heads, but to establish them as social meanings they'll have to trudge through the cultural processes by which meanings become accepted.

Stanley Fish, a professor of English and law who specializes in interpretation of both literary and legal texts, has usefully observed that we all live in "interpretive communities" which are made up of a "political, social and institutional ... mix" of constraints on acceptable interpretations.[18] The mix is subject to change, but is extremely hard to budge. And every such community is nested within other interpretive communities which affect it, so that the interpretive community of the legal profession is surrounded by the political community, the social community, and ultimately the entire interpretive community of American and perhaps international culture. It's as hard to believe that anarchists and nihilists could establish or destroy legal meanings in such an environment as it is to believe that the Esperanto Society will someday succeed in making its invented language the universal tongue of humankind. Wildly idiosyncratic interpretations by individuals are unlikely too. Quoting Fish, "[A] culture fills brains ... so that no one's interpretive acts are exclusively his own but fall to him by virtue of his position in some socially organized environment.... It follows, then, that the fear of solipsism, of the imposition by the unconstrained self of its own prejudices, is unfounded because the self does not exist apart from the communal or conventional categories of thought that enable its operations (of thinking, seeing, reading)."[19]

To acknowledge, then, that the meanings of laws, words, or anything else can be continually fragmented and reassembled into different meanings is not to conclude, as some have, that the reconstruction is solipsistic, amoral, or chaotic. The semiotics scholar Umberto Eco, renowned for showing how texts are "open" and subject to many interpretations, nevertheless acknowledges that "from the moment in which the community is pulled to agree with a given interpretation, there is, if not an objective, at least an *intersubjective* meaning which acquires a privilege over any other possible interpretation spelled out without the agreement of the community."[20] What we need to do is the basic anthropological work of observing the practices by which interpretive communities produce these artifacts called legal meanings. "Law is local knowledge," writes the anthropologist Geertz, "not placeless principle." We have become governed, he says, by enclosing ourselves in a set of meaningful signs, "webs of signification we ourselves have spun."[21] It is in taking a close look at those webs of signification and how we spin them that the methods of postmodern semiotics become useful.

The field of semiotics (a singular term with an s on the end, like physics), from the Greek term for sign, is simply the theory of signs. The kinds of signs that semiotics theorizes about include anything that makes us think of something else. Words are signs, of course, because they cause us to think of or feel or act upon things they stand for. So are symbols and pictures. Even natural phenomena are signs to us of something else, like clouds (rain!, etc.) or fire (danger!, etc.). So is the whole range of cultural artifacts and behavior, from clothing (standing for class, power, sex, etc.) to handshakes (friendship, agreement, peace, etc.). All these things in our everyday experience, in short, are signs, in the sense that they stand for something else to us.[22]

Now, if you define the term sign this broadly, you may also say that your life is one long train of signs because it's impossible to communicate, to think, to act, to experience anything except through signs. "What semiotics at this point has shown," according to one of its historians, "is that the whole of human experience—the whole of it—is mediated by signs."[23] This is one of those breathtaking reductionist insights that catches the imagination because it explains so much by so little. Economists achieve a similar gasp with their reductionist notion of homo economicus. But semiotics burrows more deeply than economists or anyone else by positing the human being as fundamentally a signifying animal: homo signans.

Semiotics theories have been with us throughout the last 2,500 years, but postmodernism seems to have unleashed a flurry of unprecedented semiotics study across scores of disciplines and around the world. A good deal of the activity involves what I would call publishing the encyclopedia of signs, describing things whose sign functions had gone unrecognized or under-recognized, looking at signs like food, fashion, wrestling, smell, music, advertising, comic strips, film techniques, etc. and asking, "what are they really telling us?" This has considerable popular appeal, and the press has picked up on it and may have given the misimpression that it is the whole of semiotics.

Fertile studies of law are being done in this category. There are works, for example, showing the meanings hidden in the teeming sign environment of the courtroom (the black robe, the elevated bench, the architecture of the space, the control of permission to speak, the vocabulary and ways of speaking, etc.), studies on the messages that legal language gives beneath the surface (power, domination, sacredness of the text, etc.), and works revealing unsuspected legal and social signs. Some of the work of scholars in Legal Realism, Feminist Legal Theory, Critical Race Theory, CLS, and Law and Economics, though not labeled "semiotics," can be seen as disclosing that the law is shot through with signs of subjectivism, patriarchy, racism, hierarchy, and economic efficiency, respectively. Writers in these areas are doing semiotics indirectly, their work expanding the social encyclopedia of signs.

Figuring out how signs do their work is the other major activity of semiotics. Here, two major schools of thought diverge. An earlier "structuralist" school attempted to locate more or less immutable rules that were somehow programmed into cultures regardless of history and social context. That attempt sank in heavy weather and has been overtaken by various postmodern approaches. The postmodern school starts instead with realistic, pragmatic views based upon the modernist notion that language and legal meaning are cultural artifacts produced in time and space through specific social institutions. The challenge is to describe how those institutions work and change.

Among the most powerful postmodern descriptions is that of Umberto Eco, professor of semiotics at the University of Bologna, medievalist, novelist, and pop-culture critic. Eco pictures each of us surrounded by an encyclopedia of signs, which stores the entire competence of human culture. But it is not an orderly encyclopedia like a set of books on a library self. It is a labyrinth, a multi-leveled, net-like or rhizome-like maze of signs with no center, in which every point can be reached from every other point. Moreover, this labyrinthian encyclopedia is constantly expanding and contracting as signs are added or forgotten over the course of history.

At every point, no one has a global vision of all the possibilities of the encyclopedia, only a local vision of the closest ones. The reader stands at a point receiving signs. And the fascinating thing is that she can explain these signs to herself only in terms of another sign which in turn is explained by another sign and so on, connecting signs in the labyrinth down a pathway of explanation. This is a key insight, remarkably postmodern, which occurred to the semiotics philosopher Peirce near the turn of the 19th century, 100 years before postmodernism. He called it, awkwardly, the process of "unlimited semiosis." Eco takes up Peirce's idea:

> [S]ignification … by means of continual shiftings which refer a sign back to another sign or string of signs, circumscribes cultural units … without ever allowing one to touch them directly, though making them accessible through other units.[24]

What Eco means here by "cultural units" are simply the things or ideas that a given culture habitually uses. For example, "snow" is a cultural unit. We would, for example, describe or make use of "snow" by using other signs (words, actions, symbols) that tell of our experience with it (cold, wet, white, danger, etc.), and after we learn to ski we may throw that group of signs away, spinning another web of signs to better tell of our experience with it. That is all that snow really "means." It has no more permanent truth than the group of signs we imagine to reflect our experience.

> Thus a cultural unit never obliges one to replace it by means of something which is not a semiotic entity, and never asks to be explained by some Platonic, psychic or object[-like] entity. Semiosis explains itself by itself; this continual circularity is the normal condition of signification.... To call this condition a 'desperate' one is to refuse the human way of signifying, a way that has proved itself fruitful insofar as only through it has cultural history developed.[25]

Depending upon a reader's historical, cultural, psychological, ideological and other circumstances, which affect her own vision and her capacity to travel the connections of the labyrinth, she produces the meaning of a text by choosing a pathway of signs. This may or may not have been the same pathway foreseen by the sender of the text or by others, though there is often a probability that it is because so many of these pathways are preconstructed by the culture and are commonly used. Unfortunately, Eco's general treatment fails to bring the specific production of legal meaning into focus, so I have taken his metaphor into the interpretive community of the law to see how it works there.

The Semiotic Web of Legal Interpretation

I've changed Eco's metaphor of the labyrinth to that of a "semiotic web," borrowing another image made popular in postmodern semiotics by Thomas Sebeok, a Peirce scholar and leading semiotician. I like the way this echoes Holmes who once referred to "the seamless web of the law." I'll offer a diagram of the web of legal interpretation below, based upon my own anthropological observations of legal practice over many years. It may be incomplete, or need revision, but it shows the pathways through the cultural web that I see habitually traveled by members of the interpretive community of the law, like a spider traveling its web, every time legal meaning is produced. Before getting to the diagram, let me recapitulate the key points that underlie it.

- The central metaphor sees the individual within a cultural web of signs, gazing at it through lenses of her own values, psychology, experience, and knowledge.
- Any individual person who says that something has meaning to her will simply be called an interpreter.
- The something that she says has meaning—it may be words or larger units of a text, or sounds, or objects, or feelings, or events in nature, anything that stands for something else—will be called a sign.
- An interpreter looking at a sign explains it to herself in terms of another sign in the web, and that sign in terms of another, and so on in a process of "unlimited semiosis," a process which ends only when the interpreter loses interest after registering the last sign within her mind, or acting in a certain way.
- The experience of the series of signs, ending in some mental or behavioral event, is the meaning the original sign has had for that interpreter on that occasion

This understanding of meaning as the experience that each of us has with the signs we read liberates us from the hoary abstractions of the label theory of language and brings us down to earth to the pragmatic world of everyday life. If, for example, I see the word STOP inside a red octagon posted on the street corner, I may explain that to myself in an instantaneous interior monologue using the sign "brake," or perhaps the signs "police" and "safety," and then apply my foot to the brakes; at that point I lose interest and drop the process of sign connecting. Next day, I may contemplate the same STOP sign through a series of interior monologue signs relating to traffic flow, commuter time, urban design, and outrageous auto insurance rates, before losing interest. Another day, I may contemplate it through dozens of signs (words, ideas, actions) relating to the topic of semiotics itself, which end only with my typing the word in this manuscript. The STOP sign caused different experiences for me on three different days, and those experiences were the meanings of the sign to me on those occasions.

At any one point, no interpreter can see all of the possible links, because the web grows and contracts over the course of history, and because every interpreter has limited competence and limiting psychological, ideological, personal and other circumstances which affect her capacity to move in the web. My neighbor, for example, who is a mathematician, may produce the meaning of the STOP sign as a part of two-dimensional octagonality manifest in nature, a meaning that I, lacking the capacity to travel those particular links of the web, could not have produced.

It would be misleading to think that the interpreter produces meanings from the web by herself or can create any meaning she wishes. She doesn't do it alone because, unlike a spider, she comes into a web with many preconstructed pathways not of her own making, and these allow her to say, to think, to be, some things and not others. Nor can the interpreter create just any meaning she wishes, for the rest of us anyway, because if she does create a private language of idiosyncratic meanings from the network of signs culturally available to her, her meanings may not be of much interest to the rest of us. The cop who tickets me or my neighbor for running the STOP sign will have no interest at all in my explanation that the sign was to me only an example of unlimited semiosis, or in my neighbor's that it made her think of octagonality. This is not to say that the STOP sign has only the cop's meaning and not ours, but that it has the cop's meaning to the cop, and perhaps to a judge; if we want them to give it our meanings instead, we have a lot of persuading to do. The social meanings of a sign are nothing more, nor less, than the meanings other interpreters are persuaded to share. And sometimes, though not always, we are persuaded to share a meaning with an author of a sign because we want to use it the way the author intended us to when he communicated it to us (as when the cop says, "pull over"); for that reason, we are sometimes interested in the author of the sign, not as the touchstone of meaning but as another's meaning that we choose to share.

In the particular part of the cultural web related to legal interpretation, my observation is that the routes that every interpreter seems always to take in producing legal meaning consist of pathways of signs relating to the cultural unit of what we call a text; pathways relating to the cultural unit of what we call the source of the text; and pathways relating to the cultural unit of what we call the views of other interpreters. For all I know, the Inuit or the Maori may take other pathways. There may be cultures in which meanings of signs are established, instead, by revelation, by intuition, by Pavlovian biological response mechanism, or some other means. But these are the steps that in our culture we seem to consider important in arriving at the meaning of a legal text. I don't suggest that the steps are taken in any specific order. They may be virtually simultaneous. But we do feel the need to define just what the text is, to wonder about its source and what weight to ascribe to that source, and to consider what other interpreters think. To the extent that other interpreters with social power endorse or acquiesce in the way we've defined the text and weighted its source, we will temporarily establish legal meaning.

In our court decisions and our other Old Story productions of legal meaning, we've ritualized our travel down these pathways in a way that gives great ceremonial fanfare to only certain parts of the web. The rituals suppress altogether the central figure of the reader, standing at a point in the web, peering inescapably through lenses of values, psychological character, and historical, cultural, and sociological circumstances. That part is hidden and denied.

We emphasize instead the search for the text and the source, as if they speak for themselves, as if discovery of them alone will produce the meaning. To a lesser extent, we acknowledge the importance of other interpreters' views, but only certain ones. Views of other judges are referred to frequently and are persuasive in part because of who the judges are, or how many there are, rather than what they've said. This explains why, even in dignified circles, interpreters spend so much time promoting or undermining the reputation of other judges, as when President Franklin Roosevelt denounced the Supreme Court in the 1930s as "nine old men," or when judges compliment one another, or rhetorically stab each other in the back in their written opinions. This also is probably the real function of stare decisis, not to show us precedents that we feel bind us, but to persuade us by arguing that other judges have held similar views in the past. Views of executive branch enforcers of laws are taken into account through the formal Old Story doctrine which looks to "contemporaneous and practical" interpretation. Opinions of political interests and the public are sometimes taken into account through the formal mechanism of friend-of-the-court briefs. There have been celebrated cases in which scores of lobbying organizations, state legislatures and attorneys general, and the Congress have all lined up to present their views in this way about the legal meaning of a statute or constitutional provision. Obviously, what's going on is not that the courts need all these friends to help them find the meaning in a legal text, but that powerful other interpreters are signaling the meanings acceptable to them. The views of the press, celebrities, and demonstrators on the courthouse steps, are certainly taken into account as well ("the felt necessities of the time, the prevalent moral and political theories, intuitions of public policy," in Holmes's words), and may sometimes be the deciding factor, but our formal rituals strongly disavow this.

The other thing the formal rituals disavow is that there is much choice once we travel down any of the pathways of text, source, and other interpreters. But, of course, the modern story of legal interpretation has shown just what a smorgasbord of choices exists. The spider web illustration on the last page of this chapter shows many of the linkages of signs routinely chosen by Anglo-American lawyers and judges in actual practice, revealing the multiple possible signs that can be combined or ignored among the pathways of the semiotic web to produce the legal meaning of any text. Our ritualized process of formal legal reasoning tries to deny it, but it is clear that at every pathway the interpreter is faced with a choice of values. Shall we adhere to the plain meaning of the words, honor a fictional original intent, and invoke the views of other judges in precedent cases? Shall we choose reason as the real text, social conditions as its source, and millions of citizens whose concerns are reflected in opinion polls as the most important other interpreters? Any choice we make will amount to implementation of our own values and a philosophy of government. Our process, in short, highlights the artifices of ritual while hiding the real values and the social power that actually shape legal interpretation.

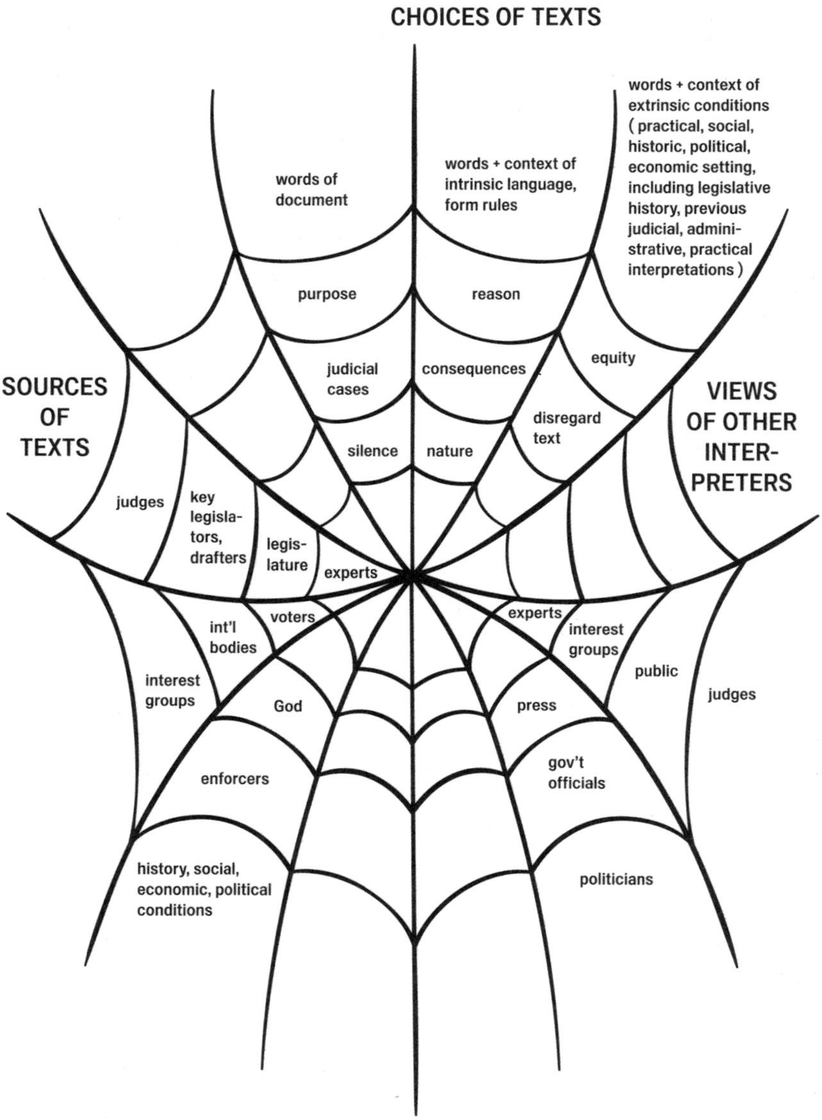
CHOICES OF TEXTS
words of document
words + context of intrinsic language, form rules
words + context of extrinsic conditions (practical, social, historic, political, economic setting, including legislative history, previous judicial, administrative, practical interpretations)
purpose
reason
judicial cases
consequences
equity
silence
nature
disregard text
SOURCES OF TEXTS
judges
key legislators, drafters
legislature
experts
VIEWS OF OTHER INTERPRETERS
voters
int'l bodies
interest groups
God
enforcers
history, social, economic, political conditions
experts
interest groups
public
judges
press
gov't officials
politicians

THE SEMIOTIC WEB OF LEGAL INTERPRETATION

Chapter 4

How Judges Fool Themselves

A judiciary that discloses what it is doing and why it does it will breed understanding. And confidence based on understanding is more enduring than confidence based on awe.

—Justice William O. Douglas[1]

Sacred Cows

The previous chapters have debunked the claim that judges find the law rather than make it. We have therefore dishonored a sacred cow and can expect resistance from the legal profession and the judges themselves. What we are up against can perhaps be suggested by a short story of authentic sacred cows.

In the state of Kerala in southern India, American anthropologist Marvin Harris noticed that many domestic cattle die young, and that male calves die at about twice the rate of females. When he interviewed the farmers, all insisted they would never deliberately kill or starve their cattle. "Every farmer ardently affirmed the legitimacy of the standard Hindu prohibition against the slaughter of domestic bovines."[2] The farmers' explanation was that the males tended inherently to sickness. Probing the nature of the sickness, Harris was told that the males were weaker because they ate less than the females. One or two farmers suggested that the males ate less because they weren't permitted to suckle their mothers for more than a few seconds. What no farmer would say was that since there was little need for traction animals in Kerala, the males were being starved to death and the females were being reared. Yet this was Harris's conclusion, a conclusion reaffirmed when he found that in other parts of India, where agricultural conditions demand more traction animals, it is the females who die young and the males who survive: in the state of Uttar Pradesh, he found an adult cattle ratio of over 200 oxen to every 100 cows. There was no allegation that Harris's informants were attempting to mislead him. On the contrary, every farmer sincerely believed that he was not shortening the life of his calves. For them, writes Harris, "the systemic relationship between ... cattle sex ratios and local ecological and economic conditions simply does not exist."

For Harris, the tale illustrates the conflict between the internal and external perspectives, the native's lived experience and the observer's data. It is a conflict that plagues anthropologists most acutely but it confronts us all whenever we try to reconcile what we see others doing with what they say they are doing, and it is precisely this conflict that faces us when we observe that judges are actually making the law but tell us they are merely finding it.[3] Like Harris's Hindu informants, our judges are entitled to respect for their sincerity. Yet from our external position we, like Harris, are entitled to be skeptical about our informants' accounts of their own behavior.

For anthropologists, this conflict between the internal and external perspectives often presents a philosophical problem of the first order because the perspectives are simply incommensurable and never the twain shall meet. I don't know whether Harris was ever able to persuade any Hindu farmers that they were killing their cattle to keep local ecological and economic conditions in balance. I'm sure he would have failed, at great personal sacrifice, to persuade the Aztecs who reigned at Tenochtitlán in the 15th century that their sacramental eating of some 20,000 people a year was due to the severe depletion of other sources of animal protein in the Valley of Mexico, as he has argued. We, as lawyers and citizens observing judges in our own society, are in a somewhat better position than the anthropologists. Our point of view and the judges' are not incommensurable: we all measure by roughly similar yardsticks of reasoning and empirical observation, so in theory we should be able to come to agreement about what's going on in judicial interpretation. And yet, listening to the judges, I am haunted by Harris's stories, by the feeling that I am listening to an internal perspective that is clung to in good faith but with a religious tenacity for which the outside observer's perspective simply does not exist.

The Internal Perspective

Many judges, though far from all, report that they actually do feel constrained by cases, statutes, regulations, doctrines and principles at every turn. The question is, can they explain why they feel that way?

Some of the more thoughtful judges have attempted it over the years, and their remarks are trenchant, certainly sincere, and almost compelling at first glance. One federal appellate judge attacks head-on the Critical Legal Studies doctrine that "'law' is but a grab bag of legal rules, some diametrically opposed to others ... [that o]n some subjective basis, judges decide what result they want to accomplish and then select the set of rules that purports to provide a rationale for their decision." He insists, to the contrary, that "legal doctrine is a real force, judges follow it, and they decide all but a small fraction of the cases ... in accordance with what they perceive to be the controlling rules."[4]

The problem, he says, is that professors like to talk only about the hard cases that provide intellectual puzzles for the classroom, whereas at least 55% of the cases that come before his court are easy ones, "dreary, boring ... doctrine-controlled, even if the doctrine involved is only deference to the findings of fact made in the trial court" or the doctrine that the precedents of one three-judge panel within the circuit are controlling on all the other panels. (The latter doctrine, he explains, is needed to avoid the chaos that would result if every change in panel composition brought a change of rule. There is nothing to do in these circumstances, he writes quoting Cardozo, "except to stand by the errors of our brethren of the week before, whether we relish them or not.") In the other 45% of the cases, in which the outcome is at least debatable, judges feel the fetters of doctrine when the judge tries to write the opinion and finds that his or her original view just "will not write," that is, it "does not adopt accepted methods of analysis and does not follow accepted rules.... So we reach a result that differs from our initial opinion and personal predilections because something that we recognize as 'law' (together with its careful exposition) demands it."[5]

The judge's trump card is the statistical evidence. He found that for the years 1981–1985 there were dissents in fewer than four percent of the cases in the 16-member Fifth Circuit. And he cites an independent study of nearly 4,000 U.S. Court of Appeals decisions involving ideologically controversial issues, which found that the judges were unanimous 83% of the time even though they were a varied group who had been appointed by presidents Kennedy, Johnson, Nixon, Ford, Carter, and Reagan. He thinks the inference obvious that the judges were guided to their unanimity by legal doctrine.

Another federal judge, in the District of Columbia Circuit, compiled his own statistics of that court for one year: Of more than 1100 cases decided, usually by three-judge panels, 94% brought no dissent. Looking only at cases decided with a full opinion by mixed panels consisting of a judge reputed to be liberal and two reputed to be conservative, or vice versa, judges in the political minority filed a dissent less than ten percent of the time. This judge, a former law professor, a Carter appointee, and a reputed liberal, found that when he himself sat on panels with two notoriously conservative judges he disagreed with them only 10% and 3% of the time respectively. He concludes that it is "fundamentally misguided" to predict cases on the basis of judges' supposed political or ideological views. At least half of the cases, he claims, are easy ones, straightforwardly controlled by relevant legal rules and clear facts, with no discernible political implications. Even in the harder cases, he argues, judges don't feel free "to write their own ideology into the law." He concedes some influence to personality, background, and view of the judicial function, but the constraints of the legal system and discipline of "the craft" impress him more: the gatekeeping doctrines that limit the cases that even reach the appellate courts, the reviewing rather than primary decision-making role of appellate judges, "the need to write an opinion ... in accord with the conventions of legal reasoning," to reconcile or distinguish precedents, deal honestly with the facts, reason logically, defend against often vigorous criticism from colleagues, withstand scholarly scrutiny, and "to reach decisions that are capable of gaining the acceptance of the public and the other branches of government."[6]

The judges make a compelling case that they are, in fact, constrained by the rule of law. How do we answer them?

Two Easy Cases

Suppose (to take the generic American laboratory toad in these experiments) there is a test of the constitutional provision that no one is eligible to be president "who shall not have attained to the Age of thirty-five Years."[7] A 25-year-old woman is put on the ballot by state authorities in a presidential primary and a political opponent brings suit to remove her name.

Suppose in a second case that a woman intentionally drives through a STOP sign, is ticketed, refuses to pay the fine, and is prosecuted.

Without more details, we will think these are easy cases, approaching 99% predictability that the hapless candidate and the driver will lose with nary a judicial dissent. But is it "the law" and "legal doctrine" that make these predictions good bets? Let us proceed, spider-like, through the semiotic web of legal interpretation presented in Chapter 3, pretending we are judges.

Choices of texts

We are first confronted with a decision of what to treat as the text of the law. The web illustration in the last chapter displays some of the standard choices available in the web of signs of Anglo-American legal tradition. Anyone familiar with the practice knows that there are no stable rules for selecting one path of the web rather than another, or some or all of them in a single case.

Homage is paid to the abstraction that constitutional texts trump legislative texts and both of these trump judicial texts, but this abstraction is no constraint on choice of texts since it can be true only after the fact. That is, only after the reader has decided which constitutional, legislative or judicial texts are relevant and has interpreted them is it possible to know whether there are any conflicts that can then be said to trump one another. The trump is the result of your interpretation, not the cause of it. (If before *Brown v. Board of Education* in 1954 a court upheld a statute requiring segregated schools, neither the decision nor the statute were said to be trumped by the Constitution because they were seen as consistent with it. When the three texts were interpreted to be in conflict after 1954, the decision and statute were said to be trumped by the Constitution.)

With legislative texts, the Old Story has a lot of stout talk about the authority of the "plain meaning" pathway that purports to follow the words alone as text, but—as the case reports demonstrate—it is employed no more than the "purpose" approach, and both compete with other choices in the web. Should we take the plain meaning view that "thirty-five years means thirty-five years," and "STOP" means "stop"? Or might we fear to tread that route, thinking that such literal-mindedness could lead us equally to conclude that since the Constitution gives Congress power only "to coin money" the word "coin" renders our paper tender worthless; or could lead us to uphold prosecution of a driver who runs a STOP sign when a flash flood has made the intersection a dangerous place to stop. These fears may lead us down the purpose route instead, and the purposes of the presidential age provision and the STOP sign may lead to different results depending upon what we decide the purposes are. Or we might decide it is better simply to disregard the most obvious text of the law, as judges frequently do: in the presidential age case by virtue of the political question doctrine (jurisdiction refused, the candidate wins her name on the ballot), in the STOP sign case on the ground that the police are too burdened to attend trial (case dismissed, driver wins). These and the other options displayed in the diagram are all alive and well in actual legal practice.

At this point, we should be disqualified for failing to clear even the first hurdle in this effort to show that doctrine controls our discretion: there is no control over our choice of texts for the presidential age provision or for the STOP sign. But let's see if we can jump the next hurdles anyway.

The words. Say that we settle upon the "plain meaning of the words" as the proper legal text; can the words alone guide our discretion? We have already rejected the "plain" or "core" meaning view of language as naive, seeing that words will have different meanings to different interpreters situated at different points and connecting different signs in the cultural web. "X years of age" can connect with different signs and result in different meanings for those who may not measure time by our calendar, such as Navaho or Hopi Americans; for waitresses who knowingly give half-price menus for "kids under 10 years of age" to small 12-year-olds who can't eat much; for winemakers whose labels of vintage year stand for "mostly of this year" (and to whom "dry" sometimes stands for "sweet"); for some in various college towns where the drinking age is "understood" to be lower on campus; for judges taking mental age rather than chronological age as the test for trial of 16-year-old defendants. Similarly, the letters "STOP" could easily be a military acronym for a weapon of horror, or may stand for a pharmaceutical product that assists smokers in breaking the nicotine habit, or would make a plausible name for a group of Rock musicians.

So words alone can't control our discretion because they never are alone, they are always embedded in various nodes or contexts of the web of signs, read by various interpreters who give them different meanings. (Even a dictionary is a particular context.)

Words + context. What about "words + context," then? Surely the words "thirty-five years of age," and "STOP " are reasonably determinate within given contexts, and their legal contexts are presidential elections and road traffic, respectively, not wine labels or Rock bands. Well, this thought does push us toward a particular section of the cultural web embodying legal contexts. But contexts, legal or otherwise, are no more self-defining than words. They are simply organizing frames, imagined orders that different interpreters place around a pathway of signs in the web.[7]

Whose context? The first indeterminacy of contextual frames, even narrowed to legal contexts, is that we don't know whose legal context to take—our own as judges, the litigants', one we think is generally shared by "the people," or some other. No rules determine the choice, and a switch of context can instantly make an easy case hard.

A judge's context: One typical judge's context connects most legal signs to another pathway of signs relating to the welfare and efficiency of the judiciary. These embrace the judicial gatekeeping doctrines that one of our judges quoted above believes control his discretion, including the political question doctrine which would allow us to refuse jurisdiction of the case challenging the 25-year-old running for president. (Candidate wins.) A litigant's context: Suppose the candidate's context links the constitutional age provision to 18th century concepts of intellectual and social maturity that are now outmoded;

today, she argues, we know 25 is as mature as 35. We could easily select this context on the traditional ground that the Constitution is not a straight jacket but a living document which must evolve with knowledge. (Candidate wins.) The people's context: But the people at large if polled would probably think it crazy to let a 25-year-old run for president, so we have little to lose by declaring that the judiciary shares the common sense of the people that 25 is not 35. (Candidate loses.)

When judges' contexts and the people's are congruent the law seems settled and the cases easy, but litigants' contexts are constantly piquing us to see pathways of the cultural web we had not previously connected, with the result that easy cases are turned into hard ones when the judges, others in the legal system, and the people at large begin to share the new contextual frame. For many years it was an easy case that apportionment of state legislative districts was a political question beyond judicial review, and an easy case that racially separate schools could be equal, because the cases were seen through judges' and many white people's contextual frames. Litigants' contexts turned the cases hard, previous contextual frames were abandoned, and now both are easy cases for the opposite result. California courts were once sobered to see a litigant's context turn an otherwise easy homicide case into a tragically hard one, when a native Japanese mother drowned her two infants in Santa Monica Bay while attempting suicide. She thought that customary Japanese notions of honor required her to keep her children with her after her death, and believed her suicide was justified by the shame of having a husband who had taken a mistress. Her act apparently would have been treated as involuntary manslaughter in Japan. Here, she initially faced the death penalty for first-degree homicide, but ultimately a plea bargain was struck, she pled "no contest" to involuntary manslaughter, and was sentenced to one year in prison. The court denied it had been influenced by the petition of 4,000 members of the Japanese community in Los Angeles, who saw the case in the Japanese context.[8] And even our easy STOP sign case turned hard recently when a woman, speeding to the hospital to give birth, protested her ticket on the ground that in her context STOP surely did not mean to endanger her baby's life.

What context? The second indeterminacy of contextual frames is that there are no rules for drawing their borders or for leaving them settled once drawn. Contexts are as complex as culture itself and there are few if any parts of the culture that judges have declined to incorporate into legal texts: practical, social, historical, political, economic, philosophical, moral, religious, mystical, psychological, scientific and other signs are all appropriated by the judiciary at one time or another, pulling legal contexts right back into the complexity of the entire cultural web. Moreover, contexts are yeasty, changing with cultural practice, sometimes slowly, sometimes overnight. If there are areas of cultural calm where the contextual frame seems settled, that is not because the frame's borders are frozen by legal doctrine but because the culture is leaving them alone.

The presidential age requirement is an easy case within its current cultural frame because no one has ever thought it important to propose a different one. But if most of the population over 25 were to die in an age-related viral epidemic, or in an epidemic brought on by global warming, the contextual frame of the Constitution's age requirement would rapidly be redrawn to include scientific, practical and political connections that would make a 25-year-old's candidacy a hard case at very least. The fact that most drivers stop at STOP signs indicates that there is a widely shared contextual frame for reading the word STOP on the highway, making STOP sign violations easy cases. But that frame is instantly redrawn by social practice in times of emergency such as floods and earthquakes, and prosecution of flood and earthquake victims for running STOP signs would present any judge with hard, not easy, cases.

Words + context, then, cannot be the tie that binds judges' discretion. Judges have too many contexts from which to choose, and no rules by which to define a context or keep it from changing. If it is true that some contexts are relatively settled and allow legal doctrine to claim it has easy cases, it is because legal doctrine is taking an easy ride on social practices that, for the moment, no one cares to challenge.

Purpose. Purposes, like "inherent structure," "coherence," "narrative chains" and similar patterns some interpreters claim to find in texts, are really a specific type of contextual frame that interpreters themselves draw around a portion of the web of signs. Therefore, the comments above about contextual frames apply here: the reader judge is confronted with the decisions of whose purpose to choose, how to define the borders of purpose from among the welter of cultural possibilities (here different purposes are easily multiplied by stating them at different levels on a ladder of abstraction), and what to do when purposes change over time.

Is the purpose of the 35-year-old age requirement to assure mature leadership, to encourage wise government, to promote the general welfare, to impose generational hierarchy, to narrow competition for the presidency, to discriminate against the young, to disqualify for several years some specific politicians known at the time of the constitutional convention, to set an arbitrary age in order to put an end to disagreements about all of the foregoing purposes? Is the purpose of traffic STOP signs to save lives, protect property, reduce speed, discourage traffic, give pedestrians a chance, prevent traffic jams, slow traffic in business districts, employ highway engineers, secure revenue from ticket fines, protect children, promote safety, or make our community a better place to live? Such purposes don't spring full-born from the texts and force themselves upon us; interpreters choose them. If the presidential age provision is an easy case it is because no one for 200 years has chosen to worry about its purpose; if someone did worry about it, say in a crisis that decimates the older population as hypothesized above, we would have a hard case, because a purpose for setting the requirement at age 35 is difficult to guess or to justify. If a STOP sign prosecution is an easy case it is because there is a widely shared contextual frame that probably includes the notion that the purpose of the signs is safety. But if evidence were adduced, as it could be, that the purpose of some STOP signs is to promote sales by slowing traffic in business districts, and of others to increase revenues from ticket fines by setting enforcement traps, then talk of purpose would make these cases hard ones. The stakes are so small in traffic cases, however, and the costs of challenge so high, that evidence of these purposes of STOP signs is never adduced.

Judicial texts. Literature on indeterminacy of case precedents is now so rich that the claim that judges are constrained by prior judicial texts no longer needs be taken seriously. The critique, given in Chapter 2, points out, among other problems, that no one knows what would constitute "following precedent" or "stare decisis," there is no true agreement on which portion of the text may be used, on how to identify any of these with certainty, on how to limit possible combinations that can lead to thousands of possible "holdings," or on which texts qualify for use. That is not to say that what we call "following precedent" is a meaningless activity, because it does serve a rhetorical, persuasive function. But it is not a constrained activity. It is more like "getting exercise" than it is like "playing baseball": almost any move counts. Therefore, if there is any case law on the presidential age provision or on STOP signs, its texts will not control our decisions.

Other possible texts. Other choices displayed in the diagram are reason, consequences, equity, nature, legislative silence (taking the failure to pass or amend legislation as a significant sign), and disregarding the text (that is, avoiding the most obvious text by omitting to mention precedents or facts, by ignoring statutes deemed obsolete, by failing to enforce laws on the books, or by invoking gatekeeping doctrines like "political question," and "justicability"; some other text, such as reason or equity, is then substituted for the obvious one). Since each of these texts is essentially unfettered on its face no discussion is needed to appreciate that none restrains the judicial reader. We have seen above how some of these choices may plausibly be applied to the presidential age case and the STOP sign case. All of the choices enjoy robust existence in Anglo-American legal practice.

Sources of texts

We next arrive at the section of the cultural web that contains signs of the sources of texts: individuals, legislators, society, nature and others whose meanings we may or may not choose to adopt as our own, assuming we can discover them. These sources do not control our discretion as judges for several reasons. First, despite much rhetorical clinging to the old-fashioned notion that author's meaning is true meaning, we do give meaning to texts in ignorance of or despite the author's intent; our actual cultural practice is to pick and choose those authors' meanings that we wish to privilege. Second, there are no rules for ranking or weighing the authorial sources that compete in every case. Third, even should we decide to honor a specific authorial intent we are rarely able to find it, because in law it is so often fictional or inaccessible.

Looking to the presidential age provision, we could choose or decline to become embroiled in the questions on which so much ink is spilled in constitutional law debates: What does it say in James Madison's notes about 35-year-old presidents? In James Madison's head? In the ratifiers' heads? In the social conditions of 1787? In the social conditions of today? In the structure of our democracy? In 200 years of case law? In the evolution of our politics? In human nature? And so on. Any of these, and others, would be legitimate choices, all respected sources of intent in our legal practice. Should we pursue them, we will find most to be unavailable or to evaporate into pure fiction, in which case we will be forced either to admit that no authorial intent exists, or (which is more customary) to construct an intent and declare we have found it. The presidential age provision, like any other provision of the Constitution, is pregnant with these issues. If they have never arisen, it is not because any legal doctrine has announced clear answers to them, but because no one has thought it important to raise them by challenging the age provision.

A similar exercise would attend any attempt to discover and honor the legislative intent of the statute authorizing STOP signs. Which of 120 state legislators' minds do we examine? Why choose the original legislature over all the subsequent ones that were silent about the statute? How do we cumulate conflicting intentions among legislators? What if their intentions differ depending upon the level of abstraction at which they are stated? Which of the selectively available and frequently fraudulent legislative history materials do we employ, and how do we weigh them? How do we treat a lack of intention with regard to unforeseen applications of the statute? Wouldn't it be more candid to assume that the real source of the statute was some amorphous cultural condition like "social needs," and to conclude that it is silly to ascribe the fiction of authorial intent to statutes in order to give them meaning? All these possibilities, and others, lurk in even a routine STOP sign case, handing us as judges leeway to do what we please with legislative intent of the traffic laws. If, again, such issues have never arisen, it is not because legal doctrine speaks with one voice about legislative intent, but because the stakes are so low in traffic cases, and the costs of challenge so high, that no one bothers.

Other interpreters' views

Finally, we come to that part of the cultural web that links us to other interpreters' understandings of the presidential age provision and of STOP signs, because as judges we are not interested in an idiosyncratic meaning of our own private language but in public meanings that communicate to others and persuade. Is this where our discretion will finally be constrained by legal doctrine?

The answer, once again, is no. An infinite variety of interpreters in society may hold strong and perhaps differing views about the meaning of the law in various contexts. Are judges constrained to limit the list of interpreters who constitute a proper audience for the law, and then to choose among the interpreters and to rank their readings relative to one another? No, legal doctrine has nothing to say about either membership in the audience nor ranking of interpreters. To simplify greatly, two basic judicial practices can be identified.

One practice seeks some general public opinion, holding (in the words of Lord Atkin in *Donoghue v. Stevenson*) that it is "an advantage to make it clear that the law … is in accordance with sound common sense."[9] One of our judges quoted above acknowledged this practice when he spoke of the need "to reach decisions that are capable of gaining the acceptance of the public and the other branches of government."[10] He feels this as a constraint on his discretion, but it is curious to call a constraint of law something you impose upon yourself and which links the law to a virtually infinite variety of practical, social, economic, political and other cultural conditions. We have already seen how these links can be traveled when judges exercise their discretion to select texts and sources, especially choice of contextual frames, purposes, and sources. They are traveled again in this practice of seeking the understanding of other interpreters, the judges becoming students of social history, of specialized cultural knowledge produced by experts, and of popular culture and its peculiar construct called common sense, with all the indeterminacy that such an effort implies.

It's my guess that popular culture today would view a 25-year-old presidential candidate as a joke, so this will be an easy case for a court which privileges the readings of popular culture. It's also my guess, however, that in a public health crisis like the one I've speculated on earlier, public opinion would change overnight and a court decision upholding the 25-year-old's candidacy would for that reason be a distinct possibility. Indeed, a political crisis far short of the one I've imagined could do the trick if it threatened civil violence. Public opinion almost always reads the law in whatever way is thought necessary to avoid violence in the streets, and the judges usually follow.

The second basic practice is to affirm that the only relevant other interpreters are the actors in the legal process, principally other judges. Formally, their views are privileged on the positivist ground that only they are authorized to find and declare the law, and that they must do so autonomously of public opinion and often in defiance of it. Informally, their views are privileged because every judge is part of a professional culture of shared values. Their views may be known from their formal statements, such as judicial texts, issued in their official capacities through traditional legal discourse, in which case we are simply returned to the indeterminacy of legal texts which this chapter has been at pains to demonstrate. Or, their views may be known informally through collegial channels of local judicial culture, and in this rather invisible, greatly underestimated wellspring we have a formidable force for production of legal meaning. The informal culture of the judiciary, like that of any bureaucracy, has its own traditions and concerns centering on its institutional welfare, its power, and the self-esteem of its personnel. Judges who go along with local judicial culture (few opt to be mavericks) may indeed feel a contextual frame imposed upon their discretionary choices, as described earlier. But it is curious to call this a constraint of legal doctrine when it is self-selected and is composed not of legal doctrine but of group behavior designed to secure the welfare of a bureaucratic structure which happens to be a judiciary. Moreover, every judge as a member of the group has a discretionary hand in fashioning the group's behavior.

How would informal judicial culture view the presidential age and STOP sign cases? My guess is that it would find them trivial annoyances, resent having them clutter the docket, and seek ways to deal with them summarily without giving any real thought to their facts or law. Various techniques are available to this end. And should the cases become politically controversial in times of crisis and develop into hard cases, the instinct of judicial culture would likely be to avoid controversy through the political question or some other gatekeeping method, and if that does not succeed, to switch frames and privilege some view of popular culture instead.

The judge

We've completed our trip through the web of texts, sources and other interpreters and found that none limits discretion because each offers us multiple options and many of the options are as unbounded as cultural complexity itself. We are left with the central figure of the web, the judge, situated in precisely those nodes of history, culture, and psychology of which legal doctrine claims to be independent, reading the signs of the web through the lenses of his or her own values.

Sophisticated statistical studies in the political science literature confirm the obvious that personal values are at work in the judges' heads. Political scientists have built a strongly explanatory model based upon extensive statistical evidence showing that what drives the decisions of U.S. Supreme Court justices is their ideology, thus confirming what the Legal Realists had long proclaimed.[11] In federal trial courts, liberal and conservative judicial decisions correlate strongly with the judges' political party, the appointing president, and the geographical locale of the court. In the federal appellate courts, party affiliation and appointing president likewise are strong predictors of liberal or conservative results in non-unanimous, controversial cases. The study which one of our judges cited for showing an 83% unanimity rate among nearly 4,000 decisions also revealed that in those civil rights and liberties cases which were non-unanimous the judges appointed by Kennedy, Johnson or Carter voted for the liberal result more than 60% of the time, while appointees of Nixon, Ford and Reagan voted for the liberal result only 26% of the time. When Carter and Reagan appointees jointly participated in cases but disagreed, the Carter judges voted for the liberal outcome 95% of the time and the Reagan judges 5%.[12]

How, then, in the midst of all this obvious subjectivity do appellate judges nevertheless arrive at 83% and higher rates of unanimity? This is how:

First, we've seen that judges will often read the signs of the law in a contextual frame that is widely shared in the culture. It would be surprising if judges did not share many of the social beliefs of their own time and place. If no one else is pondering the potential instability of the 35-year-age requirement for presidents, judges will not likely ponder it either. A good deal of the judges' unanimity is no doubt rooted in these common cultural assumptions.[13]

Second, the informal culture of the judiciary is a powerful force for consensus of values rooted not in legal doctrine but in the welfare of the judiciary. Ascending to the bench, both liberals and conservatives come to share the ideology of the robe. Culturally, law interpreters have always been a privileged caste that has acquired its power by claiming to possess esoteric and exclusive knowledge of legitimate authority, by locating that authority in objective sources autonomous from society, by speaking a mystifying language, and by restricting membership. In the United States, access to this privileged caste has been limited predominantly to politically connected white males of the middle and upper classes. Even the relatively few women and racial minorities who have been admitted to the judicial club have previously received the same education in the catechism of traditional legal interpretation, and all have had a number of years in law practice. All share a common interest in maintaining the institutionalized influence of the judiciary. You would not expect much diversity or iconoclasm in such a group, nor do you get them. You would expect adherence to group modes of behavior, and loyalty to the systems that support the group's status and power, and these are what you get, dressed up as legal doctrine.[14]

Virtually every mechanism that our judges mention as a constraint on their discretion is not a doctrine of external law, but a group norm that protects the judicial culture, to wit:

- The "need to write an opinion … in accord with the conventions of legal reasoning," like the need "to adopt accepted methods of analysis," is simply a desire to conform to the style of traditional legal discourse, a style which does not determine results but does reaffirm the social hegemony of the discourse.
- The need to defend against criticism from colleagues, and the need for "careful exposition," are desires to persuade the members of the judicial club.
- The emphasis on gatekeeping doctrines that limit the cases reaching the appellate courts highlights the judicial bureaucracy's needs to regulate its work flow and to avoid controversy when possible.
- The need to defer to the findings of fact made in the trial court is a desire for judicial efficiency and for collegiality with lower court judges.
- The rule that the first panel's decisions are precedental within the circuit does not constrain judges for precedents are indeterminate texts, nor would its absence lead to chaos (it does not in civil-law countries which explicitly disavow case precedents), but it does reflect the judges' agreement to control work flow and to maintain the appearance of harmony on which the social myth of the objectivity of law partly depends.

Finally, the rate of unanimous and dissenting opinions is not accepted in political science literature as a good measure of doctrinal consensus because it masks substantial disagreement.[15] A number of mechanisms allow judicial culture to suppress its disagreements:

- Judges negotiate doctrine through interpersonal give-and-take, circulation of drafts, and conferences, like a legislative committee.
- Those who disagree hesitate to undertake the time-consuming burden of writing dissents.
- On some courts, for efficiency, judges rotate decision-making in certain cases, agreeing in advance to sign one another's opinions.
- Literature on group behavior indicates that smallness of a group subdues individuality. You must be bolder to dissent on a three-judge panel where you will be alone than on a larger court where you may have allies.
- Visiting judges, widely used to supplement perennially overburdened regular judges, file many fewer dissents than the others, perhaps because of time constraints or because it is even more difficult psychologically for outsiders (particularly lower-court judges sitting with higher-court judges) to muster the will to dissent.
- Some cases are actually doctrinally inconsistent, the inconsistencies obscured by the surface fact that all were unanimously decided. Unpublished opinions no doubt hide more extensive doctrinal inconsistencies.
- A judge who might otherwise dissent may be content to join unpublished opinions, thinking that the harm done will be done quietly and limited to these parties so it's not worthwhile to write a dissent.

Conclusion

In summary, what makes easy cases easy is not legal doctrine but shared social and professional values. Indeed, legal doctrine is a veritable instrument for instability, always offering multiple, unconstrained choices of texts, sources and other interpreters' views. The judges are sincere in reporting their experience of constraints, because social and professional constraints are very real. But the judges have fooled themselves into believing that these constraints of culture and judicial bureaucracy are somehow matters of legal doctrine.

It should not surprise us that judges fall into this self-deception. Few of them have the time to attempt deep introspection about their own mental processes. Few have any training or experience in language analysis or interpretation theory outside of the superficial catechism taught in law school and reinforced in law practice. Few are inclined even to address the issue, since their personal success and institutional power often depend upon the myth of fixed law and judicial objectivity. The judges' self-deception appears to rest on the same mechanisms that enable both tribal shamans and Western psychiatrists genuinely to believe in their own methods despite lack of empirical evidence of their effectiveness.[16] Moreover, we know that self-deception is a basic psychological mechanism for most of us in everyday life.[17] Given these conditions, we should not expect judges to overcome their self-deception, but that should not stop the rest of us from leading the sacred cow of legal objectivity out to a tranquil and distant pasture.

Part Two
The Practice

Chapter 5

How Statutes Get Their Meaning: The Speed Limit Laws

A statute is an instrument of government partaking of its practical purposes but also of its infirmities and limitations, of its awkward and groping efforts.

—Justice Felix Frankfurter[1]

For two decades there was a law on the books that affected virtually every American every day, that saved lives and gasoline, but that was resented, resisted and finally scrapped due to popular antagonism. This was the 55 mile-per-hour national speed limit set by Congress. Enacted in 1974 as a gas-saving measure in response to a foreign oil embargo (vehicles burn less gas per mile at slower speeds), the law also appeared to reduce highway mortality and so had the backing of an array of safety advocates and insurers. Despite the benefits, much of the driving public, accustomed to speeds of 65, 70 and higher, was never enamored of 55 and disobeyed it. Enforcement was spotty. As the gas crisis waned, resistance grew, particularly among the political representatives of western states where long stretches of country highways seemed to beckon for higher speeds. The statute was weakened in 1987 to allow 65 mph in rural areas, then in 1995 it was repealed altogether. Its 20-year saga is a nice illustration of the way statutes are instruments of government, practical yet infirm, awkward and groping, whose fate depends upon the many interpreters who interpret them.

Congress, of course, has no authority to set local speed limits *within* the states. Instead, in 1974 it made federal highway funds contingent upon state speed limits of 55. The key language of the federal statute read:

> The Secretary of Transportation shall not approve any project … in any State which has a maximum speed limit on any public highway within its jurisdiction in excess of fifty-five miles per hour....

Nearly all states complied by adopting statutes changing their speed laws. By these statutes, the states made 55 miles per hour the law. Or did they?

First Judge

To keep this starkly clear, let's take as our language the minimalist version of these laws, which was posted along the roadside: "55 MAXIMUM SPEED."

Assume the year is 1990. The 1974 law is still on the books. Consider a hypothetical reader who is a positivist judge who believes in the Old Story about interpretation, faced with a motorist who was ticketed for going 60. The defendant, age 20, resident alien from Asia, appears to be poor and uneducated. He was driving a remodeled 1952 Ford pick-up truck. There is no indication that the truck was in unsafe condition. We'd like more information than is normally available about the judge's value lenses, but we know that he fits the typical profile of the Republican governor's appointees to the bench over the last eight years: white, male, over age 50, and a former public prosecutor. He considers himself in the political and social mainstream, perhaps leaning a little toward the "law and order" side. Social stability and respect for authority are among his highest social and personal values. While he considers himself free of racial and class prejudice, he believes the road to success for minorities and the poor is paved only with individualism and hard work, Horatio Alger style.

He believes, perhaps by introspection, perhaps by habit and intuition, that these values will be best promoted in this case if he sticks to what he thinks of as the plain meaning of the statutory text, honors the authority of the legislative source, and follows the views of the police, prosecutor, and other judges as the most important other interpreters.

He decides that the text "55 maximum speed" has a plain meaning reflected in every dictionary and in the basic language competence of the general population. Since the meaning is unambiguous, he declines to examine any extrinsic evidence of purpose such as legislative history.

It is enough for him to note that the statute was duly enacted by the authoritative source of social policy in a representative government, the state legislature.

He knows that other interpreters here include the highway police, the prosecutor and other judges, and wants to be mindful of their views. The patrol officer and prosecutor, he surmises, must have had good reason to charge this particular defendant because they rarely bring cases for violations so close to the line as 60 miles per hour. He knows that some other judges have found defendants guilty in similar circumstances, though there are no reported appellate decisions because the fines were too small to make appeal worthwhile.

For him, this is an open and shut case. Despite defendant's protest that "no one goes 55 any more," he finds him guilty and imposes a fine.

Second Judge

A different judge could easily arrive at a different result, though she would be following the same steps. We needn't even make her a Legal Realist. Let's say she also wears the value lenses of a mainstream positivist who believes in the Old Story and is also concerned about social stability. She is middle aged, and one of the small number of women and even smaller number of Latinos on the bench, appointed by a previous Democratic governor after a career in immigration law and personal injury litigation. She has a practical rather than authoritarian cast of mind, is especially sensitive to survival of the judiciary, and believes that the judicial system is too weak to control large social disputes. To her, the judiciary fulfills its role best when it does justice for individuals in particular cases. These values are with her, perhaps by introspection, perhaps by habit and intuition, at every step she takes to produce the meaning of the statute.

She feels that the text "55 maximum speed" must be read in its social context, since words necessarily take meaning from the contexts in which they appear. So the real text is words + context, and the context for her is not the general dictionary of the English language but the specific context of reducing speed to save fuel and lives, which the legislative history reveals were the purposes of the statute.

The judge is not disrespectful of the state legislature, but she finds that the basic source of the 55 mile-per-hour rule was the federal Congress whose intention was to save fuel at the height of the Arab oil embargo in the early 1970s, and also to save lives. She takes judicial notice of the social facts that the oil crisis has passed and that statistics on fatalities are in dispute because of uneven enforcement across the nation.

She is wary of this particular officer and the prosecutor as other interpreters in this case, suspicious of their virtually unprecedented zeal in bringing charges against a driver doing only 60 miles per hour. She thinks they may be "out to get him" for some other reason, and knows that the police are often harder on the poor and immigrants than on affluent Anglos. She is more impressed with various other interpreters: She looks to the chief of the highway patrol who called a press conference to denounce the 55 limit not only as "unenforceable" but also "dangerous" because the slower drivers cause accidents. She looks to the press officer for the highway patrol who was quoted in the newspaper saying that "the people themselves have set the speed limit." As administrators charged with implementation, their practical interpretations of the statute are entitled to great weight in her mind. She is also keenly aware from watching the news that most state governments are engaged in a winning battle with the Federal Highway Traffic Safety Administration. FHTSA has withheld millions of dollars from states that have failed to enforce the 55 limit, but in each instance the states have secured legislation from Congress forgiving the failures. The chorus of state governments opposing the 55 limit, and ratification of their position by Congress in subsequent legislation, are strong extrinsic evidence that the state and federal authors of the 55 mile-per-hour law themselves do not believe its purpose will be fulfilled by strict enforcement. These authors apparently agree that, in the words of a state legislator quoted in the news, it is time to recognize that the, people have "voted with their gas pedals" for a higher speed. Indeed, the legislative history of the 1987 amendment to the federal statute raising the speed to 65 on rural interstates indicates that Congress was trying to let western and mid-western states, whose highways are mainly rural interstates, off the hook of FHTSA enforcement. The history also discloses that Congress silently acquiesced to clear evidence that the 55 limit was not, and would not be, enforced in the big cities.

As for other judicial interpreters, the judge discovers that only a few similar cases have been brought or upheld, all in the early days of the statute when the police were emphasizing strict enforcement. She feels confident that many other judges will share her view that the words must be read in social context, citing a long list of precedents, beginning with the "mischief rule" in *Heydon's Case*, and the U.S. Supreme Court's famous 1892 decision in *Holy Trinity Church*, which similarly disregard "literal" or "dictionary" meanings in order to achieve the statutory purpose. Citing copious case authority, she knows other judges will agree that legislative history is entitled to great weight and that judicial deference is owed to the practical interpretations of administrators and legislators.

She finds that the law is *not* working to achieve its intended purposes and informs the prosecutor that unless he dismisses the charges quietly she will throw the case out on grounds of arbitrary and discriminatory enforcement, repeal of the statute by implication, the classic canon of construction *cessante ratione legis, cessat et ipsa lex* ("the reason of the law ceasing, the law itself also ceases"), or all of these traditional positivist doctrines.

Highway Patrol Officer

Consider next what the interpreter who is a highway patrol officer might do with the 55 mile-per-hour statute.

He might take as his text not simply the words but the context of practical law enforcement. That context includes, among other things, calibration of radar and speedometers, the number of speeders, drivers creating the greatest danger, and other enforcement actions in progress. The highway patrol has formal and informal policies on these questions and trains its officers accordingly. A call to a training officer at state headquarters, for example, elicits the admission that officers are instructed to allow a margin of three miles per hour for expected errors in their radar equipment, so the actual speed limit applied is at least 58 miles per hour. (Widespread rumor has it that there is an agency-wide policy of not ticketing anyone going up to 62 miles per hour, but there has been no official admission of this.) The officer also has his own discretionary policies on enforcement, within agency guidelines, and these sometimes differ according to his mood. For him, then, the text of the law includes not only the words "55 maximum speed" but their enforcement context as well. The source of that text is not only the state legislature but also the police agency that employs him and the actual conditions on the highway. The most important views of other interpreters for him are not those of the judges or legislators but of drivers on the highway, and of his supervisors and colleagues in the patrol all of whom share the view of the chief of the agency who has denounced the 55 speed limit as "unenforceable" and "unsafe." The personal value lenses through which our officer considers these texts, sources, and other interpreters include his tough belief in "law and order," concern for his own safety, and desire for good evaluations from his supervisors. He never tickets any drivers unless they are exceeding 62, and tickets drivers traveling between 63 and 70 only if they are committing other dangerous maneuvers at the same time. He tickets most drivers exceeding 70.

An Average Driver

Finally, consider the average citizen who drives 65 miles per hour on the freeways day in, day out. How does she derive the meaning of the signs reading "55 MAXIMUM SPEED" as she whizzes by? She probably takes as her text the practical conditions on the road, reason, social custom, daily driving practices, or the well-known enforcement practices of the highway patrol, and figures that these override the dictionary meaning of 55 miles per hour. There is nothing outrageous about this: Her common sense tells her that a lot of language in society isn't taken literally, such as, "How are you?" or, "Come for dinner at 7 o'clock." Indeed, we're ostracized if we take such things at face value: we're expected to say "Fine!" though we're suffering miserably, and to show up for dinner after 7 o'clock, not expecting to put on the feed bags until 8 or so. Our citizen takes the highway patrol and the behavior of nearly all other drivers as the source of that common-sense text, and she quite accurately believes the patrol officers and other drivers to be the most important other interpreters in considering how her own interpretation is likely to be received. She sees all this through the value lenses of a mature, honest citizen, concerned about both her safety and her time, happy to obey the law but savvy that the real law is found in life, not in books.

Conclusion

If your reaction to all this is to say that I've simply told you about four interpreters, three of whom decided to ignore the law, you're probably the prisoner of the Old Story and its untenable assumptions. Don't assume that "the law" is restricted to "law in books." Law in the statute books isn't terribly important, except to printers and librarians, until it becomes part of law in action. And then it is often not the most important part. The law that counts is the law that gets you ticketed, fined, sent to jail—why would you be interested in anything else? And that law, in the matter of speed limits, is not found in books or on roadway signs reading "55 MAXIMUM SPEED. That law is found in behavior of the other drivers, the highway patrol, prosecutors, judges, state and federal politicians, and the news media. If you insist that all I'm trying to say is that the real law isn't enforced, look again. Don't be trapped into the assumption handed down by centuries of priestly interpreters that the law is something enshrined in a written text. Compare what you are calling the "real" law with the modernist, anthropological observation of our actual cultural behavior that I am describing. Whose law is more real?

Perhaps you acknowledge that the real law isn't enshrined in the written text "55 MAXIMUM SPEED," but you nevertheless protest that three of the interpreters I've told you about were doing something other than interpreting the meaning of that text. In this you may still be captured by the old assumption that "meaning" is a thing or a thought that can be discovered through word labels. Recall our anthropological observation about the semiotic process. When people say that a sign "means" something, they are really recounting an experience: the first sign has made them think of another, and that of another, and so on in a chain of signs that ends when the person registers a final sign in thought or behavior. Here, all four interpreters took the same initial sign ("55 MAXIMUM SPEED") and linked it to other signs in a series of mental experiences ending in a final behavior (respectively finding defendant guilty, throwing the case out, writing traffic tickets only at certain higher speeds, and driving 65).

In linking signs all interpreters took the same steps that seem always to be followed in our culture to make socially acceptable meanings: Looking through their own value lenses, they selected a text or texts, attributed the text to some source, and considered the views of other interpreters. Then they produced the meaning in their final thoughts or behavior about the series of signs they had linked. Their meanings differed because at each step the interpreters were faced with multiple legitimate choices offered by the encyclopedic cultural web of signs in which they found themselves embedded as displayed in the web illustration in Chapter 3. Moral, political and social values were at stake in every choice but were largely undisclosed because the myths of the Old Story about legal interpretation keep values hidden. In the end, the meanings decided upon by each reader were those acceptable to other interpreters with social power. For all but the first judge mentioned above, those other interpreters were, above all, the millions of drivers individually empowered to impose their reading of "55" as "60+" simply by stepping on the gas pedals of their modernist automotive machines; and it's doubtful that even the first judge would be able to resist this overwhelming power of reader-drivers except in quiet, isolated cases. Normally, social power to make legal meanings is not so widely distributed, but whether distributed to the masses or to elites it is always social power that ultimately establishes the meaning of the law.

Chapter 6

How the Constitution Gets Its Meaning: Brown v. Board of Education

We are under a Constitution, but the Constitution is what the judges say it is.

—Charles Evans Hughes, Governor of New York,
Later Chief Justice of the United States[1]

Parts of the American Constitution are written in the kinds of phrases that look good chiseled into the stone pediments of government buildings and have the ring of revealed wisdom. From these lapidary texts, judges, citizens, politicians and other interpreters produce meanings fraught with dramatic consequences. Abortion, religion, equality, the death penalty, criminal justice, criticism of the government, and a host of other explosive social issues swirl around the interpretation of short, cryptic phrases. Interpretation of the Equal Protection Clause in *Brown v. Board of Education* in 1954, perhaps the most discussed judicial decision of the last 100 years, illustrates how the Supreme Court as the key interpreter of the Constitution is able to produce such potent meanings from so few words. (You can find *Brown* reprinted in the Appendix.)

The Court's Opinion

On the surface, Chief Justice Warren's opinion for the unanimous Court works through a traditional positivist analysis to arrive at its conclusion that racially segregated schools violate the Equal Protection Clause. It's true that the opinion has been criticized for having too much social science and not enough law. What the critics have in mind is its unusual brevity and clarity (Warren held the heretical belief that an opinion on such a sensitive subject should be readable by the general public), its somewhat sparse citation of legal documents and judicial precedents, and its reference to social science and psychological research in one footnote. But these are differences in degree, not in kind, from the usual Supreme Court opinion. *Brown* actually follows a standard formula from the Old Story about legal interpretation. Paraphrased and distilled, Warren's analysis flows this way:

Brown and the three cases joined with it for decision arise from different states and different facts, but all present the common question whether racially segregated public schools, solely by virtue of being segregated, deprive the black plaintiffs of the equal protection that the 14th Amendment guarantees them.

The first place to look to resolve the question is to the original intent when the Amendment was adopted in 1868. Evidence of that intent is found in Congressional debates, in the states' ratification processes, in then-existing practices of racial segregation, and in the recorded views of the Amendment's proponents and opponents. We delayed decision in Brown and its companion cases for several months in order to get additional arguments from the parties on precisely this historical evidence. The evidence, however, turns out to be inconclusive. Adding to the unclarity is the fact that public education was not yet well established, particularly in the south, in 1868. In other words, public education is not something the authors would have been thinking about since it barely existed at the time, so naturally there is little evidence available about the Amendment's intended effect on schools.

The next place to look for the meaning of the Equal Protection Clause is in the judicial precedents construing it. The early cases start off with strong, broad interpretations prohibiting all racial discrimination. Plessy v. Ferguson which established the "separate but equal" doctrine came late, in 1896, and involved transportation, not education. The cases involving the "separate but equal" doctrine in public education have been mixed in results, and none directly challenged whether the Plessy doctrine applies to public education. Brown and its companion cases now make that challenge.

To resolve the question, we cannot "turn back the clock" to 1868 or 1896. The question is whether in the context of public education today segregation denies equal protection of the laws. It does. Today, compulsory public education is extraordinarily important for the functioning of our democratic society and for individual success in life. At school, students pick up intangible educational qualities which aid their success. At segregated schools, black students suffer psychological feelings of inferiority by virtue of the segregation alone, which affects their opportunity to learn and affects "their hearts and minds in a way unlikely ever to be undone." This conclusion is backed up by two of the Court's recent precedents overturning segregation in graduate schools, by the trial court's findings in the

Brown case, and by modern psychological and sociological research. Therefore, separate educational facilities are inherently unequal and laws supporting them violate the 14th Amendment.

In sum, Warren first makes the traditional assumption that the meaning is in the text. Next, he assumes that the meaning the authors originally intended would be the one that counts. But that meaning, on the specific question of segregated schools, is unrecoverable because the historical and judicial evidence of it is unclear. Then, he assumes without discussion that whatever else the Equal Protection Clause means it must mean that state laws may not fall more harshly on one race than on another solely because of race. It is unclear whether Warren thinks this is so as a matter of the plain meaning of the Clause, a matter of the authors' original intent, or both. He says, ambivalently, that we can't "turn back the clock." That may be a rejection of original intent in favor of today's plain meaning ("equal" plainly does not mean "inferior" and inferiority must be gauged as it exists today), but earlier he had sought original intent so it's doubtful that he's rejecting it now. Instead, unsuccessful in his attempt to find original intent on the specific issue of school segregation, he appears now to move up the ladder of abstraction to the broad principle of racial equality, and finds the original intent on that principle was to prohibit laws that make one race inferior to another. Whether he is finding that principle in plain meaning or in original intent, both are standard Old-Story techniques for discovering the meaning hidden in a text. Having found that meaning, Warren's final job is a positivist, mechanical application of the meaning to today's facts. He establishes the facts—showing harsh inequalities in the intangible effects of the educational environment—in traditional fashion through judicial evidence (judicial notice of social facts, the Court's findings in precedents on graduate education, the trial court's findings in *Brown*) and social science evidence. While the social sciences relied upon here, psychology and sociology, are sometimes criticized as soft (and critics have questioned the evidence in *Brown* on that ground), the Old Story about legal interpretation has routinely employed social evidence, especially history, economics, and judges' personal knowledge of social facts, as extrinsic evidence of purpose of the text and reasonableness of the interpretation. So there is nothing new in *Brown's* borrowing from social science.

In the final paragraph, the Court announces delay in the full effect of its decision until the parties can reargue how best to formulate implementing decrees.

That's what you see on the surface of Warren's opinion. Beneath the surface, the opinion was working through the semiotic web of legal interpretation diagrammed in Chapter 3, expressing important values through its choices of texts, sources of texts, and views of other interpreters to be accepted, and in this way establishing a persuasive meaning of the Equal Protection Clause.

The Justices' Culture, Psychology, and Values

It's impossible to give here a full-blown picture of the historical, cultural, sociological and psychological circumstances that shaped the value lenses of each of the nine justices who joined in *Brown*. The single best source for such a picture is Richard Kluger's masterful, rich book about the case, *Simple Justice,* on which I rely heavily for this chapter.[2] Some salient points may be mentioned.

All the justices were in their 50s and 60s at the time of the decision, each born near the turn of the century. By virtue of their historical moment, each was a witness to the rapid social changes brought by modernism, to the Russian Revolution, to the traumas of the two world wars and the great economic depression, to the massive migration from country to city, and to the immense transformation in the role of blacks in society. The black population had largely remained in the rural states that once held them slaves. But between 1915 and 1930, drawn by the labor shortage created by World War I, the closing of the immigration gates to many Europeans, and industrial expansion, nearly 100,000 blacks migrated every year from South to North. Again during and after World War II, labor scarcity drew blacks North and gave them incomes that, while shockingly behind those of whites, added up to significant economic power. Blacks fought superbly in both wars and gained personal power and independence in the process, despite cruel treatment in segregated armies. Franklin Roosevelt brought them into his political coalition, winning them away from their traditional alliance with the party of Lincoln, and they shared in the New Deal's relief and work programs. Harry Truman, from conviction, and perhaps with an eye on black voters in important swing states in the industrial North, pushed the toughest civil rights program since Reconstruction. He appointed a Committee on Civil Rights composed of prominent black and white citizens in 1946, and then backed its call for anti-poll-tax and anti-lynching laws, equality in housing, a Fair Employment Practices Commission, and vigorous enforcement of anti-discrimination laws. He named blacks to key posts in the government and ordered the armed forces to integrate.

Culturally, the justices had lived all their lives in an openly racist society, though as the decades went by the racism was increasingly pierced by strong voices of moral protest. North and South, pop culture commonly deprecated blacks as "niggers," "coons," and worse. Some Ivy League scholars caught up in social Darwinism labeled blacks an intellectually and morally inferior race. Many economists saw them as a source of cheap labor naturally suited to warm climates. Southern mobs lynched them with impunity, not only in the stealth of night but once even in a town theater with tickets sold for the rights to shoot the swaying body from the orchestra seats. Northern mobs, especially union workers competing for jobs, bullied, beat, and slaughtered them on numerous infamous occasions. Most labor unions, not to mention professional groups like the American Bar Association, were closed to blacks. They were kept from voting by poll taxes, literacy tests, and dozens of other cunning devices. South and North, depending upon the state and town, blacks were forbidden to set foot in areas reserved for white eating, white sleeping, white defecating, white entertaining, white traveling, white walking, white sitting, white resting, white playing, white swimming, white housing, and, of course, white schooling.

Through it all, a counterpoint of moral protest was constantly raised. W.E.B. Du Bois, Jane Addams, John Dewey, Lincoln Steffens, Marcus Garvey, Rabbi Stephen S. Wise, Franz Boas, Clarence Darrow, Charles Houston, Nathan Margold, A. Philip Randolph, Ralph Bunche, Langston Hughes, Kenneth Clark, Gunnar Myrdal, Eleanor Roosevelt, Richard Wright, Ralph Ellison, and Thurgood Marshall were among the thousands of prominent outspoken voices of conscience heard by the justices during the course of their lives. There were, moreover, the great symbolic challenges to racism that could not have escaped the justices: among them, Jesse Owens' triumph at the Olympics of 1936, Jackie Robinson's breakthrough into professional baseball in 1946, opera star Marian Anderson's performance on the steps of the Lincoln Memorial in 1939 under the auspices of the Roosevelt Administration after her concert at Constitution Hall had been cancelled by the Daughters of the American Revolution who owned the building. Not least, the justices had witnessed repeated legal attacks on racism mounted ever since 1915 by the National Association for the Advancement of Colored People and in recent decades the Court had sustained many of the challenges, including those against discrimination in primary elections, interstate trains and buses, real estate covenants, and graduate schools. More than just precedents, such cases made the anguish and irrationalities of racism vivid to the justices in the jargon of their own judicial subculture.

Psychologically, the influences on each justice can be described only in a full biography. Thumb-nail sketches, drawn mainly from the material in Kluger's book, look like this:

Earl Warren, white, male, 62, grew up in California, the son of a poor Norwegian immigrant, took a law degree, then rose through judicial politics as a district attorney, attorney general, and finally two-time governor of California. His long political record had been that of an active, anti-corruption, law and order type, with a mix of progressive views (labor, public works,) and oppressive ones (round-up of Japanese-Americans during the War). A smiling bear, honest, un-intellectual, Republican, Warren was so popular with the voters that even the Democrats endorsed his second run for governor. He was on the Republican ticket as Vice-President with Dewey in 1948. He competed with Eisenhower for the top slot in 1952, and there was talk later that the latter promised him a seat on the Court if he would deliver the California delegates to Eisenhower, which he did. When Chief Justice Vinson, who was prepared to uphold segregation in *Brown*, died in 1953, Eisenhower named Warren as Chief Justice. He joined the Court after it had already been deliberating on *Brown* for more than a year and had delayed decision for a second round of arguments. He studied the briefs, heard the second round, and at the next conference of justices stated that he thought the separate but equal doctrine was grounded in the notion that blacks were an inferior race, a notion unacceptable "in this day and age." That gave the fifth clear vote of the nine justices to strike down segregation. From that moment, he put his personal political charm to work on the others to achieve a unanimous Court.

Hugo Black, white, male, 65, from Alabama, appointed by Roosevelt, former little-person's lawyer, local police judge and politician who had briefly joined the Ku Klux Klan for expediency, later a leading New Deal Senator, then one of the staunchest liberal and humanitarian members of the Court (he was the only justice to attend the Marian Anderson concert in 1939) who sided frequently with blacks and individual rights. Black favored outlawing school segregation on principle as soon as *Brown* was argued, though he told the other justices there would be riots in the South.

William O. Douglas, white, male, 53, from Washington state, appointed by Roosevelt, former Yale law professor, Roosevelt's first head of the Securities and Exchange Commission, individualist and outdoorsman, bright, quick, cold, impatient with his colleagues' pettifogging legal techniques, a Legal Realist keenly aware of the Court as a political body, and certain that the Court's key role was to protect individual liberties. In favor of desegregation from the outset, Douglas is reported to have said at a conference of the justices that the question is "very simple for me."

Harold Burton, white, male, 64, former city attorney and mayor of Cleveland, later a moderate Republican Senator from Ohio who supported progressive domestic legislation and the move to establish the United Nations, appointed to the Court by Truman in an a rare attempt to appear non-partisan. Burton's voting record on the Court often but not always favored black plaintiffs. Reputed to be a mild, fair, open-minded, and humble man, Burton wrote to Frankfurter at the beginning of the *Brown* proceedings that the "separate but equal" doctrine might have made sense 50 years previously when "the lives of negroes and whites were then and there in fact separately cast and lived." But times had changed and segregation could no longer be equal "in a society that is lived and shared so jointly by all races as ours is now."

Sherman Minton, white, male, 62, from Indiana, once called "an almost pathological Democrat" by Justice Frankfurter. After one term in the Senate during the New Deal where he befriended then-Senator Truman, Minton served on the federal appellate bench until Truman named him to the Supreme Court in 1949. As a judge, his intelligence was widely disparaged and his record on civil liberties and race cases was considered poor by civil libertarians, though he had taken some liberal stances when in the Senate. His opinions were mainly distinguished by a dogged belief that the powers of the legislative and executive branches should be upheld however exercised. Justice Reed and others expected Minton to help block desegregation of schools, but Minton surprised them by denouncing segregation as unreasonable at the first conference on *Brown*, siding with Black, Douglas and Burton.

Felix Frankfurter, white, male, 69, born in Vienna, immigrated to New York, a Legal Realist, the only Jewish law professor at Harvard at a time when Harvard-set quotas against Jews, and in 1954 the only Jewish justice on the Court, appointed to the Court by Roosevelt after serving in the New Deal's "brain trust." Intellectual, avid social reformer and civil libertarian, adviser to the NAACP early in his career, Frankfurter had sided with black rights in virtually every case he had heard, yet on the bench he grew increasingly conservative over the years and obsessed with upholding the Court's image of objectivity. As a judge, he said he was involuntarily "the symbol of the Jew," an outsider who had to restrain himself and avoid divisiveness, and he pushed the Court to sidestep controversy and to defer to the will of the more political branches. To guard the Court's influence and prestige, he would cast his opinions in arcane, objective-sounding scholasticism and emphasize that a judge had be "above the battle.... We must assume in him not only personal impartiality but intellectual disinterestedness." Yet no one was a greater politician within the Court, nor had a more realistic appraisal of judges' actual motives, than Frankfurter. He constantly lobbied his colleagues for desired results, and secretly reported private conversations from the justices' inner sanctum to his former law clerk Philip Elman, even (unethically) while Elman was an attorney in the Solicitor General's Office and therefore a party to many of the cases. Using code names for his brethren, he would tell Elman, for instance, that Douglas voted to hear a certain obscene-mail case "to satisfy his lifelong ambition to put the word 'fuck' in the U.S. Reports," while Black, despite his public absolutist position on free speech, was a prude who was ready to send the same defendant to jail for life. Fearful that a divided decision in *Brown* would weaken the Court and further divide the country, Frankfurter worked to delay any decision until either the political process would tackle desegregation or the justices would reach unanimity. When Chief Justice Vinson, opposed to desegregation and an obstacle to a unanimous opinion, died suddenly while the case was pending, Elman found Frankfurter in high spirits on the way to the funeral: "Phil," he exclaimed, "this is the first solid piece of evidence I've ever had that there really is a God." Ultimately, Frankfurter delayed long enough to get a unified Court in *Brown*, and later wrote to Judge Learned Hand: "If the 'great libertarians' [Black and Douglas, who favored immediate action] had had their way, we would have been in the soup."

Robert Jackson, white, male, 60, from upstate New York, wealthy, patrician, country-gentleman lawyer, bright, a beautiful prose stylist, appointed to the Court by Roosevelt, had ambitions to be President or Chief Justice. He served as Solicitor General and Attorney General before Roosevelt put him on the Court, and after the war Truman borrowed him from his Court duties to prosecute the Nazi defendants at the Nuremberg Trials, which he did with ardent insistence on the fairness of American judicial procedures and the moral righteousness of the indictments which were based, in part, on natural law concepts. But he was unpredictable on domestic civil liberties issues, and ambivalent about *Brown* when it was first argued. He said he couldn't see how the Court could abandon *Plessy* after 60 years without harming its cherished reputation as a non-political body, though he had openly abandoned stare decisis on other occasions. He reportedly wished the Court could condemn segregation but declare itself powerless to do anything about it and urge the political processes of Congress to resolve it.

Tom Clark, white, male, Texan, 53, the son of a hard-core white supremacist, came to the Justice Department in Washington during the New Deal through political connections where, during the war years, he helped direct the round-up of Japanese-Americans on the West Coast. Truman, whom he had backed for vice-president at the Democratic Convention in 1944, appointed him Attorney General upon assuming the Presidency. As Attorney General, he was Truman's leading anti-communist witch-hunter (compiling the first Attorney General's "pink list" of suspected communists), but had also pushed the Administration's civil rights program and brought the Justice Department into *Shelley v. Kraemer*, the housing discrimination case, on the side of blacks. When Truman appointed him to fill a vacancy on the Court in 1949, he was widely regarded as little more than the President's political crony. Clark was not ready to overturn school segregation when *Brown* was argued, and feared violence in the south, but changed his mind when he saw a consensus developing on the Court under Chief Justice Warren's urging.

Stanley Reed, white, male, 68, from the Kentucky tobacco country, former railroad and tobacco company lawyer, drawn to Washington by Hoover, appointed Solicitor General by Roosevelt where he defended the New Deal's programs, later named to the Court by Roosevelt. Reed had always voted for blacks in the major racial cases, but told his colleagues he opposed desegregation. In 1953, he very reluctantly went along with the Court's decision enforcing a disused District of Columbia ordinance that prohibited segregation in restaurants. According to Kluger, "Reed, an austere and very proper Southern gentleman, lived with his wife at the Mayflower Hotel in downtown Washington, and the couple did not cook in.... The Justice was reported to have exclaimed, upon returning from the conference at which the ... vote was taken: 'Why—why, this means that a nigra can walk into the restaurant at the Mayflower Hotel and sit down to eat at the table right next to Mrs. Reed!'" Reed wanted to dissent in *Brown* but was finally dissuaded by Warren. His clerk later recounted: "I think he was really troubled by the possible consequences of his position. Because he was a Southerner, even a lone dissent by him would give a lot of people grist for making trouble. For the good of the country, he put aside his own basis for dissent."

These sketches of the justices reveal nothing so crude as a set of predictors based upon race, gender, age, political party, geographical region or the president who appointed them. The chips don't fall into those piles so neatly in any one case, though political scientists have shown that some such factors do have some predictive power over the long run. Rather, the sketches suggest that each justice, filtering the question in *Brown* through his own complex set of experiences and values, answered it essentially by deciding what he thought was the best social policy rather than by deciding that the law dictated a result. Black and Douglas had witnessed and personally identified with the struggles of the underdogs in the 20th century, and built strong philosophical beliefs around those struggles. They probably felt compelled as a matter of conscience to adopt a policy of "integration now." Warren, Burton, and Minton, whose philosophical commitments were made of less steely stuff, nevertheless had been activist politicians of a somewhat progressive stripe, believing that with political leadership America changes for the better. To them, we may surmise, it was simply enlightened common sense to acknowledge the enormous social and economic changes in the role of blacks during their lifetimes, to conclude that times had changed and "in this day and age" a workable school integration policy was the only pragmatic, forward-looking policy for the country. Frankfurter, though ideologically committed to civil liberties and racial equality early in his life, later was even more ideologically committed to the image of the Court as the impartial and nearly sacred fountainhead of justice. His policy was to protect the authority of the Court above all, by delaying, in hopes that the political process would take the matter out of the Court's hands or that the Court would at least speak without dissents in order to add credibility to the decision. Jackson seemed to follow a similar policy for reasons of his own that are unclear. Clark and Reed, so far as we can tell, had no sympathy with the idea of integrated schools and would have been happier if *Brown* had gone the other way, but in the end adopted the overriding policy of making the Court's policy unanimous in order to ease the threat of violent resistance in the South.

Each of the justice's policies was produced the same way meanings are always produced, by picking a text (equity for Black and Douglas; today's social context for Warren, Burton and Minton; Frankfurter and Jackson choosing to disregard the text), considering its source, and weighing the views of other interpreters, but there is no space here to analyze them. We'll look, instead, at the way Warren's opinion for the unanimous Court produced the meaning of the Constitution by considering the text, source, and the views of other interpreters.

In Search of a Text

A glance at the diagram in Chapter 3 will refresh your memory of some of the textual pathways available to our interpreters in the semiotic web of legal interpretation. Warren could have linked the Equal Protection Clause to underlying texts of equity, as Black and Douglas probably would have done; nature or natural law, as Jackson did in part when prosecuting the Nazi war crimes at Nuremberg; original purpose; the words of the Clause plus their context historically or today; the words of the Clause alone; judicial precedents; or other possible texts. What he did was to consider and reject two or three possibilities and finally settled upon a text of words of the Clause as inserted in the context of today's social conditions.

The 14th Amendment's words themselves ("nor shall any State ... deny to any person within its jurisdiction the equal protection of the laws") are not even discussed in the opinion, except in a footnote excerpt quoting another case. Evidently, it was taken for granted that the words are too vague for the plain meaning approach to carry them even to first base. Indeed, the unimportance of the Constitution's literal text is made clear in *Boiling v. Sharpe*, decided the same day as *Brown*, in which the Court overturned segregation in District of Columbia schools. It was thought that the District, not being a "state," could not be brought within the 14th Amendment's language, so the 5th Amendment, which does not speak of equal protection but which forbids the federal government from denying "due process," was applied instead, reaching the same result. The Court found the clauses to overlap, "both stemming from our American ideal of fairness...." In other words, two different phrases of the Constitution could, at least sometimes, mean exactly the same thing.

The initial hunt for the text in *Brown*, then, is in the historical context surrounding the words' adoption. A year earlier, the Court had ordered reargument precisely to gather more of this evidence. Lawyers for the black plaintiffs faced a swamp of beasts. There had been murky maneuvering in Congress over the Civil Rights Act of 1866, which many in Congress believed would have eliminated segregated schools but for an amendment which removed the words that would have done it. When the first section of the 14th Amendment was adopted two years later in part (some said only) to underpin the Act of 1866, it arguably therefore went no further than that Act. Worse, 24 of the 37 states in 1868 had permitted or required segregated schools, yet none of the ratifying legislatures devoted any significant debate to the question of schools. Congress itself had permitted segregated schools in the District of Columbia before and after the Amendment was adopted. Defendants in *Brown* claimed the clear inference was that hardly anybody in the state legislatures or Congress thought the Amendment required desegregation of schools. Plaintiffs' historians argued, however, that the broad spirit of the 14th Amendment as part of the Radical Republicans' humanitarian program of racial equality surely embraced the concept of integrated schools originally, but that spirit had been subverted in Reconstruction politics in the years following its adoption. There was also the historical fact that the public school movement was new in the country, and in the South had barely taken root at all, so it was rather moot to search for specific intentions about segregation in an arena that was virtually non-existent. Finally, there was no evidence on the historical actors' intentions about the future; they may have contemplated a concept of equal protection that evolved to combat the new ways society has of producing inequality. Looking at all this evidence, several justices thought it ran against the plaintiffs, and none thought it helped them greatly. If the Court had wanted to uphold segregated schools, using history as the text could have helped. The Court, however, didn't want that result, so it neutralized the historical evidence, calling it "inconclusive." That characterization is not unfair. But notice how the Court elides the fact that most of the justices believed the historical evidence did show a conclusive intent to permit segregated schools, yet were prepared to strike down segregation anyway. In truth, from the beginning the Court was not much interested in using history as the text. The reargument on the historical evidence was a delaying tactic initiated by Frankfurter when he saw that after the first arguments there was not yet a consensus on the Court. With reargument, the Court gained another year to work out a unanimous policy.

A more candid Court might have said something like this:

We think it unwise to pretend to let historical evidence of original intent determine the outcome of this case. The notion of original intent is quite problematical in the first place. It is almost always a fictional creation, given that intentions may be stated differently depending upon their level of generality, the authors may not have foreseen the circumstances of today, their real intentions may have been politically or personally motivated and entirely irrelevant to the questions we face, evidence of their intentions is poorly recorded and inaccessible as a practical matter, and when, as here, there are numerous authors we have no rules for deciding just who counts as an author, whose intention counts most, or how we might achieve the metaphysically impossible task of melding many intentions into one. In the second place, even if we were to look at historical evidence in search of just a general sense of our past, we would want to justify our reasons for doing so. Whether to engage in such a search is always a matter of competing social values and philosophies of government. Seeking the past has been justified on the grounds that it encourages social stability, protects settled expectations, taps the wisdom of our ancestors, is required by our "social contract," or produces a reverent devotion in the populace for the sacred text of the Constitution. Such concerns are not to be disregarded lightly. But the fact is this Court and the nation have turned them aside when we have thought them outweighed by competing values. We have not wanted our Constitution to become a straightjacket for succeeding generations. We have seen it as a living document capable of fitting the changing needs of a rapidly changing society. We have not been eager to honor ignominious chapters in our nation's political history, nor to privilege from past centuries a morality that we now find cruel or barbaric. So with Brown. Aside from the futile, fictional nature of any attempt to reconstruct the original intent of the 14th Amendment, we believe it inappropriate to honor an unfortunate political history and a 19th century morality in a matter in which our society and moral beliefs have been so fundamentally transformed over the last hundred years.

The Court, however, saying no such thing and moving on in search of another text to privilege, turns to the case law. Again its approach is to neutralize the proferred texts. Starting on a civil liberties note, the opinion declares that the first cases interpreting the 14th Amendment forbade "all state-imposed discriminations against the Negro race." It footnotes four cases for the statement, without mentioning that despite some strong language on equality the cases were read and implemented mainly to the disadvantage of blacks; perhaps for this reason the Court doesn't lean on them more heavily. Next, *Plessy*, which established the "separate but equal doctrine" 60 years before and in the minds of most was the dragon to be slain, is lightly treated as irrelevant because it came long after adoption of the Amendment and dealt with transportation, not education. Warren's opinion then faces what Frankfurter had characterized in oral arguments as "a long course of decisions" that had "settled" the issue in favor of segregated schools. Warren focuses on just eight cases, two of which are virtually ignored (a standard option in the semiotic web) by being shuffled to the footnotes, and six of which are found not to have squarely faced the question of whether separate schools, even though equal in tangible factors like physical facilities, nevertheless deprive children of equal intangible educational opportunities. What Warren has done with *Plessy* and these other eight precedents is simply take advantage of the fact that there is no litmus test for finding the holding of a case. By recharacterizing the facts and the level of abstraction at which he states the holdings, he is able to render toothless what many lawyers, including most justices on the Court, had long believed to be a biting line of precedent supporting segregated schools. Had he wanted to reach a different result, he could easily have privileged a different reading of the precedents. Instead, through standard Old-Story connections in the semiotic web, he is able to arrive at the conclusion that the precedents are weightless.

A more candid Court might have said something like this:

It is true that there is a line of precedents that many have believed uphold racial segregation of schools. It is also true that it is possible to dissect the facts and reasoning of those precedents and find that they never squarely faced the issue presented here. But reading the same precedents broadly or narrowly can become a transparently disingenuous judicial game which undermines the faith of citizens in the seriousness with which we take our task. Perhaps the most straightforward and least controversial thing that can be said of our precedents is this: Many decisions have permitted segregation to exist in many forms, including school seg-

regation, for many years; our more recent decisions have resulted in the dismantling of segregation in primary elections, interstate transportation, real estate covenants, and graduate schools. Our decisions are therefore mixed but moving away from segregation. The precedents neither bind us nor help us any further than that. Chief Justice Vanderbilt once observed that the certainty that is said to be produced by stare decisis "is not an end in itself.... [It] is desirable only insofar as it operates to produce the maximum good and the minimum harm and thereby to advance justice.... [C]ourts have frequently and wisely departed from precedent." And Justice Douglas has added that, "The place of stare decisis in constitutional law is ... tenuous.... [A judge cannot let] men long dead and unaware of the problem of the age in which he lives do his thinking for him." So we must do our own thinking in this case, weighing the good, the harm, and the justice of school segregation in our age.

The Court, however, saying no such thing, continues its search for a text to privilege and at last finds it in the Equal Protection Clause inserted in the context of public education in American life today. We noted earlier the ambivalence of Warren's statement that "we cannot turn the clock back" 86 years to the time the Amendment was adopted or 58 years to *Plessy*. That could be a rejection of original intent in favor of today's plain meaning. It could be an assertion that the original intent of the Amendment was to prevent inferior treatment of one race, or to keep equality evolving with the times. In any event, he assumes a self-evident meaning that "equal" cannot embrace treating one race "inferior" to another. That meaning was not at all plain, of course, to racists, eugenicists, social Darwinists, and the like. They, like sexists, hold that equality means treating things equally according to their nature, thus treating inferiors (in their eyes, members of certain races, or women) inferiorly—or at least differently. This sort of thinking was commonplace popular culture in 1954, not infrequently accompanied by righteous claims of beneficent intentions: "You don't do the cat a favor by training it to be a dog."

If Warren had wanted to privilege such a reading of the Equal Protection Clause instead of the one he did, many in the country would have found it plain. Indeed, even President Eisenhower's views ran along those lines. Warren, however, handles such views by silence. He then takes his reading that "equal protection" means "not inferior" and inserts it into the social context of today to give content to the term "inferior." And today's context is one in which public education is of extraordinary importance to the individual and to society, one whose intangible educational qualities are available only in the same schools that whites attend, and one in which racial separation alone "generates a feeling of inferiority ... that may affect [the students'] hearts and minds in a way unlikely ever to be undone." It follows inexorably that separate is today inferior, which is unequal.

This part of Warren's opinion is the most candid. He might have more candidly acknowledged that for many the plain meaning of equality does not rule out different and even inferior treatment of others, and mounted a clearer rejection of this apartheid philosophy. He might have reviewed the 20th century history of education and of the blacks in American life more fully, reflecting more of the tragedy, hope, and change actually experienced by his generation. He might have more candidly reflected the controversies over the psychological and sociological evidence cited in footnote 11 for the proposition that separate is inferior, and might have given the proposition a more eloquent defense by appealing, say, to the values underlying the golden rule of treating others as we would be treated ourselves ("*who among us would trade skins and think ourselves equally treated?*"). But his evidence is laid out and his values are close to the surface, close to his own actual beliefs, and resonate with widely shared values that are easily grasped. He has found a text here that is rooted in the experience and values of everyday modern life, and has presented it rather straightforwardly.

The Sources of Warren's Text

The sources of that text are multiple. The source for the proposition that "equal protection" means "not inferior" may be the Congress, state legislators and other authors of the 1868 Amendment, or may be the Court itself. Warren finesses the point. The finesse means he chooses not to give special weight to the original authors, which works in tandem with his decision not to privilege original intent as the text. Obviously, he and the others justices fear the historical intent speaks against the result they want to reach, so they play it pianissimo. His sources for the proposition that separate is inferior, which is unequal in today's context, are, first, broad judicial notice of the historical, social conditions of education; second, the Court itself, speaking in its two precedents on graduate school education; third, the lower courts in the Kansas and Delaware cases involved in *Brown*; and fourth, the six psychologists and sociologists cited in footnote 11. All are well-trodden pathways in the semiotic web (though the scholars' evidence less than the others), designed to encourage respect for the meaning arrived at by showing that it emanated from sources that are respected independently.

Other Interpreters

Every time a court mentions a source of a text it is also mentioning another interpreter and usually seeking to persuade you because you respect that other reader's views. Thus, as we've just noted, Warren's opinion mentions other interpreters who are the sources of its text (judges, scholars) in this way. We also know, however, that the Court was extraordinarily concerned with views of other interpreters who are never mentioned and, as always when confronted by interpreters with social power, the Court strived to shape its decision to secure their acquiescence.

From the beginning, white segregationists were powerful other interpreters. The justices feared that an order to integrate the schools would provoke civil violence in the South (indeed, events proved them right, and not just in the South, when *Brown* entered its implementation phase). The decision to include the Kansas case and make its complainant the lead plaintiff was designed to mollify Southerners by acknowledging problems outside the South as well. The justices' indecision after first arguments in 1952, and the Frankfurter plan to delay by asking for reargument, were instilled by their fear of violence and hope that the political process would rescue them from facing the decision. Warren's muted decision, firm and sensible but lacking in grand moral rhetoric or condemnation of the segregationists, and not even explicitly overruling *Plessy* entirely, further reflected that fear. The additional delay in 1954 for reargument on implementation decrees, and the approval of gradual desegregation "with all deliberate speed," were likewise undertaken with a nervous look over the shoulder at segregationists. Philip Elman, Frankfurter's former clerk then in the Solicitor General's office and writing the brief for the United States in *Brown*, learned in his telephone chats with his former boss that the justices' great fear was violent resistance to a sudden order from the Court to integrate overnight. They were looking for a way to desegregate gradually. Elman's brief proposed gradual desegregation, overseen by district courts with an eye to local conditions. Says Elman:

> So that is why I made this "indefensible" argument in … the 1952 brief. None of this was based on what I thought was right.… I was simply counting votes on the Supreme Court … even though many people think that "with all deliberate speed" was a disaster. It broke the logjam.

And not least, of course, the unanimity of the *Brown* decision, as we know, was gained not because of the inevitability of legal doctrine but because those opposed to the decision, like Reed and Clark, wanted to ease the threat of civil disobedience.

The Court was alive to interpreters on the other side of the issue too. Over their lifetimes, the protests of thousands of prominent citizens, and of humble citizens whose family members had been lynched, killed in race riots, or treated like property or animals, rang in the justices' ears. The views of the Truman Committee on Civil Rights, of those who desegregated the armed forces in 1948, and of other government policymakers during the Roosevelt and Truman years had had their impact upon most of the justices. The views of the National Association for the Advancement of Colored People, whose lawyers represented the black plaintiffs, were expressed in many forums in addition to the Court. Official friends of the Court whose views were submitted in formal briefs included the Eisenhower Administration's Justice Department (though Eisenhower himself was unenthusiastic), the American Jewish Congress, the American Civil Liberties Union, the American Federation of Teachers, the Congress of Industrial Organizations, and the American Veterans Committee. A majority of the justices agreed anyway with these views of the integrationist interpreters of the Constitutional text. But it would not have been easy or perhaps even possible for the justices to interpret the text the way they did without the support and influence of these other interpreters. With their help, a majority of the justices produced the meaning in 1954 that the Equal Protection Clause forbids racially separate schools, and then persuaded their colleagues to join in the decision.

True to the old myth that the Court finds the law oblivious to public opinion, Warren's decision mentions neither the justices' fears of those who would disobey nor their sympathy with those who voiced the anguish of blacks. A more candid Court might have said something like this:

We are keenly conscious that we do not decide our cases in a social vacuum, that the public cares passionately about much of what we do here. In requiring integration of schools, we realize that we unsettle cultural habits that are deeply ingrained and passionately defended in many places by political majorities. For that reason, we have proceeded slowly and cautiously in this case. For that reason, the members of the Court who were initially skeptical speak with us in one voice to say to the country that angry differences must now be set aside and treated with the balm of reconciliation, lest we inflict new wounds even more dangerous to us all. For that reason, we will strive to assure that implementation of our decision is no less pragmatic and sensitive than it is resolute. In this spirit, the federal judiciary will do its part, and we look to the executive and legislative branches to help achieve a smooth transition by also being responsive to practical needs of local school districts on the one hand while leaving no doubt on the other that the law will be fully enforced. Some will question why this Court, a committee of nine in black robes unaccountable to the electorate, should wield such power to reorder fundamental social arrangements in a democracy. We will not purvey the old myth that we are merely reading the Constitutional text, as if its details were written in invisible ink discernable only to the judicial eye. Nor will we claim the mantle of Platonic guardians, wiser than other citizens, who know what is best for the country. The answer really depends upon one's philosophy of government. Of the many philosophies that have been offered to justify our system of judicial review, two seem to reflect the American experience particularly well. The first has been with us from the beginning of the republic: the notion that the government works best and most democratically when power is dispersed among three branches and among the states and federal government, each unit checking and balancing the others. Our decision today, taking action on a critical issue where there is a deadlock of political power among the states and the federal executive and legislative branches, illustrates the continuing vitality of that concept of government. The second philosophy is also vindicated by today's decision. It holds that the courts have a special function in a democracy which they are particularly designed to perform and the other branches are particularly poor at performing, namely, to protect individuals and minorities from being crushed by political majorities. In our role as guarantor of that protection, we today shield a minority against political majorities that would deny them the right to an equal education solely because of the color of their skin. Every citizen wants this protection. Most realize that the only way to be certain the protection will be there for them is to guarantee that it is there for all.

Conclusion

In the end, did the integrationist or segregationist interpreters prove to be the more powerful interpreters of the Constitution?[3] More than fifty years after *Brown*, despite significant changes in American politics, society, and education, most schools are still attended by predominantly separate racial groups. Equal educational and other social resources are still not equally available to racial minorities, despite some progress. For the Supreme Court isn't the only interpreter of the Constitution. After it made its decision, the federal executive branch, the Congress, the lower courts, the school boards, the states, the politicians, the real estate brokers, the taxpayers, the parents, the press, and many other interpreters of the Equal Protection Clause went to work in thousands of towns and cities across the country giving the Constitution, and the Court's decision, their own meanings. In everyday life, the law in action turns out to have the meaning that the complex power structure of American society wants it to have. That power structure broadly succeeded in stymying *Brown's* integration of the schools, so that when the Supreme Court itself appeared to undermine *Brown* in 2007 it was essentially putting an official imprimatur on a result already worked out by society. That year, the Court handed down *Parents Involved in Community Schools v. Seattle School District*, holding 5 to 4 that school boards could not integrate elementary or secondary schools through assigning students by race.[4]

Chief Justice Roberts, writing for four justices and claiming to be "faithful to the heritage of *Brown*," said that race could not be used as a criterion in any circumstances, even to integrate the schools. Justice Kennedy joined the four but wrote a separate opinion allowing race-based assignments in rare instances. The years had brought new justices to the Court, and the Roberts bloc of four staunch political conservatives were now taking their turn at the interpretation game on the most famous case of the 20th century. They simply dipped into the bag of Old Story tricks and pulled out a new text for *Brown*: a transcript of one sentence uttered in the 1950s oral argument by Robert L. Carter, a lawyer for the black schoolchildren, seeming to take a flat position against any race-based assignment of students to schools. The *New York Times* legal analyst, writing under the apt headline "The Same Words, but Differing Views," quoted Carter, now a senior federal judge, objecting that Roberts had used his words out of context and "[stood] the argument on its head." William T. Coleman, Jr., another lawyer for the plaintiffs in *Brown*, called Roberts's interpretation "dirty pool," and a third, Columbia law professor Jack Greenberg, called it "preposterous." Greenberg added: "You can't really say that five justices are so smart that they can read the law and precedents and four others can't. Something else is going on."[5]

Of course something else is going on. This chapter, and this book, have been at pains to describe what that something else is.

Chapter 7

How Case Precedents Get Their Meaning: *Palsgraf v. Long Island Railroad*[1]

[T]o determine to be loyal to precedents, and to the principles back of the precedents, does not carry us far upon the road.

—Judge Benjamin Cardozo[2]

If there is one case whose acquaintance is made by every law student, that case is *Palsgraf v. Long Island Railroad.* Introduced in the Torts course, *Palsgraf* is generally taken as the premier statement of the doctrine of foreseeability: the notion that persons are not liable for the injuries they negligently cause to others if they could not have reasonably foreseen the consequences of their acts. In this instance, Helen Palsgraf was waiting for a train in Brooklyn one day in 1924 when an explosion at the station knocked some heavy scales down upon her. The explosion was caused by fireworks concealed in a newspaper carried by a passenger running to board another train. Two guards working for the railroad had attempted to help the man aboard, one pulling, the other pushing, causing the fireworks to fall to the rails and explode. Mrs. Palsgraf sued the railroad for negligence, won a jury verdict, and won the first appeal. But New York's highest court, in an opinion by Chief Judge Benjamin Cardozo, reversed. The employees' shoving and hauling may have been negligent, but there was no liability, said the court, because they could not have foreseen that the innocent package wrapped in newspaper would unleash such destruction and injure Mrs. Palsgraf. Cardozo wrote for a majority of four; three judges dissented. (You will find the majority opinion reprinted in the Appendix.)

I'll omit detailed analysis of the dissent and other judges, focusing only upon the opinion by Cardozo, then and now a luminous name in American legal history. What we'll find is that the opinion illustrates the way judges always construct the meaning of cases before them from the usual subjective selection of texts, sources, and other interpreters' views. Although Cardozo was a disciple of Holmes and a noted modernist who paved the way for Legal Realism, he did not shrink from wrapping his views in the guise of the Old Story in order to shape the law the way he thought it ought to be shaped. Here, he constructed the meaning (let's call it "no liability without foreseeability") by declaring that the relevant texts were precedents, treatises, and reason; by privileging, as sources of those texts, judges, scholars, human nature, and historical evolution; and by honoring the views of certain other interpreters, namely, certain judges and scholars, society in general, and business people, all the while conscious that his own illustrious reputation allowed him virtually to impose his views without solicitous regard for others.

Cardozo's Lenses: Culture, Psychology, Values

Cardozo's intellectualism, epigrammatic prose, grand vision, and forceful personality combined to earn him the renown of a "great judge" during his years on the New York Court of Appeals long before he replaced Oliver Wendell Holmes on the U.S. Supreme Court. Many of his decisions were celebrated as modern, forward-looking departures from the common law, none more so than his 1916 opinion in *MacPherson v. Buick Motor Co.* which made manufacturers of defective automobiles liable to the ultimate buyers who are injured by them. His book, *The Nature of the Judicial Process*, based on lectures at Yale in 1921, assured his fame as a legal thinker. In it, he confessed the fundamentally subjective nature of judging. I have quoted him in Chapter 2, but his words are worth repeating here:

> There is in each of us a stream of tendency, whether you choose to call it philosophy or not, which gives coherence and direction to thought and action. Judges cannot escape that current any more than other mortals.... We may try to see things as objectively as we please. None the less, we can never see them with any eyes except our own.[3]

And more:

> What is it that I do when I decide a case? To what sources of information do I appeal for guidance? In what proportions do I permit them to contribute to the result? In what proportions ought they to contribute? If a precedent is applicable, when do I refuse to follow it? If no precedent is applicable, how do I reach the rule that will

> make a precedent for the future? If I am seeking logical consistency, the symmetry of the legal structure, how far shall I seek it? At what point shall the quest be halted by some discrepant custom, by some consideration of the social welfare, by my own or the common standards of justice and morals? Into that strange compound which is brewed daily in the caldron of the courts, all these ingredients enter in varying proportions. I am not concerned to inquire whether judges ought to be allowed to brew such a compound at all. I take judge-made law as one of the existing realities of life. There, before us, is the brew. Not a judge on the bench but had a hand in the making.[4]

Yet, for all that, Cardozo was anything but a loose cannon on the bench. Quite the contrary. The caldrons in which he stirred the brew sat in mahogany club rooms, not out on street corner soup kitchens of social turmoil. He appears to have been a man of starchy collars and a gaze that could crack marble at 50 paces. Professor (later federal appellate judge) John Noonan, who wrote an important, poignant essay on *Palsgraf* in his book *Persons and Masks of the Law*, points to several things about Cardozo that seemed to make the judicial mask fit him perfectly. First, he was a bachelor all his life, and never had children. Noonan wonders about the different "emotional context" this would give a judge dealing with accidents like Helen Palsgraf's; I would add that it is all the easier to live one's life story through the law when one is, in effect, wedded to it. Second, Cardozo was the son of a notoriously corrupt lower court judge who owed his position to Tammany Hall's Boss Tweed and who resigned under threat of impeachment. Cardozo-son was always anxious to distance himself from Cardozo-father, committing himself to a life of pure legal and ethical principle, and disdaining too close an interest in the human situation of the parties before him lest he reveal personal biases. Third, Cardozo was ambitious to make a grandiose mark on the law by striving, in his own words, "for consistency, for certainty, for uniformity of plan and structure." And his principal vehicle, off the bench, for doing so was the American Law Institute, the organization of law professors, lawyers, and judges which publishes the "Restatements" of the law. Cardozo was a founding officer of the ALI. Its task, he stated, was no less than to "bring certainty and order out of the wilderness of precedent."[5]

It was his work with the ALI that apparently put the gleam in Cardozo's value lenses as he considered Helen Palsgraf's case. We learn from Noonan that the ALI had noticed the case while it was on appeal, and invited Cardozo to attend a scholarly debate about it, which he did. The group was split but by a close vote adopted the rule of "no liability without foreseeability." Cardozo, who didn't vote in the ALI meeting, did vote later against Helen Palsgraf. A year after his decision, the ALI used *Palsgraf*, without name and thinly disguised, as the official illustration of its rule on foreseeability. If in this instance Cardozo was driven by his thirst for certainty and structure, or by his desire to put his personal imprimatur on the Restatement, he was driven by other values at other times.

Cardozo was a witness to the rise of populism, socialism, and the progressive movement, and was more than a little familiar with ideas for protecting people from the harsher effects of the industrial revolution. Worker's compensation plans to cover on-the-job injuries had swept the nation in the decades before *Palsgraf*. With the yeast of such schemes in the air, Cardozo could have found his way to rule in Mrs. Palsgraf's favor had he wanted to. This was the judge, after all, who in *Macpherson v. Buick Motor Co.* tossed a large shot of firewater into the brew of tort liability. He might have taken *Macpherson*, as it was later taken by other courts, further in the direction of pushing large enterprises that injure consumers to buy insurance and spread the costs among their customers. He might have hooked into the ancient line of cases imposing strict liability without negligence for inherently dangerous instruments. More modestly, he might have joined the position of the dissenters that "we endeavor to make a rule in each case that will be practical and in keeping with the general understanding of mankind." But these values were not paramount for Cardozo at the time. He seemed to be thinking about the Restatement.

Cardozo's Texts[6]

Facts. Since the theory of precedent calls for rules to be combined with the concrete facts of a case, the judge always faces the initial task of selecting the facts. Present a few isolated facts like platters at a dinner party, and you assure that everyone sees those few as the text to be feasted upon. Write an encyclopedia of facts and you privilege a text of details that others will later rework in a hundred ways. Give a bare bones sketch, and you make the facts virtually disappear from the text. It is this latter, minimalist approach Cardozo follows, devoting only his brief opening paragraph to the facts, and that in the laconic, clipped (and sometimes stilted) prose for which he was famous. "A train stopped at the station, bound for another place." "The fireworks when they fell exploded." "The scales struck the plaintiff, causing injuries for which she sues." Etc. This is consistent with Cardozo's values. He's eager to create order out of wilderness, to lay down a broad principle worthy of the Restatement. Too many facts could later obscure or limit the rule. Had he had a different goal, he could have easily emphasized facts suggesting this is a railroad case, or a dangerous instruments case, or an explosives case, or a consumer case, or an insurance case, or a case about the cost of dispute resolution for the poor.

Noonan tells us that Mrs. Palsgraf, a 43-year-old single parent of three children, janitor of her apartment, and day worker earning $416 a year, was taking her two teenage daughters to the beach on a hot August day in New York City when the accident occurred. Court fees and doctors' bills came to more than half her annual wages. The Long Island Railroad, on the other hand, had assets of $114 million, and carried 80 million passengers a year. In the year Mrs. Palsgraf was injured, again according to Noonan, railroads in the United States "killed 6,617 persons and injured 143,739.... The global figures suggested that the maiming and killing of passengers was a necessary by-product of the running of railroads." Such facts could have laid a foundation for a *MacPherson-like* or other rule based on calculations of overall social costs and benefits, and to Noonan such facts are an important part of the text because, for him, the case is about social policy and people. For Cardozo, however, the case is about an abstract principle, so he never lets such facts in the door.

Precedents and treatises. Here is where Cardozo locates the core text of the case. In the second and fourth long paragraphs of the opinion, he cites 21 cases, nine scholarly treatises, and two law review articles for the proposition that there is no liability without foreseeability. He states it in various ways (there must be "notice," the hazard must be "apparent to the eye of ordinary vigilance," etc.) and uses the Latinate "prevision" rather than the Anglo-Saxon "foreseeability," but the point is clear and the function of the paragraphs is to persuade us that the point emerges from the cases and treatises. And it does persuade—if we are loyal to the Old Story faith that these are the kinds of texts in which law is found, and if we don't challenge Cardozo's analysis of the texts too closely. It would be child's play, of course, to show how any lawyer (Cardozo himself, for that matter) seeking a different result could have used the same precedents and scholarship to reach it: Notice that, with two exceptions, Cardozo never actually ties any of the authorities directly to the foreseeability proposition, but cites them for broader abstractions, such as "negligence in the air will not do." Narrower readings of them can conclude that they don't answer the foreseeability question. The two exceptions, the article by Seavey and the *Boronkay* case in the fourth paragraph, are tied directly to the proposition that the risk must be one "to others within the range of apprehension," but a different reading of those authorities yields a different conclusion. Notice that he dismisses the contrary five cases and two scholarly authorities as dealing with marginal categories of "ancient forms of liability," or "imminently dangerous acts" or "transferred intent," silently rejecting the option of nurturing those categories here. Notice that he cites cases from outside New York, which technically have no force in his jurisdiction. Notice that he relies on treatises rather heavily, which are private texts without official standing. Like most judges, Cardozo feels no duty to anticipate such objections. More basically, he feels no need to justify his use of cases and treatises in the first place. The principal philosophy that justifies their use is the philosophy of the Old Story that the law is discovered in such texts. We modernists know better, know that such texts are merely materials with which the judicial artist creates the law, and we ask that their use be justified on the basis of some openly stated philosophy of government or judging. The modernist Cardozo knows better too, but suppresses any mention of the philosophies at stake, letting the Old Story carry him on the road to his result.

Reason. The other text for Cardozo is reason. He employs common-law reasoning by analogy in the third paragraph to show us that any other rule but the foreseeability rule "will involve us, and swiftly too, in a maze of contradictions." The guard who stumbles over a can of dynamite hidden in a bundle of newspapers, or a valise, and the person who jostles one's neighbor in a crowd and dislodges a bomb, are used to illustrate the unreasonable results of requiring "extravagant prevision" as the norm of social conduct. Again, the function of the paragraph is to persuade, and it does its job because the hypothetical results do seem so unreasonable. But there are other analogies (say, analogies to *Macpherson*, or to dangerous instruments), and other types of reason (say, the calculation of social costs and benefits of a rule of liability regardless of foreseeability), which Cardozo treats with silence, once again suppressing the social values in his choice of texts.

The Texts' Sources

To select precedents and treatises as primary texts for your case is implicitly to privilege judges and scholars as the sources of those texts. Cardozo even gives the names of the judges each time he quotes from a precedent. To those who accept the Old Story on faith, this is as it should be and is persuasive because judges and scholars are master interpreters of the law. To modernists who know that judges are mortals who, try as they please, never see things with any eyes but their own, it is an open question whether judges and scholars should be privileged in any case. What are their personal characteristics and philosophies? How did they get on the bench or into academia? Do they represent an elitist stratum of American society? Did they write when social conditions were different? Has their wisdom held up over time? What philosophy of government suggests that we should feel bound or influenced by them today? These are some of the values silently pushing and pulling beneath the surface of Cardozo's sources.

The source for Cardozo's text of reason, though, is human nature itself. At the end of the third paragraph's exercise in reasoning by analogy, he concludes: "Life will have to be made over, and human nature transformed, before prevision so extravagant can be accepted as the norm of conduct, the customary standard to which behavior must conform." Human nature is always a powerfully persuasive source. We all know how futile it is for the law to be fundamentally out of sync with human nature, so at first glance Cardozo hits home here. What he elides, of course, is that human nature need not be made over in order for the law to impose liability without foreseeability. The law may set up schemes to mitigate human disasters precisely because we know that our natural, unprescient negligence cannot be made over: witness worker's compensation plans, absolute liability for dangerous activities, or the very concept of insurance.

The final source for his texts is historical evolution. In his fifth paragraph, Cardozo finds "confirmation" of the foreseeability rule in "history and development" of the law of negligence from medieval to modern times. In a Darwinian metaphor, he speaks of liability for damage to others as "a plant of later growth," which "emerged out of the legal soil," and was thought of as an "offshoot of the parent stock," all leading to the conclusion that the plaintiff must show a breach of duty owed directly to himself, something absent if the plaintiff was unforeseeable. In other words, it is the natural, inevitable evolution of law itself which is the source of the rule, so we must accede to it. Now, in intellectual circles of Cardozo's day, Darwinian metaphors for social phenomena were not as likely to be taken for charlatanism as they are today. But even then there were skeptics who pointed to the danger of believing that such links could be made, or if made could not be changed by human intervention. Cardozo might also have turned the metaphor to work a different result by announcing that liability in the Palsgraf situation is the next step in the natural evolution of liability law. He declines these options. He knows that by packaging judges, scholars, human nature, and natural evolution, he has put together a formidable, persuasive bunch of sources for the texts in which he says he found the foreseeability rule.

Other Interpreters

Cardozo, not without good reason, thought more highly of his own views than those of most other interpreters, with the exception of his mentor Holmes. He knew that his reputation allowed him to dominate others like a giant sequoia in a forest of pines. His prose style alone, which rings of the Oracle of Delphi ("The risk reasonably to be perceived defines the duty to be obeyed, and duty imports relation") is evidence of a superior attitude. Yet, like all judges hoping that their decisions will not tarnish their names and wanting to influence the law beyond their tenure on the bench, Cardozo had to be sure that the meaning he produced in the case before him would be acceptable to a sufficient number of other powerful interpreters.

The other interpreters Cardozo clearly took into account were the judges and scholars whose works he cited in the opinion, and the members of the ALI who debated the case. Arguably, he took into account general public opinion when he said that a different rule would require human life to be made over and the customary norm of conduct changed. While the public was not likely to be aware of a small tort case like Helen Palsgraf's, an appeal to the common sense of the public always puts judges on firm ground with other influential interpreters. He must have taken into account the views of the railroads and business community. At least, the meaning he produced in Palsgraf was likely to reassure those sectors that the highest court in New York state was not under the influence of creeping socialism. Views Cardozo had to have taken into consideration but then calculated he could successfully disregard include the views of the jury, trial judge and appellate court who decided for Mrs. Palsgraf; views of the minority members of the ALI in the debate on the case; views of the three dissenting judges on his own court; and, perhaps, views of progressive social and legal thinkers who, had they known of the case, may have seen an opportunity for protection of consumers and the poor against the engines of industrialism and the inaccessibility of the legal system.

Conclusion

The point of all this is not to show that the meaning Cardozo produced from the Palsgraf situation was wrong and Noonan's or another's right. Those judgments depend upon your values. The point, rather, is that Cardozo was able to produce a publicly acceptable meaning by assembling texts, sources, and views of other interpreters into a persuasive picture, all the while hiding the choices of values being made. Such are the rituals of our tribe.

How ironic that Cardozo, the great legal modernist, would resort to such obfuscation. His colleague Judge Andrews, writing for the three dissenters, was more honest. For Andrews, the question was not one of foreseeability but of whether the defendant's negligence was the proximate cause of plaintiff's injury. And what we mean by the word proximate he wrote, "is that because of convenience, of public policy, of a rough sense of justice, the law arbitrarily declines to trace a series of events beyond a certain point. This is not logic. It is practical politics. It is all a question of expediency. There are no fixed rules to govern our judgment.... There is in truth little to guide us other than common sense." It would be hard to find a better example of the modernist, Legal Realist view. Cardozo, of course, was merely the first interpreter of the *Palsgraf* situation. Thousands of subsequent interpreters—lawyers, judges, professors—have been producing the meaning of *Palsgraf* in the same way since 1928 and yielding a rich variety of permutations. Tort professors like to joke that Cardozo's opinion in *Palsgraf* is the most famous and least followed precedent in American law.

Chapter 8

Post-Scripts

P.S. for Law Students

As a law student, you're one of a select group of academic achievers who surely should know when you're being indoctrinated. And yet, generation after generation, most law students fail to spot it. Your professors tell the Old Story with such a facile blend of confidence and mystery—and you are so dazzled and worn out—that you follow them over the brink and into the myth that law is found, not made.

It's not that the professors are out to deceive you deliberately. Many of them were indoctrinated themselves, never studied the Legal Realists or their successors, and idealistically believe that the Old Story is a noble one. Others are too busy keeping up with the mechanics of the Old Story as applied to some specialized field to worry about whether it's all built upon false premises. Most of them also find it easier to follow the orthodoxy as set out in casebooks and curricula. Even the modernists and postmodernists on the faculty can find it tough to know what to teach if they tear the Old Story out of their course materials.

Unfortunately, the illuminati of your school are going to grade you on your ability to think inside the box of the Old Story, so you have little choice but to learn it. The trick for you is to go in and out of the box without getting trapped inside. This can be done if you stay alert, and it's very liberating. Once you pierce through the Old Story indoctrination that is going on in most of your courses, law school becomes easier. Gone is the confusion about what the rule is or what a case really stands for: the answer is always "could be." Gone is the control the professor has to make you seem foolish, because you can always reach into the Old Story's bag of tricks yourself and make a plausible retort, or else shoot the professor a horse dose of Legal Realism: "Don't you think the result would be different if the judge weren't such a mossback conservative (or flaming liberal, or morally anesthetized fence-sitter, or …)?" Or, "Professor, since there is no official definition of what constitutes a holding of a case, then doesn't that turn all holdings into possible dicta and all dicta into possible holdings, so that the whole notion of stare decisis is just a lot of applesauce?" That sort of thing.

In my own classes where I tell the story I've told in this book, I find students usually divide into three camps. Some feel the scales fall from their eyes, sense a breath of fresh air blow across their stifling law books, and become skeptical critics of legal education and the law. They feel empowered as legal analysts. More, they feel the liberty, in fact the obligation, to re-engage their consciences that law school has suppressed. So, this insight actually enables them to make law and life more value-based, not less.

A second group is comprised of disappointed idealists. They acknowledge the reality of human subjectivity in interpreting the law, but they still yearn for the ideal of the "rule of law" rather than rule by human beings. Candor about what's really going on, they fear, would just encourage more bias, ideology and politics, so we'd better keep it quiet. As a disappointed idealist myself, I share their yearning. But it is naive and dangerous to believe there will be less subjectivity if we cover it up. Since *all* interpretation is unavoidably subjective at some point, there is not less but merely different subjectivity and it is imposed by people who are obscure and manipulative about what they are doing rather than transparent and forthright. I myself cannot reconcile such a coverup with the values of egalitarianism and democratic government.

The third group of students is unfazed. They see the notion that the law is made, not found, as blasé common sense already shared widely by the public. These students are content to be learning the tricks of the trade even if the tricks are something of a sham, because society accepts that as the way the legal system works. They will be only too glad to make a lucrative living by continuing the professional tradition of the Old Story.

The choice is yours.

P.S. for Lawyers

You run into a colleague who regales you with news of an interesting new case he has just filed. What's the first question you ask him? Right: "Who's the judge?" You don't need any theory of semiotics or Legal Realism to teach you that the law depends upon the interpreter. Your practical litigation experience has made you into a de facto Legal Realist.

I have some concern that the cynics among you could see this book as just a hornbook for the sort of Machiavellian manipulation that gives lawyers, and Machiavelli too, a bad name. But the libraries are bursting with more comprehensive manuals than this one for that purpose. I'm hoping, instead, that the practicing bar will use the analysis and examples here to shear away some of the overgrowth of doctrine, words and mystifying nonsense in the legal jungle, to clear a path so that attorneys, clients, litigants, judges and the public can see what actually is a stake in each legal battle and how the outcome will actually be determined.

You can help clear this path by the way you talk to clients, write your briefs, argue to judges, and behave in public. You can be part of the mystifying tradition, or part of the wedge of enlightenment.

P.S. for Judges

You are the official speakers of the official discourse, the official readers of the official texts. So you have enormous power to make the change from the Old Story to the new. If you change, all will follow.

Why change? Because the official discourse is false. We've known that for more than a century, thanks to the light shone by Holmes, Pound, Cardozo and others. Yet their light flickers dimly in judicial opinions today, barely kept burning by a few on the bench. After a hundred years, one would think the judiciary would have transformed itself, would have discarded the manipulative doctrines of the Old Story, would be weighing competing values in cases candidly with no pretense that the law is certain and judges value-free.

Instead, the liturgy of the Old Story continues to be invoked in case after case. And at the first sign that interest groups are questioning the decisions of a judge, alarms race through the bench and the flag of judicial objectivity is raised. In a recent example, the president of the judges' association in one of our large states declaimed to his colleagues in his inaugural address: "After the political interest groups remove all the learned judges who decide cases based upon the law and the facts and the Constitution, the only remaining judges will simply be bellwethers of the latest political fashion.... Our freedoms, and the country's very existence, are at stake."

The feeling is no doubt sincere, but the thinking is a fossil, circa 1908. It sounds just like the reaction of bench and bar that year to President Theodore Roosevelt's message to Congress about judges. As Cardozo recounts it in *The Nature Of The Judicial Process*, Roosevelt asserted that,

> Every time [judges] interpret contract, property, vested rights, due process of law, liberty, they necessarily enact into law parts of a system of social philosophy.... The decisions of the courts on economic and social questions depend upon their economic and social philosophy; and for the peaceful progress of our people during the twentieth century we shall owe most to those judges who hold to a twentieth century economic and social philosophy....

Cardozo reports that "this statement when made aroused a storm of criticism. It betrayed ignorance, they said, of the nature of the judicial process. The business of the judge, they told us, was to discover objective truth." But the ideal of objective truth, Cardozo maintained, "is beyond the reach of human faculties to attain." In addition to social and economic forces that shape judges' opinions, there are "other forces, the likes and the dislikes, the predilections and the prejudices, the complex of instincts and emotions and habits and convictions.... There has been a certain lack of candor in much of the discussion of the theme, or rather in the refusal to discuss it, as if judges must lose respect and confidence by the reminder that they are subject to human limitations.... None the less, if there is anything of reality in my analysis of the judicial process, they do not stand aloof on these chill and distant heights; and we shall not help the cause of truth by acting and speaking as if they do."

None of this denies that our freedoms depend to an important extent upon an independent judiciary. Lacking a powerful and independent judiciary, we would lack much of the means to resist accumulation of autocratic power, and to protect individual and minority rights against the mob. But the myth of judicial objectivity is a weak reed upon which to rest so much. The architects of the federal and state constitutions rested judicial independence upon harder-headed arrangements: by giving the judiciary significant power separate from the other branches, by making it difficult to remove judges, by conferring immunity for their decisions, and by giving them long terms. These measures, though imperfect, have in fact achieved meaningful judicial independence. The life-term for federal judges is perhaps the most protective measure, while the four- to six-year terms common for state trial judges seem insufficient. Too, the periodic elections to which most states subject their judges to assure democratic accountability could threaten judicial independence unless serious campaign finance reform is forthcoming so that elections are not, in effect, just bought by money. These are the grounds on which to battle for judicial independence, not the chimera of judicial objectivity.

I have said above that the judiciary should be weighing competing values candidly with no pretense that the law is certain and judges value-free. You should have no fear that this is a call to abandon closely reasoned judicial decisions and instead to write speeches suitable for the floor of the legislature. The nature of the judicial task would not even allow it. Unlike legislators, you judges undertake the task of resolving disputes between specific parties about how certain rules apply to their specific facts. There is no way to accomplish this except by taking parties, facts and rules seriously, and reasoning closely about them, a skill that you and your colleagues have polished into a fine craft and made the hallmark of excellence of our judiciary. Maintaining that craft as you add candor to it, you come face to face with the value choices you are making and you justify those choices with similar tight reasoning, reasoning that convinces yourself, and the public, that this is a decision deserving respect.

P.S. for Journalists

You journalists, skeptics by profession, are not easily fooled, and for the most part you have not been taken in by the rhetoric of the law. Mr. Dooley, the fictional Irish bartender of *Chicago Tribune* columnist Finley Peter Dunne, observed in the 1890s that "th' Supreme Court follows th' iliction returns," and even before that and ever after the press has told the bald facts about judicial behavior. News stories on major court decisions frequently, and properly, refer to liberal/conservative/centrist line-ups of the judges. Cases where economic or cultural interests conflict are often, and properly, reported in the media as a clash of interest groups rather than a dispute of legal technicalities. And when in the year 2000 the U.S. Supreme Court took Mr. Dooley a step further and actually determined the election returns along partisan lines in *Bush v. Gore*, the Fourth Estate did not shrink from spotlighting the decision as raw politics. Time and again the press has proved Thomas Jefferson right when he said that it would be better to have newspapers without a government than a government without newspapers.

Sometimes, though, even reporters get taken in by the Old Story. Intense political battles over nominations to the court have been going on since George Washington's appointments, and the tradition of nominees testifying before the Senate began in 1925. Many nominees have been rejected for political reasons. Yet Chief Justice nominee John Roberts slipped one past much of the media when he told his Senate confirmation hearing in 2005 that "Judges are like umpires. Umpires don't make the rules. They apply them." It was the pure Old Story packaged in as clever a spin as ever came out of a political campaign: pithy, emotionally appealing, and false. How many news reports balanced the spin by pointing out that, unlike umpires, judges may officially change the rules as they go? Or that the law is a murky Sargasso Sea compared with the few, clear rules of baseball? Or that even among umpires there are strict and liberal constructionists? Roberts's sophomoric metaphor could perhaps pass for judicial wisdom in the political theater of the Senate Judiciary Committee, but it is surprising that he was able to palm it off to anyone in the press

Outside the judicial arena it is even more difficult to know when you're being spun by attorneys or officials who say the law is this or the law is that. They wave a zoning ordinance, a contract, an agency rule, a legislator's statement, and make categorical legal claims that sound plausible. They may not even think they are spinning an interpretation. How are you to know how solid the claim is? One thing you can do is scan Chapter One of this book and find which of the Old Story techniques is being relied on, then find its opposing techniques and see for yourself how the interpretation can be contradicted. The technique with the most powerful interpreters behind it is the one likely to hold up.

Some in the press may be reluctant to accept this book's message that legal techniques themselves do not lead to clear answers about the law. The press, after all, has an institutional interest in claiming "clear law" as a bulwark to protect its First Amendment rights, to shield reporters' sources, or to avoid prosecution for publishing government secrets, among other things. But the slightest familiarity with the history of the First Amendment and these other issues shows that the law is no bulwark, that it permits breaches in the name of law. The bulwark, if there is one, lies in acceptance of the importance of press freedoms by the public, by opinion elites, and by individual human beings who are interpreting the laws. If they are convinced of it, the law will follow. The *culture* of free press best ensures freedom for the Fourth Estate.

So it is with every legal issue, as this book has been at pains to demonstrate: the law is whatever the most powerful interpreters say it is. We've seen that the highway speed limit was not set by the federal 55 mile-per-hour statute but by drivers with with their feet on the gas pedals. Equality in schools has been determined not by *Brown v. Board of Education* but by the myriad contentious interest groups interpreting *Brown*. The parameters of torture under international law have not been established in an authoritative memorandum by the U.S. Justice Department because other powerful readers of international law do not accept its analysis. Abortion, the right to bear arms, the death penalty, criminal justice, protection of the environment, campaign finance and other momentous issues loom as legal questions, yet the law will follow the winners of the culture wars on these questions. It is by reporting on these culture wars that the press can inform us what the law is, and what it will be.

P.S. for Citizens

During the time that two recent nominees to the U.S. Supreme Court were assuring the Senate Judiciary Committee that their personal views would not affect their judicial decisions and were irrelevant, a poll showed that 61% of the American public thought that the Senate ought to consider the personal views of nominees to the Court. The citizens were not hoodwinked. They exercised their common sense. This book has shown why that common sense is correct. It follows that if you care about your future and public policy you should make every effort to assure that judges sharing your values are seated on the bench This means speaking out, organizing, educating, lobbying. It means criticizing judicial decisions that undermine your values.

But little good will be accomplished if judicial politics becomes just another vulgar spectacle of money and narrow partisanship. First, money must be kept out of the judicial process—as it should be kept out of all politics—by public financing of judicial elections and strict limits on expenditures in campaigns for judicial appointments. Second, the public debate needs to be lifted out of the simple-minded shallows in which each side accuses the other of supporting "activist" judges. *Every* judge is unavoidably an activist for *some* set of values. Acknowledging that the judiciary, like the executive and legislative, is a political branch of government, will favor neither liberal nor conservative interests. Both sides will, as they already do, participate in political efforts to turn the judiciary their way. But citizens on the right, citizens on the left, and those in between need to articulate why judges supporting their values would be best not just for their narrow interests but for the rest of us, for the common good. What are the pragmatic consequences for the country? *There* is the ground for debate in a democracy.

Finally, savvy citizens across the political spectrum should recognize that everyone has a common interest in putting judges on the bench who are committed at a minimum to the one principle that distinguishes the judiciary from the legislative or executive branches of government: that it is the special role of the judiciary to protect individuals from arbitrary power and to protect minorities from being crushed by majorities. The principle is as much at the heart of our democracy as the principle of majority rule. The judiciary is particularly suited to this role while the other branches are not. Indeed, it is hard to justify the existence of the judiciary unless it provides this protection. And whatever our political and philosophical beliefs, we all want this protection to be there for us when the day comes that we are the target of the boot or the mob. It will not be there for us unless we assure it is there for others.

Appendix

Brown v. Board of Education
Palsgraf v. Long Island Railroad

Brown, et al. v. Board of Education of Topeka, et al.

No. 1

Supreme Court of the United States

347 U.S. 483 (1954)

MR. CHIEF JUSTICE WARREN delivered the opinion of the Court.

These cases come to us from the States of Kansas, South Carolina, Virginia, and Delaware. They are premised on different facts and different local conditions, but a common legal question justifies their consideration together in this consolidated opinion.[1]

In the South Carolina case, *Briggs v. Elliott,* the plaintiffs are Negro children of both elementary and high school age residing in Clarendon County. They brought this action in the United States District Court for the Eastern District of South Carolina to enjoin enforcement of provisions in the state constitution

1. In the Kansas case, *Brown v. Board of Education,* the plaintiffs are Negro children of elementary school age residing in Topeka. They brought this action in the United States District Court for the District of Kansas to enjoin enforcement of a Kansas statute which permits, but does not require, cities of more than 15,000 population to maintain separate school facilities for Negro and white students. Kan. Gen. Stat. §72-1724 (1949). Pursuant to that authority, the Topeka Board of Education elected to establish segregated elementary schools. Other public schools in the community, however, are operated on a nonsegregated basis. The three judge District Court, convened under 28 U. S. C. §§2281 and 2284, found that segregation in public education has a detrimental effect upon Negro children, but denied relief on the ground that the Negro and white schools were substantially equal with respect to buildings, transportation, curricula, and educational qualifications of teachers. 98 F.Supp. 797. The case is here on direct appeal under 28 U. S. C. §1253.

and statutory code which require the segregation of Negroes and whites in public schools. S. C. Const., Art. XI, §7; S. C. Code §5377 (1942). The three judge District Court, convened under 28 U. S. C. §§2281 and 2284, denied the requested relief. The court found that the Negro schools were inferior to the white schools and ordered the defendants to begin immediately to equalize the facilities. But the court sustained the validity of the contested provisions and denied the plaintiffs admission to the white schools during the equalization program. 98 F.Supp. 529. This Court vacated the District Court's judgment and remanded the case for the purpose of obtaining the court's views on a report filed by the defendants concerning the progress made in the equalization program. 342 U.S. 350. On remand, the District Court found that substantial equality had been achieved except for buildings and that the defendants were proceeding to rectify this inequality as well. 103 F.Supp. 920. The case is again here on direct appeal under 28 U. S. C. §1253.

In the Virginia. case, *Davis v. County School Board,* the plaintiffs are Negro children of high school age residing in Prince Edward County. They brought this action in the United States District Court for the Eastern District of Virginia to enjoin enforcement of provisions in the state constitution and statutory code which require the segregation of Negroes and whites in public schools. Va. Const., §140; Va. Code §22-221 (1950). The three judge District Court, convened under 28 U. S. C. §§2281 and 2284, denied the requested relief. The court found the Negro school inferior in physical plant, curricula, and transportation, and ordered the defendants forthwith to provide substantially equal curricula and transportation and to "proceed with all reasonable diligence and dispatch to remove" the inequality in physical plant. But, as in the South Carolina case, the court sustained the validity of the contested provisions and denied the plaintiffs admission to the white schools during the equalization program. 103 F.Supp. 337. The case is here on direct appeal under 28 U. S. C. §1253.

In the Delaware case, *Gebhart v. Belton,* the plaintiffs are Negro children of both elementary and high school age residing in New Castle County. They brought this action in the Delaware Court of Chancery to enjoin enforcement of provisions in the state constitution and statutory code which require the segregation of Negroes and whites in public schools. Del. Const., Art. X, §2; Del. Rev. Code §2631 (1935). The Chancellor gave judgment for the plaintiffs and ordered their immediate admission to schools previously attended only by white children, on the ground that the Negro schools were inferior with respect to teacher training, pupil-teacher ratio, extracurricular activities, physical plant, and time and distance involved in travel. 87 A. 2d 862. The Chancellor also found that segregation itself results in an inferior education for Negro children (see note 10, *infra),* but did not rest his decision on that ground. *Id.,* at 865. The Chancellor's decree was affirmed by the Supreme Court of

Delaware, which intimated, however, that the defendants might be able to obtain a modification of the decree after equalization of the Negro and white schools had been accomplished. 91 A. 2d 137, 152. The defendants, contending only that the Delaware courts had erred in ordering the immediate admission of the Negro plaintiffs to the white schools, applied to this Court for certiorari. The writ was granted, 344 U.S. 891. The plaintiffs, who were successful below, did not submit a cross petition.

In each of the cases, minors of the Negro race, through their legal representatives, seek the aid of the courts in obtaining admission to the public schools of their community on a nonsegregated basis. In each instance, they had been denied admission to schools attended by white children under laws requiring or permitting segregation according to race. This segregation was alleged to deprive the plaintiffs of the equal protection of the laws under the Fourteenth Amendment. In each of the cases other than the Delaware case, a three judge federal district court denied relief to the plaintiffs on the so-called "separate but equal" doctrine announced by this Court in *Plessy v. Ferguson,* 163 U.S. 537. Under that doctrine, equality of treatment is accorded when the races are provided substantially equal facilities, even though these facilities be separate. In the Delaware case, the Supreme Court of Delaware adhered to that doctrine, but ordered that the plaintiffs be admitted to the white schools because of their superiority to the Negro schools.

The plaintiffs contend'd that segregated public schools are not "equal" and cannot be made "equal," and that hence they are deprived of the equal protection of the laws. Because of the obvious importance of the question presented, the Court took jurisdiction. [2] Argument was heard in the 1952 Term, and reargument was heard this Term on certain questions propounded by the Court.[3]

Reargument was largely devoted to the circumstances surrounding the adoption of the Fourteenth Amendment in 1868. It covered exhaustively consideration of the Amendment in Congress, ratification by the states, then existing practices [***878] in racial segregation, and the views of proponents and opponents of the Amendment. This discussion and our own investigation convince us that, although these sources cast some light, it is not enough to resolve the problem with which we are faced. At best, they are inconclusive. The most avid proponents of the post-War Amendments undoubtedly intended them to remove all legal distinctions among "all persons born or naturalized in the

2. 344 U.S. 1, 141, 891.

3. 345 U.S. 972. The Attorney General of the United States participated both Terms as *amicus curiae.*

United States." Their opponents, just as certainly, were antagonistic to both the letter and the spirit of the Amendments and wished them to have the most limited effect. What others in Congress and the state legislatures had in mind cannot be determined with any degree of certainty.

An additional reason for the inconclusive nature of the Amendment's history, with respect to segregated schools, is the status of public education at that time. [4] In the South, the movement toward free common schools, supported by general taxation, had not yet taken hold. Education of white children was largely in the hands of private groups. Education of Negroes was almost nonexistent, and practically all of the race were illiterate. In fact, any education of Negroes was forbidden by law in some states. Today, in contrast, many Negroes have achieved outstanding success in the arts and sciences as well as in the business and professional world. It is true that public school education at the time of the Amendment had advanced further in the North, but the effect of the Amendment on Northern States was generally ignored in the congressional debates. Even in the North, the conditions of public education did not approximate those existing today. The curriculum was usually rudimentary; ungraded schools were common in rural areas; the school term was but three months a year in many states; and compulsory school attendance was virtually unknown. As a consequence, it is not surprising that there should be so little in the history of the Fourteenth Amendment relating to its intended effect on public education.

In the first cases in this Court construing the Fourteenth Amendment, decided shortly after its adoption, the Court interpreted it as proscribing all stateimposed

4. For a general study of the development of public education prior to the Amendment, see Butts and Cremin, A History of Education in American Culture (1953), Pts. I, II; Cubberley, Public Education in the United States (1934 ed.), cc. II–XII. School practices current at the time of the adoption of the Fourteenth Amendment are described in Butts and Cremin, *supra*, at 269–275; Cubberley, *supra*, at 288–339, 408–431; Knight, Public Education in the South (1922), cc. VIII, IX. See also H. Ex. Doc. No. 315, 41st Cong., 2d Sess. (1871). Although the demand for free public schools followed substantially the same pattern in both the North and the South, the development in the South did not begin to gain momentum until about 1850, some twenty years after that in the North. The reasons for the somewhat slower development in the South (e. g., the rural character of the South and the different regional attitudes toward state assistance) are well explained in Cubberley, *supra*, at 408–423. In the country as a whole, but particularly in the South, the War virtually stopped all progress in public education. *Id.*, at 427–428. The low status of Negro education in all sections of the country, both before and immediately after the War, is described in Beale, A History of Freedom of Teaching in American Schools (1941), 112–132, 175–195. Compulsory school attendance laws were not generally adopted until after the ratification of the Fourteenth Amendment, and it was not until 1918 that such laws were in force in all the states. Cubberley, *supra*, at 563–565.

discriminations against the Negro race.[5] The doctrine of "separate but equal" did not make its appearance in this Court until 1896 in the case of *Plessy v. Ferguson*, supra, involving not education but transportation.[6] American courts have since labored with the doctrine for over half a century. In this Court, there have been six cases involving the "separate but equal" doctrine in the field of public education.[7] In *Cumming v. County Board of Education*, 175 U.S. 528, and *Gong Lum v. Rice*, 275 U.S. 78, the validity of the doctrine itself was not challenged.[8] In more recent cases, all on the graduate school [*4921 level, inequality was found in that specific benefits enjoyed by white students were denied to Negro students of the same educational qualifications. *Missouri ex rel. Gaines v. Canada*, 305 U.S. 337; *Sipuel v. Oklahoma*, 332 U.S. 631; *Sweatt v. Painter*, 339 U.S. 629; *McLaurin v. Oklahoma State Regents*, 339 U.S. 637. In none of these cases was it necessary to re-

---

5. *Slaughter-House Cases,* 16 Wall. 36, 6772 (1873); *Strauder v. West Virginia, 100 U.S.* 303, 307–308 (1880):

> "It ordains that no State shall deprive any person of life, liberty, or property, without due process of law, or deny to any person within its jurisdiction the equal protection of the laws. What is this but declaring that the law in the States shall be the same for the black as for the white; that all persons, whether colored or white, shall stand equal before the laws of the States, and, in regard to the colored race, for whose protection the amendment was primarily designed, that no discrimination shall be made against them by law because of their color? The words of the amendment, it is true, are prohibitory, but they contain a necessary implication of a positive immunity, or right, most valuable to the colored race,—the right to exemption from unfriendly legislation against them distinctively as colored,—exemption from legal discriminations, implying inferiority in civil society, lessening the security of their enjoyment of the rights which others enjoy, and discriminations which are steps towards reducing them to the condition of a subject race."

See also *Virginia v. Rives, 100 U.S.* 313, 318 (1880); *Ex parte Virginia, 100 U.S.* 339, 344–345 (1880).

6. The doctrine apparently originated in *Roberts v. City of Boston,* 59 Mass. 198, 206 (1850), upholding school segregation against attack as being violative of a state constitutional guarantee of equality. Segregation in Boston public schools was eliminated in 1855. Mass. Acts 1855, c. 256. But elsewhere in the North segregation in public education has persisted in some communities until recent years. It is apparent that such segregation has long been a nationwide problem, not merely one of sectional concern.

7. See also *Berea College v. Kentucky, 211* U.S. 45 (1908).

8. In the *Cumming* case, Negro taxpayers sought an injunction requiring the defendant school board to discontinue the operation of a high school for white children until the board resumed operation of a high school for Negro children. Similarly, in the *Gong Lum* case, the plaintiff, a child of Chinese descent, contended only that state authorities had misapplied the doctrine by classifying him with Negro children and requiring him to attend a Negro school.

examine the doctrine to grant relief to the Negro plaintiff. And in *Sweatt v. Painter*, supra, the Court expressly reserved decision on the question whether *Plessy v. Ferguson* should be held inapplicable to public education.

In the instant cases, that question is directly presented. Here, unlike *Sweatt v. Painter*, there are findings below that the Negro and white schools involved have been equalized, or are being equalized, with respect to buildings, curricula, qualifications and salaries of teachers, and other "tangible" factors.[9] Our decision, therefore, cannot turn on merely a comparison of these tangible factors in the Negro and white schools involved in each of the cases. We must look instead to the effect of segregation itself on public education.

In approaching this problem, we cannot turn the clock back to 1868 when the Amendment was adopted, or even to 1896 when *Plessy v. Ferguson* was written. We must consider public education in the light of its full development and its present place in American life throughout the Nation. Only in this way can it be determined if segregation in public schools deprives these plaintiffs of the equal protection of the laws.

Today, education is perhaps the most important function of state and local governments. Compulsory school attendance laws and the great expenditures for education both demonstrate our recognition of the importance of education to our democratic society. It is required in the performance of our most basic public responsibilities, even service in the armed forces. It is the very foundation of good citizenship. Today it is a principal instrument in awakening the child to cultural values, in preparing him for later professional training, and in helping him to adjust normally to his environment. In these days, it is doubtful that any child may reasonably be expected to succeed in life if he is denied the opportunity of an education. Such an opportunity, where the state has undertaken to provide it, is a right which must be made available to all on equal terms.

We come then to the question presented: Does segregation of children in public schools solely on the basis of race, even though the physical facilities and other "tangible" factors may be equal, deprive the children of the minority group of equal educational opportunities? We believe that it does.

---

9. In the Kansas case, the court below found substantial equality as to all such factors. 98 F.Supp. 797, 798. In the South Carolina case, the court below found that the defendants were proceeding "promptly and in good faith to comply with the court's decree." 103 F.Supp. 920, 921. In the Virginia case, the court below noted that the equalization program was already "afoot and progressing" (103 F.Supp. 337, 341); since then, we have been advised, in the Virginia Attorney General's brief on reargument, that the program has now been completed. In the Delaware case, the court below similarly noted that the state's equalization program was well underway. 91 A. 2d 137, 149.

In *Sweatt v. Painter, supra,* in finding that a segregated law school for Negroes could not provide them equal educational opportunities, this Court relied in large part on "those qualities which are incapable of objective measurement but which make for greatness in a law school." In *McLaurin v. Oklahoma State Regents, supra,* the Court, in requiring that a Negro admitted to a white graduate school be treated like all other students, again resorted to intangible considerations: " ... his ability to study, to engage in discussions and exchange views with other students., and, in general, to learn his profession." Such considerations apply with added force to children in grade and high schools. To separate them from others of similar age and qualifications solely because of their race generates a feeling of inferiority as to their status in the community that may affect their hearts and minds in a way unlikely ever to be undone. The effect of this separation on their educational opportunities was well stated by a finding in the Kansas case by a court which nevertheless felt compelled to rule against the Negro plaintiffs:

> "Segregation of white and colored children in public schools has a detrimental effect upon the colored children. The impact is greater when it has the sanction of the law; for the policy of separating the races is usually interpreted as denoting the inferiority of the negro group. A sense of inferiority affects the motivation of a child to learn. Segregation with the sanction of law, therefore, has a tendency to [retard] the educational and mental development of negro children and to deprive them of some of the benefits they would receive in a racial[ly] integrated school system."[10]

Whatever may have been the extent of psychological knowledge at the time of *Plessy v. Ferguson,* this finding is amply supported by modem authority.[11] Any language in *Plessy v. Ferguson* contrary to this finding is rejected.

---

10. A similar finding was made in the Delaware case: "I conclude from the testimony that in our Delaware society, State-imposed segregation in education itself results in the Negro children, as a class, receiving educational opportunities which are substantially inferior to those available to white children otherwise similarly situated." 87 A. 2d 862, 865.

11. K. B. Clark, Effect of Prejudice and Discrimination on Personality Development (Midcentury White House Conference on Children and Youth, 1950); Witmer and Kotinsky, Personality in the Making (1952), c. VI; Deutscher and Chein, The Psychological Effects of Enforced Segregation: A Survey of Social Science Opinion, 26 J. Psychol. 259 (1948); Chein, What are the Psychological Effects of Segregation Under Conditions of Equal Facilities?, 3 Int. J. Opinion and Attitude Res. 229 (1949); Brameld, Educational Costs, in Discrimination and National Welfare (Maclver, ed., 1949), 44–48; Frazier, The Negro in the United States (11949),674–68 1. And see generally Myrdal, An American Dilemma (1944).

We conclude that in the field of public education the doctrine of "separate but equal" has no place. Separate educational facilities are inherently unequal. Therefore, we hold that the plaintiff, and others similarly situated for whom the actions have been brought are, by reason of the segregation complained of, deprived of the equal protection of the laws guaranteed by the Fourteenth Amendment. This disposition makes unnecessary any discussion whether such segregation also violates the Due Process Clause of the Fourteenth Amendment.[12]

Because these are class actions, because of the wide applicability of this decision, and because of the great variety of local conditions., the formulation of decrees in these cases presents problems of considerable complexity. On reargu,ment, the consideration of appropriate relief was necessarily subordinated to the primary question—the constitutionality of segregation in public education. We have now announced that such segregation is a denial of the equal protection of the laws. In order that we may have the full assistance of the parties in formulating decrees, the cases will be restored to the docket, and the parties are requested to present further argument on Questions 4 and 5 previously propounded by the Court for the reargument this Term.[13] The Attorney General '[*49M"of the United States is again. invited to participate. The Attorneys General of the states requiring or permitting segregation in public

---

12. See *Bolling v. Sharpe, post, p. 497,* concerning the Due Process Clause of the Fifth Amendment.

13. "4. Assuming it is decided that segregation in public schools violates the Fourteenth Amendment

> "(a) would a decree necessarily follow providing that, within the limits set by normal geographic school districting, Negro children should forthwith be admitted to schools of their choice, or
>
> "(b) may this Court, in the exercise of its equity powers, permit an effective gradual adjustment to be brought about from existing segregated systems to a system not based on color distinctions?
>
> "5. On the assumption on which questions 4 *(a)* and (b) are based, and assuming further that this Court will exercise its equity powers to the end described in question 4 (b),
>
> "(a) should this Court formulate detailed decrees in these cases;
>
> "(b) if so, what specific issues should the decrees reach;
>
> "(c) should this Court appoint a special master to hear evidence with a view to recommending specific terms for such decrees;
>
> "(d) should this Court remand to the courts of first instance with directions to frame decrees in these cases, and if so what general directions should the decrees of this Court include and what procedures should the courts of first instance follow in arriving at the specific terms of more detailed decrees?"

education will also be permitted to appear as *amici curiae upon* request to do so by September 15, 1954, and submission of briefs by October 1, 1954.[14]

It is so ordered.

Helen Palsgraf, Respondent, v. The Long Island Railroad Company, Appellant Court of Appeals of New York

248 N.Y. 339; 162 N.E. 99 (1928)

JUDGES:

Cardozo, Ch. J. Pound, Lehman and Kellogg, JJ., concur with Cardozo, Ch. J.; Andrews, J., dissents in opinion in which Crane and O'Brien, JJ., concur.

Plaintiff was standing on a platform of defendant's railroad after buying a ticket to go to Rockaway Beach. A train stopped at the station, bound for another place. Two men ran forward to catch it. One of the men reached the platform of the car without mishap, though the train was already moving. The other man, carrying a package, jumped aboard the car, but seemed unsteady as if about to fall. A guard on the car, who had held the door open, reached forward to help him in, and another guard on the platform pushed him from behind. In this act, the package was dislodged, and fell upon the rails. It was a package of small size, about fifteen inches long, and was covered by a newspaper. In fact it contained fireworks, but there was nothing in its appearance to give notice of its contents. The fireworks when they fell exploded. The shock of the explosion threw down some scales at the other end of the platform, many feet away. The scales struck the plaintiff, causing injuries for which she sues.

The conduct of the defendant's guard, if a wrong in its relation to the holder of the package, was not a wrong in its relation to the plaintiff, standing far away. Relatively to her it was not negligence at all. Nothing in the situation gave notice that the falling package had in it the potency of peril to persons thus removed. Negligence is not actionable unless it involves the invasion of a legally protected interest, the violation of a right. "Proof of negligence in the air, so to speak, will not do" (Pollock, Torts [11th ed.], p. 455; *Martin v. Herzog*, 228 N. Y. 164, 170; cf. Salmond, Torts [6th ed.], p. 24). "Negligence is the absence of care, according to the circumstances" (Willes, J., in *Vaughan v. Taff Vale Ry. Co.*, 5 H. & N. 679, 688; 1 Beven, Negligence [4th ed.], 7; *Paul v. Consol. Fireworks Co.*, 212 N. Y. 117; *Adams v. Bullock*, 227 N. Y. 208, 211; *Parrott v. Wells-Fargo Co.*, 15 Wall. [U.S.] 524). The plaintiff as she stood upon the platform of the station might claim to be protected against intentional invasion

14. See Rule 42, Revised Rules of this Court (effective July 1, 1954).

of her bodily security. Such invasion is not charged. She might claim to be protected against unintentional invasion by conduct involving in the thought of reasonable men an unreasonable hazard that such invasion would ensue. These, from the point of view of the law, were the bounds of her immunity, with perhaps some rare exceptions, survivals for the most part of ancient forms of liability, where conduct is held to be at the peril of the actor (*Sullivan v. Dunham*, 161 N. Y. 290). If no hazard was apparent to the eye of ordinary vigilance, an act innocent and harmless, at least to outward seeming, with reference to her, did not take to itself the quality of a tort because it happened to be a wrong, though apparently not one involving the risk of bodily insecurity, with reference to some one else. "In every instance, before negligence can be predicated of a given act, back of the act must be sought and found a duty to the individual complaining, the observance of which would have averted or avoided the injury" (McSherry, C. J., in *W. Va. Central R. Co. v. State*, 96 Md. 652, 666; cf. *Norfolk & Western Ry. Co. v. Wood*, 99 Va. 156, 158, 159; *Hughes v. Boston & Maine R. R. Co.*, 71 N. H. 279, 284; *U S. Express Co. v. Everest*, 72 Kan. 517; *Emry v. Roanoke Nav. Co.*, 111 N. C. 94, 95; *Vaughan v. Transit Dev. Co.*, 222 N. Y. 79; *Losee v. Clute*, 51 N. Y. 494; *DiCaprio v. N. Y. C. R. R. Co.*, 231 N. Y. 94; 1 Shearman & Redfield on Negligence, §8, and cases cited; Cooley on Torts [3d ed.], p. 1411; Jaggard on Torts, vol. 2, p. 826; Wharton, Negligence, §24; Bohlen, Studies in the Law of Torts, p. 601). "The ideas of negligence and duty are strictly correlative" (Bowen, L. J., in *Thomas v. Quartermaine*, 18 Q. B. D. 685, 694). The plaintiff sues in her own right for a wrong personal to her, and not as the vicarious beneficiary of a breach of duty to another.

A different conclusion will involve us, and swiftly too, in a maze of contradictions. A guard stumbles over a package which has been left upon a platform. It seems to be a bundle of newspapers. It turns out to be a can of dynamite. To the eye of ordinary vigilance, the bundle is abandoned waste, which may be kicked or trod on with impunity. Is a passenger at the other end of the platform protected by the law against the unsuspected hazard concealed beneath the waste? If not, is the result to be any different, so far as the distant passenger is concerned, when the guard stumbles over a valise which a truckman or a porter has left upon the walk? The passenger far away, if the victim of a wrong at all, has a cause of action, not derivative, but original and primary. His claim to be protected against invasion of his bodily security is neither greater nor less because the act resulting in the invasion is a wrong to another far removed. In this case, the rights that are said to have been violated, the interests said to have been invaded, are not even of the same order. The man was not injured in his person nor even put in danger. The purpose of the act, as well as its effect, was to make his person safe. If there was a wrong to him at all, which may very well be doubted, it was a wrong to a property interest only, the safety of his package. Out of this wrong to property, which threatened injury to nothing else, there has passed, we are told, to the plaintiff by derivation or succession a right of action for the invasion of an interest of another order, the right to bodily security. The diversity of interests emphasizes the futility of the effort to build the plaintiffs right upon the basis of a wrong to some one else. The gain is one of emphasis, for a like result would follow if the interests were the same. Even then, the orbit of the danger as disclosed to the eye of reasonable vigilance would be the orbit of the duty. One who jostles one's neighbor in a crowd does not invade the rights of others standing at the outer fringe when the unintended contact casts a bomb upon the ground. The wrongdoer as to them is the man who carries the bomb, not the one who explodes it without suspicion of the danger. Life will have to be made over, and human nature transformed, before prevision so extravagant can be accepted as the norm of conduct, the customary standard to which behavior must conform.

The argument for the plaintiff is built upon the shifting meanings of such words as "wrong" and "wrongful," and shares their instability. What the plaintiff must show is "a wrong" to herself, *i.e.*, a violation of her own right, and not merely a wrong to some one else, nor conduct "wrongful" because unsocial, but not "a wrong" to any one. We are told that one who drives at reckless speed through a crowded city street is guilty of a negligent act and, therefore, of a wrongful one irrespective of the consequences. Negligent the act is, and wrongful in the sense that it is unsocial, but wrongful and unsocial in relation to other travelers, only because the eye of vigilance perceives the risk of damage. If the same act were to be committed on a speedway or a race course, it would lose its wrongful quality. The risk reasonably to be perceived defines the duty to be obeyed, and risk imports relation; it is risk to another or to others within the range of apprehension (Seavey, Negligence, Subjective or Objective, 41 H. L. Rv. 6; *Boronkay v. Robinson & Carpenter,* 247 N. Y. 365). This does not mean, of course, that one who launches a destructive force is always relieved of liability if the force, though known to be destructive, pursues an unexpected path. "It was not necessary that the defendant should have had notice of the particular method in which an accident would occur, if the possibility of an accident was clear to the ordinarily prudent eye" (*Munsey v. Webb,* 231 U.S. 150, 156; *Condran v. Park & Tilford,* 213 N. Y. 341, 345; *Robert v. U. S. E. F. Corp.,* 240 N. Y. 474, 477). Some acts, such as shooting, are so imminently dangerous to any one who may come within reach of the missile, however unexpectedly, as to impose a duty of prevision not far from that of an insurer. Even today, and much oftener in earlier stages of the law, one acts sometimes at one's peril (Jeremiah Smith, Tort and Absolute Liability, 30 H. L. Rv. 328; Street, Foundations of Legal Liability, vol. 1, pp. 77, 78). Under this head, it may be, fall certain cases of what is known as transferred intent, an act willfully dangerous to A resulting by misadventure in injury to B (*Talmage v.*

Smith, 101 Mich. 370, 374) [*345] These cases aside, wrong is defined in terms of the natural or probable, at least when unintentional (*Parrot v. Wells-Fargo Co. [The Nitro-Glycerine Case],* 15 Wall. [U.S.] 524). The range of reasonable apprehension is at times a question for the court, and at times, if varying inferences are possible, a question for the jury. Here, by concession, there was nothing in the situation to suggest to the most cautious mind that the parcel wrapped in newspaper would spread wreckage through the station. If the guard had thrown it down knowingly and willfully, he would not have threatened the plaintiffs safety, so far as appearances could warn him. His conduct would not have involved, even then, an unreasonable probability of invasion of her bodily security. Liability can be no greater where the act is inadvertent.

Negligence, like risk, is thus a term of relation. Negligence in the abstract, apart from things related, is surely not a tort, if indeed it is understandable at all (Bowen, L. J., in *Thomas v. Quartermaine,* 18 Q. B. D. 685, 694). Negligence is not a tort unless it results in the commission of a wrong, and the commission of a wrongimports the violation of a right, in this case, we are told, the right to be protected against interference with one's bodily security. But bodily security is protected, not against all forms of interference or aggression, but only against some. One who seeks redress at law does not make out a cause of action by showing without more that there has been damage to his person. If the harm was not willful, he must show that the act as to him had possibilities of danger so many and apparent as to entitle him to be protected against the doing of it though the harm was unintended. Affront to personality is still the keynote of the wrong. Confirmation of this view will be found in the history and development of the action on the case. Negligence as a basis of civil liability was unknown to mediaeval law (8 Holdsworth, History of English Law, p. 449; Street, Foundations of Legal Liability, vol. 1, pp. 189, 190). For damage to the person, the sole remedy was trespass, and trespass did not lie in the absence of aggression, and that direct and personal (Holdsworth, op. cit. p. 453; Street, op. cit. vol. 3, pp. 258, 260, vol. 1, pp. 71, 74.) Liability for other damage, as where a servant without orders from the master does or omits something to the damage of another, is a plant of later growth (Holdsworth, op. cit. 450, 457; Wigmore, Responsibility for Tortious Acts, vol. 3, Essays in Anglo-American Legal History, 520, 523, 526, 533). When it emerged out of the legal soil, it was thought of as a variant of trespass, an offshoot of the parent stock. This appears in the form of action, which was known as trespass on the case (Holdsworth, op. cit. p. 449; cf. *Scott v. Shepard, 2* Wm. Black. 892; Green, Rationale of Proximate Cause, p. 19). The victim does not sue derivatively, or by right of subrogation, to vindicate an interest invaded in the person of another. Thus to view his cause of action is to ignore the fundamental difference between tort and crime (Holland, Jurisprudence [12th ed.], p. 328). He sues for breach of a duty owing to himself.

The law of causation, remote or proximate, is thus foreign to the case before us. The question of liability is always anterior to the question of the measure of the consequences that go with liability. If there is no tort to be redressed, there is no occasion to consider what damage might be recovered if there were a finding of a tort. We may assume, without deciding, that negligence, not at large or in the abstract, but in relation to the plaintiff, would entail liability for any and all consequences, however novel or extraordinary (*Bird v. St. Paul F. & M. Ins. Co.*, 224 N. Y. 47, 54; *Ehrgott v. Mayor, etc., of N Y.*, 96 N. Y. *264; Smith v. London & S. W. Ry. Co.*, L. R. 6 C. P. 14; 1 Beven, Negligence, 106; Street, op. cit. vol. 1, p. 90; Green, Rationale of Proximate Cause, pp. 88, 118; cf. *Matter of Polemis, L.* R. 1921, 3 K. B. 560; 44 Law Quarterly Review, 142).

There is room for argument that a distinction is to be drawn according to the diversity of interests invaded by the act, as where conduct negligent in that it threatens an insignificant invasion of an interest in property results in an unforseeable invasion of an interest of another order, as, e.g., one of bodily security. Perhaps other distinctions may be necessary. We do not go into the question now. The consequences to be followed must first be rooted in a wrong.

The judgment of the Appellate Division and that of the Trial Term should be reversed, and the complaint dismissed, with costs in all courts.

NOTES

Chapter 1: The Old Story

1. The quotations at the head of the chapter are from William Blackstone, *Commentaries on the Laws of England, (1765–69)* (London: Cavendish Publishing, 2001), I: 69, III: 396.

2. For pieces or versions of the old story see among others: Fathers of the English Dominican Province, trans., *St. Thomas Aquinas, Summa Theologica (1266–73),* (Chicago: Encyclopedia Britannica, 1971), Second Part, Question 96, Article 6; William Blackstone, *Commentaries on the Laws of England (1765–69)* (London: Cavendish Publishing, 2001), I: 59–62, 87–91; John Austin, *Lectures on Jurisprudence,* 5th ed., rev. and ed. Robert Campbell, (1885, reprint, Verlag Detlev Auvermann KG, Glashütten im Tamus, 1972), II: 989; Francis Lieber, *Legal and Political Hermeneutics* (1839, reprint, St. Louis: G. I. Jones, 1963) (despite some modern insights, Lieber still tells the old story); Sedgwick, *Treatise on the Rules of Interpretation and Application of Statutory and Constitutional Law* (New York: J.S. Voorhies, 1857); Joseph Story, *Commentaries on the Constitution of the United States* (Cambridge, Mass: Brown, Shattuck, 1833).

3. *See,* Edwin W. Patterson, "The Interpretation and Construction of Contracts," *Columbia Law Review* 64 (1964): 833; Raoul Berger, *Government by Judiciary* (Cambridge, Mass.: Harvard University Press, 1977); American Law Institute, *Restatement of the Law, Contracts (Second)* (St. Paul: American Law Institute Publishers, 1981), Sections 200–223 (the structure and assumptions of the old story are still maintained in this restatement, though they creak under the weight of the annotators' modernist insights); Norman A. Singer, ed., *Sutherland Statutory Construction* (St. Paul: Thomson/West, 2000) (the evolution from the first edition in 1891 to today shows signs of creeping modernism and even postmodernism in the Sutherland treatise, but it is still a bulwark of the old story); John D. Calamari & Joseph M. Perillo, *Contracts,* 3d ed., (St. Paul: West Publishing Co., 1987) Sections 3-1 to 3-18 (reports the old story, warning in Section 3-16 that, "It would be a mistake, however, to suppose that the courts follow any of these rules blindly, literally or consistently"); Horace B. Read, John W. MacDonald, Jefferson B. Fordham & William J. Pierce, *Materials on Legislation,* 4th ed., (Mineola: The Foundation Press, 1982); Francis Bennion, *Statutory Interpretation* (London: Butterworth, 1984); Jack Davies, *Legislative Law and Process in a Nutshell,* 2d ed., (St. Paul: West 1986); Rupert Cross, John Bell & George Engle, *Statutory Interpretation,* 2d ed. (London: Butterworth, 1987); Rupert Cross & J.W. Harris, *Precedent in English Law,* 4th ed., (Oxford: Clarendon, 1991).

The Law Is in the Text

4. Both Augustine and Aquinas referred to natural law as "written in the hearts of men." *See,* Fathers of the English Dominican Province, trans., *St. Thomas Aquinas, Summa Theologica (1266–73),* (Chicago: Encyclopedia Britannica, 1971), Second Part, Question 96, Article 6; Second Part, Question 94, Article 6.

There Are Rules for Finding the Meaning in Statutes, Constitutions, Contracts, and Other Texts that Attempt to Guide Future Conduct

1. Follow the plain meaning of the words.

5. The statement of an English judge in 1346 that "we cannot carry the statute further than the words of it say" is in Waghan v. Anon., Year Book 20 Edward III, ii. 198 (1346).

6. The U. S. Supreme Court's declaration in 1916 that where the language is plain "the duty of interpretation does not arise," came in Caminetti v. United States, 242 U.S. 470 (1916).

7. The Supreme Court of Ohio's statement: State v. Krutz 502 N.E.2d 210, 211 (Ohio 1986).

8. Frankfurter's warning that the judiciary should not "usurp a power which our democracy has lodged in its elected legislature," is from Felix Frankfurter, "Some Reflections on the Reading of Statutes," *Columbia Law Review* 47 (1947): 527, 533.

9. It was the Indiana Supreme Court that coined the line, "The courts shall declare that the legislature meant what it said," in Spencer v. State, 5 Indiana 41 (1853). It was Holmes, who sometimes espoused an objective theory of law, who declared, "We do not inquire what the legislature meant; we ask only what the statute means." Oliver Wendell Holmes, "The Theory of Legal Interpretation," *Harvard Law Review* 12 (1899): 417, 419. The line has given comfort to plain meaning adherents of the old school, but Holmes never believed that statutes had plain meanings.

10. In constitutional interpretation, the reference to the Constitution's "majestic generalities" belongs to Justice Robert Jackson, West Virginia State Board of Education v. Barnette, 319 U.S. 624, 639 (1943).

11. The federal judge who claimed that no one would expect the Supreme Court to twist the Presidential age provision into a call for "sufficient maturity" was Irving R. Kaufman, U.S. Court of Appeals for the 2d Circuit, writing in, "What Did the Founding Fathers Intend?," *New York Times Magazine*, Feb. 23, 1986, pp. 42, 68.

12. The Contracts hornbook referring to the "staggering" number of plain meaning cases is John D. Calamari & Joseph M. Perillo, *Contracts,* 3d ed., (St. Paul: West Publishing Co., 1987), 167, note 22.

13. That critics admit words are sometimes the best evidence of minds' contents, see Arthur L. Corbin, "The Interpretation of Words and the Parole Evidence Rule," *Cornell Law Quarterly* 50 (1965): 161, 172.

14. Judge Hand's phrase about the "twenty bishops" came in Hotchkiss v. National City Bank, 200 F. 287, 293 (S.D.N.Y. 1911).

2. If the words are ambiguous, apply intrinsic canons (rules) of construction that help clarify the internal workings of the language of the law.

15. I've drawn the list of canons primarily from the Field Code "maxims of jurisprudence" in California Civil Code Sections 3509–3548 (West 1997); Norman A. Singer, ed., *Suther-*

land Statutory Construction, (St. Paul: Thomson/West, 2000), Sections 46.01–47.38; Edwin W. Patterson, "The Interpretation and Construction of Contracts," *Columbia Law Review* 64 (1964): 833; American Law Institute, *Restatement of the Law, Contracts (Second)* (1981, St. Paul: American Law Institute Publishers), Sections 202, 203, 206.

16. The "tomato is a vegetable" case under the second canon is Nix v. Hedden, 149 U.S. 304 (1893), and worth reading to catch the flavor of American eating habits at the turn of the century.

3. If ambiguity persists, look for extrinsic evidence of the purpose the authors intended.

17. The mischief rule is found in Heydon's Case, "Exchequer," 76 Eng. Rep. 637 (1584).

18. "Usage of trade" is defined in *Uniform Laws Annotated, Uniform Commercial Code* (St. Paul: West Publishing Co., 1976), Section l-205 (2).

19. The "rabbit" case is Smith v. Wilson, 110 Eng. Rep. 266 (1832).

20. The "rabbi" case is Fisher v. Congregation B'Nai Yitzhok, 110 A. 2d 881 (1955).

21. For the frequency of resort to legislative history, see Jorge L. Carro & Andrew R. Brann, "The U.S. Supreme Court and the Use of Legislative Histories: A Statistical Analysis," *Jurimetrics* 22 (1982): 294, 298.

22. For examples of cases using extensive evidence of the Constitutional framers' intentions, *see* Dred Scott v. Sandford, 19 Howard 393 (1857), and Powell v. McCormack, 395 U.S. 486 (1969).

23. The Parole Evidence Rule and its limitations are set out in American Law Institute, *Restatement of the Law, Contracts (Second)* (St. Paul: American Law Institute Publishers, 1981), sections 213–214. *See also*, John D. Calamari & Joseph M. Perillo, *Contracts*, 3d ed., (St. Paul: West Publishing Co., 1987) and Arthur L. Corbin, "The Interpretation of Words and the Parole Evidence Rule," *Cornell Law Quarterly* 50 (1965): 161.

24. On "course of performance" as practical construction of contracts, see *Uniform Laws Annotated, Uniform Commercial Code* (St. Paul: West Publishing Co., 1976), Section 2-208.

25. On "contemporaneous and practical construction" of statutes, *see* Norman A. Singer, ed., *Sutherland Statutory Construction* (St. Paul: Thomson/West, 2000), Sections 49.01 *et seq.*

26. The case deferring to the federal agency's 34-year practical construction is Empire State Highway Transportation Association v. Federal Maritime Board, 291 F.2d 336 (D.C. Cir. 1961).

27. The Hound of the Baskervilles opinion was Montana Wilderness Association v. United States Forest Service (U.S. Court of Appeals Ninth Circuit, slip opinion May 14, 1981, *reprinted in* William N. Eskridge, Jr. & Phillip P. Frickey, *Cases and Materials on Legislation* (St. Paul: West Publishing Co., 1988), 743, *modified in* 655 F. 2d 951 (1981).

4. Always be certain that your interpretation is reasonable.

28. Compare William Blackstone, *Commentaries on the Laws of England, (1765–69)* (London: Cavendish Publishing, 2001), I: 70: "And hence it is that our lawyers are with justice so copious in their encomiums on the reason of the common law, that they tell us, that the law is the perfection of reason, that it always intends to conform thereto, and that what is not reason is not law."

29. Donoghue v. Stevenson, 1932 App. Case 562.

30. A celebrated statement of the "golden rule" of statutory interpretation is Baron Parke's in Perrys v. Skinner, 2 M. & W. 471, 476 (1937).

31. Blackstone's reference to the rule using the example of the law against drawing blood in the streets of Bologna is found in *Commentaries*, I: 69.

32. A typical statement that courts may not "make a new contract for the parties" may be found in Rodolitz v. Neptune Paper Products, Inc., 239 N. E. 2d 628, 630 (1968).

33. The Restatement's assumptions that the parties and language will be "reasonable," are found in American Law Institute, *Restatement of the Law, Contracts (Second)* (St. Paul: American Law Institute Publishers, 1981), Sections 230, 233, 235, 236.

34. The UCC's prohibition of unconscionable contracts is in *Uniform Laws Annotated, Uniform Commercial Code* (St. Paul: West Publishing Co., 1976), Section 2-302.

There Are Rules for Finding the Meaning in the Texts of Judicial Precedents

35. Typical descriptions of how to read precedents, and the need for stare decisis to assure stability, predictability, the justice of treating like cases alike, objective judging, and efficiency, can be found in many sources, including: Rupert Cross & J.W. Harris, *Precedent in English Law*, 4th ed., (Oxford: Clarendon Press, 1991); P. S. Atiyah & Robert S. Summers, *Form and Substance in Anglo-American Law*, (Oxford: Clarendon Press, 1987), Chapter 5; Edgar Bodenheimer, John Bilyeu Oakley, & Jean C. Love, *An Introduction to the Anglo-American Legal System*, 2d ed., (St. Paul: West Publishing Co., 1988); John Delaney, *How to Brief a Case* (Bogota, N.J.: Delaney Publications, 1987); Helene & Marshall Shapo, *Law School without Fear: Strategies for Success* (Westbury, NY: Foundation Press, 1996). A benchmark analysis of stare decisis is Arthur L. Goodhart's "Determining the Ratio Decidendi of a Case," *Yale Law Journal* 40 (1930): 161.

36. The Blackstone quotation at the end of the chapter is found in his *Commentaries on the Laws of England, (1765–69)* (London: Cavendish Publishing, 2001), II: 376.

Chapter 2: The Modern Story

1. The quotation at the head of the chapter is from Oliver Wendell Holmes, Jr., *The Common Law* (Boston: Little Brown, 1881), 1.

The Modernist Revolution

2. Among the many sources from which the story of 20th century modernism can be gathered, some interesting ones are: Jose Ortega y Gasset, *El Tema de Nuestro Tiempo* (1923, reprint, Madrid: Revista de Occidente, 1966); Harry Elmer Barnes, *Living in the Twentieth Century* (Indianapolis: Bobbs-Merrill, 1928); John Herman Randall, Jr., *The Making of the Modern Mind* (New York: Houghton Mifflin, 1940); Werner Heisenberg, *Physics and Philosophy: The Revolution in Modern Science* (New York: Harper, 1958); Floyd W. Matson, *The Broken Image: Man, Science and Society* (New York: Braziller, 1964), *The Idea of the Modern in Literature & the Arts* (New York: Horizon Press, 1967); Norman F. Cantor & Michael S. Werthman, eds., *The History of Popular Culture* (New York: MacMillan, 1968); Lewis Mumford, *The Myth of the Machine: The Pentagon of Power* (New York: Harcourt Brace Jovanovich, 1970); Stephen Kern, *The Culture of Time and Space* (Cambridge, Mass.: Harvard University Press, 1983).

3. Virginia Woolf's joke about human nature changing in December of 1910 is quoted in Irving Howe, ed., *The Idea of the Modern in Literature & the Arts* (New York: Horizon Press, 1967), 15 without reference to the source.

4. The statement from the Humanist Manifesto appears in Paul Kurtz, ed., *The Humanist Manifestos I and II* (Buffalo: Prometheus Books, 1985).

5. The two words that I say in the text "sum up" modernism—"subjective" and "pragmatic"—sometimes pulled in opposite directions. The pull of pragmatism led some toward a new kind of objectivism. The pragmatic notion was that we should only accept as true our experience of the world, and this must be carefully—objectively—measured and reported, so that we can then better engineer our world the way we want it to be. As Matson recounts in *The Broken Image*, cited above, this injected a renewed spirit of scientific positivism in science, philosophy, psychology, and the social sciences (and, I would add, arts and architecture). It also produced a glorification of the machine, homo habilis' greatest tool. The tension between this and the subjectivist spirit of modernism, which cut against scientific positivism and agonized about the domination of humans by machines, was severe but not always irreconcilable. It occasionally co-existed even in individual personalities. This is true, for instance, of the philosopher Peirce, a highly subjective pragmatist who nevertheless sometimes claimed to anchor his views in some external objective truth. Freud, who certainly helped make the 20th century seem a subjective place and whose thinking and practice "more nearly resemble[d] those of a poet than of a scientific mechanist," nevertheless, "never abandoned the hope that his concepts could be "reduced to the categories of physical science" (Matson, 183). And Malevich, the Russian abstract suprematist painter, wrote to a friend in 1913: "We have come as far as the rejection of reason, but ... another kind of reason has grown in us which ... can be called beyond reason which also has law, construction and sense, and only by learning this shall we have work based on the law of the truly new 'beyond reason.'" (Maurice Tuchman, *The Spiritual in Art: Abstract Painting* (Los Angeles: L.A. County Museum of Art, 1986). Other celebrated modernists have traversed the continuum from objective to subjective beliefs (though few have traveled the opposite direction), and their trips have been taken as symbolic by their adherents. Ludwig Wittgenstein is notorious for making such a trip between the logical positivism of his *Tractatus Logico-Philosophicus* in 1922 and the musings of his *Philosophical Investigations* published in 1953, but the phenomenon can be observed equally in the biographies of many others—such as Le Corbusier, who was designing mass-produced "machines for living" (houses) in the 1920s and emotional, anti-rational forms like the chapel at Ronchamp in 1950.

6. The quotation from Kafka's diary in the text can be found in an appendix to Franz Kafka, *The Trial* (New York: Schocken Books, 1984), 275.

7. The historian of ideas quoted on the impact of Einstein's relativity theory is Floyd W. Matson, *The Broken Image: Man, Science and Society* (New York: Braziller, 1964), 121. Matson, in turn, is quoting Lincoln Barnett, *The Universe and Dr. Einstein* (New York: Mentor Books, 1958), 19.

8. Matson (at 129) also quotes the Heisenberg passage about man "confronting himself alone," from Werner Heisenberg, *The Physicist's Conception of Nature* (New York: Harcourt Brace Jovanovich, 1958), 24.

9. For materials underlying the references in the penultimate paragraph of the section, *see* Charles Sanders Peirce, *Collected Papers*, Charles Hartshorne, Paul Weiss, & Arthur Burks, eds., (Cambridge, Mass: Harvard University Press, 1931–66); Ferdinand de Saussure, *Course in General Linguistics*, (London: Peter Owen, 1966); Octavio Paz, *Marcel Duchamp* (New York: Seaver Books, 1978); Calvin Tomkins, *The Bride and the Bachelors* (New York: Penguin Books, 1976); William James, *Pragmatism*, Bruce Kuklick, ed., (Indianapolis: Hackett Publishing, 1981), *Essays in Radical Empiricism* (Glouster, Mass: P. Smith,

1967); John Dewey, *Reconstruction in Philosophy* (Boston: Beacon Press, 1920), *Human Nature and Conduct* (New York: H. Holt, 1922). Peirce is quoted by James K. Feibleman, *An Introduction to Peirce's Philosophy* (London: George Allen & Unwin, 1960), 199. The 1906 James lecture in New York is mentioned in Margaret Knight, *William James* (London: Penguin Books, 1950), 54.

Thought Window

10. *See* the spirited autobiographies of the modernists Margaret Mead, *Blackberry Winter* (New York: William Morrow, 1972); and Lewis Mumford, *Sketches From Life* (New York: Dial Press, 1982).

11. A noted historian bolsters the point I make in the text about relativism and absolutism: "[H]istory suggests that the damage done to humanity by the relativist is far less than the damage done by the absolutist.... As a historian, I confess to a certain amusement when I hear the Judeo-Christian tradition praised as the source of our concern for human rights. In fact, the great religious ages were notable for their indifference to human rights in the contemporary sense. They were notorious not only for acquiescence in poverty, inequality, exploitation and oppression but for enthusiastic justifications of slavery, persecution, abandonment of small children, torture, genocide.... Human rights is not a religious idea. It is a secular idea, the product of the last four centuries of Western history. It was the age of equality that brought about the disappearance of such religious appurtenances as the auto-da-fe and burning at the stake, the abolition of torture and of public executions, the emancipation of the slaves.... The basic human rights documents—the American Declaration of Independence and the French Declaration of the Rights of Man—were written by political, not by religious, leaders.... Most of the organized killing now going on is the consequence of absolutism: Protestants and Catholics killing each other in Ireland; Muslims and Jews killing each other in the Middle East; Sunnites and Shiites killing each other in the Persian Gulf; Buddhists and Hindus killing each other in Ceylon; Hindus and Sikhs killing each other in India; Christians and Muslims killing each other in Armenia and Azerbaijan; Buddhists and Communists killing each other in Tibet.... Nor does relativism necessarily regard all claims to truth as equal or believe that judgment is no more than the expression of personal preference. For our relative values are not matters of whim and happenstance. History has given them to us.... People with a different history will have different values. But we believe that our own are better for us. They work for us; and, for that reason, we live and die by them.... Absolutism is abstract, monistic, deductive, a historical, solemn, and it is intimately bound up with deference to authority. Relativism is concrete, pluralistic, inductive, historical, skeptical and intimately bound up with deference to experience." Arthur Schlesinger, Jr., "The Opening of the American Mind," *The New York Times Book Review*, July 23, 1989, p. 1.

Legal Modernism

12. Holmes's influential early commentaries were *The Common Law* (Boston: Little Brown, 1881), and "The Path of the Law," *Harvard Law Review* 10 (1897): 457.

13. The quotation from Roscoe Pound is in his "The Need of a Sociological Jurisprudence," *The Green Bag* 19 (1907): 607, 612. *See also* his "Mechanical Jurisprudence," *Columbia Law Review* 8 (1908): 605, and "The Scope and Purpose of Sociological Jurisprudence," *Harvard Law Review* 25 (1912): 140.

14. On the Legal Realists, *see* Wilfred E. Rumble, Jr., *American Legal Realism: Skepticism,*

Reform and the Judicial Process (Ithaca, N.Y.: Cornell University Press, 1968); William Twining, *Karl Llewellyn and the Realist Movement* (London: Weidenfield and Nicholsen, 1973); Robert S. Summers, *Instrumentalism and American Legal Theory* (Ithaca, N.Y. and London: Cornell University Press, 1982); Gary J. Aichele, *Legal Realism and Twentieth Century American Jurisprudence: The Changing Consensus* (PhD dissertation, University of Virginia, 1983); Richard A. Posner, *Overcoming Law* (Cambridge Mass. and London: Harvard University Press, 1995), Chapter 19.

Of Realists' works themselves and their direct predecessors, *see especially*: Joseph W. Bingham, Jr. "What is Law?," *Michigan Law Review* 11 (1912): 1; Benjamin N. Cardozo, *The Nature of the Judicial Process* (New Haven: Yale University Press, 1921); *The Growth of the Law* (New Haven: Yale University Press, 1924); Joseph C. Hutcheson, Jr., "The Judgment Intuitive: The Function of the 'Hunch' in Judicial Decision," *Cornell Law Quarterly* 14 (1929): 274; Jerome Frank, *Law and the Modern Mind* (New York: Coward-McCann, 1930), *Courts on Trial: Myth and Reality in American Justice* (Princeton: Princeton University Press, 1949) ; Karl N. Llewellyn, "A Realistic Jurisprudence—The Next Step," *Columbia Law Review* 30 (1930): 431, "Some Realism About Realism," *Harvard Law Review* 44 (1931): 1222, "Remarks on the Theory of Appellate Decision and the Rules or Canons About How Statutes Are to be Construed," *Vanderbilt Law Review* 3 (1950): 395; Max Radin, "Statutory Interpretation," *Harvard Law Review* 43 (1930): 863; Felix S. Cohen, "Transcendental Nonsense and the Functional Approach," *Columbia Law Review*, 35 (1935): 809; Fred Rodell, *Woe Unto You, Lawyers!* (New York: Reynal and Hitchcock, 1939). For a discussion of links between Legal Realism and Critical Legal Studies, see Gary Peller, "The Metaphysics of American Law," *California Law Review* 73 (1985): 1151.

The Law Is Not in the Text, but in Experience

15. The long quotation from Holmes is from his "The Path of the Law," *Harvard Law Review* 10 (1897): 457, 465–66, 468.

16. The famous line from Justice Fortescue is recorded in *Year Book 36 Henry VI*, (1458) ff 25b-26.

17. Holmes's even more famous quip that "It is revolting to have no better reason for a rule of law than that so it was laid down in the time of Henry IV," is again found in his "Path of the Law," at 469.

18. Pound's distinction between law in books and law in action is found in his "Law in Books and Law in Action," *American Law Review* 44 (1910): 12.

19. The Cardozo paragraph beginning, "We are reminded by William James in a telling page," is in Benjamin N. Cardozo, *The Nature of the Judicial Process* (New Haven: Yale University Press, 1921), 12.

20. For evidence of law's long control by castes of patriarchal strongmen and priestly interpreters *see*: Henry Sumner Maine, *Ancient Law* (1880, reprint, New Brunswick: Transaction Publishers, 2002); Arthur S. Diamond, *The Evolution of Law and Order* (London: Watts & Co., 1951), *Primitive Law, Past and Present* (London: Methuen, 1971); Samuel Noah Kramer, *The Sumerians* (Chicago: University of Chicago Press, 1963); Harold J. Berman, *Law and Revolution* (Cambridge, Mass.: Harvard University Press, 1983) (Berman is unsympathetic to what he would see as the "cynicism about law" expressed in my text, and also points out that at various times and places law served to challenge, rather than reinforce, dominant elites. But of his list of "ten basic characteristics of law in the West," he ac-

knowledges that four have remained intact since the 11-12th century era that he considers formative. These are that (1) law is autonomous from politics and other social institutions, (2) it is "still entrusted to the cultivation of professional legal specialists," (3) legal training centers flourish in which law is "conceptualized" and "systematized," and (4) "such legal learning still constitutes a meta-law by which the legal institutions and rules are evaluated and explained." The four features describe, of course, characteristics of what I am referring to as the caste of priestly interpreters.); Gerda Learner, *The Creation of Patriarchy* (New York and Oxford: Oxford University Press, 1986); Peter Goodrich, *Reading the Law* (Oxford: Basil Blackwell, 1986), *Legal Discourse* (New York: St. Martin's Press, 1987).

21. The quotation that "The code establishes the social power of a priestly group of interpreters of the law ..." is from Goodrich's important work just cited, *Reading the Law*, at 27–28.

22. The quotation about secularization of the law is from A. Glucksmann, *The Master Thinkers* (1980) quoted in *Reading the Law* at 5.

23. On various periods with priestly castes that arguably took the techniques to the "high-water mark," *see* Frederick Pollock & Frederick W. Maitland, *The History of English Law Before the Time of Edward* (1895, reprint, Union, N.J.: Lawbook Exchange, 1966); Berman's *Law and Revolution*, just cited; Ronald K. L. Collins & David M. Skover, "Paratexts," *Stanford Law Review* 44 (1992): 504; Andrew Borkowski, *Textbook on Roman Law*, 2d ed., (Oxford: Oxford University Press, 1997); Mary Ann Glendon, Michael W. Gordon & Christopher Osakwe, *Comparative Legal Traditions* (St. Paul: West Publishing Co., 1982); and Goodrich's two books, just cited.

24. Roman law's examination of the liability of a ball thrower whose ball hit the hand of a barber whose razor slit the neck of a slave he was shaving can be found in *The Digest of Justinian*, Theodor Mommesen *et al.*, eds., (Philadelphia: University of Philadelphia Press, 1985) 1: Book 9, Chapter 2, paragraph 11.

25. Blackstone's cavalier admission that the reasons for some laws cannot be remembered "at this distance of time" comes in his *Commentaries on the Laws of England, (1765–69)* (London: Cavendish Publishing, 2001), I: 70.

There Are No Categorical Rules for Finding Meaning in Statutes, Constitutions, Contracts, and Other Texts that Attempt to Guide Future Conduct

1. There can be no rule that plain meaning must be followed, because words have no plain meaning.

26. Referential or essentialist theories of language (what I've called "label theories") are discussed in Bernard Harrison, *An Introduction to the Philosophy of Language* (London: Macmillan, 1979). Although such theories still thrive in certain philosophical circles, various modernist critiques have in the view of many rendered these theories untenable, replacing them with a notion that "meaning is use," a shorthand way of saying that the meaning of words depends upon their use in transient social, historical, theoretical, and other human contexts. Words are used by people to do things, as well as to refer, and what they "refer" to when they refer at all is their human context, not to some immutable external reality.

A few well-known, or especially insightful, sources from which this modernist view of language can be gleaned (though with significant differences among themselves) are Charles Sanders Peirce, *Collected Papers*, Charles Hartshorne, Paul Weiss, & Arthur Burks, eds., (Cambridge, Mass: Harvard University Press, 1931–66); Ivor A. Ogden & Charles K.

Richards, *The Meaning of Meaning* (New York: Harcourt Brace, 1923); Felix S. Cohen, "Field Theory and Judicial Logic," *Yale Law Journal* 59 (1950): 238; Benjamin Lee Whorf, *Language, Thought, and Reality* (New York: The Technology Press and John Wiley & Sons, 1956); Ludwig Wittgenstein, *Philosophical Investigations* trans. G.E.M. Anscombe, 2d ed., (Oxford: Basil Blackwell, 1958); Richard Rorty, *Philosophy and the Mirror of Nature* (Princeton: Princeton University Press, 1979); Umberto Eco, *Semiotics and the Philosophy of Language* (Bloomington: University of Indiana Press, 1984), "How Culture Conditions the Colours We See," in Marshall Blonsky ed., *On Signs* (Baltimore: Johns Hopkins University Press, 1985), 157; Stanley Fish, *Is There a Text in This Class?* (Cambridge, Mass: Harvard University Press, 1980), *Doing What Comes Naturally* (Durham, North Carolina: Duke University Press, 1989).

Of course, the assertion that language has a plain meaning need not depend upon a referential philosophy of language. The assertion may amount to a more modest claim that in a given social context much language will have some relatively settled meaning. It may be that H. L. A. Hart meant nothing more than this when he laid down his notorious dictum that legal language often possesses a core of certainty surrounded by a penumbra of doubt. *See* Herbert L. A. Hart, *The Concept of Law* (Oxford: Clarendon Press, 1961). But that claim, which could be sensible and pragmatic (after all, we do communicate regularly with one another on the basis of shared contexts and meanings), needs to be alive to the facts that it is the context that is determining the meaning; that contexts and cores, especially in law, are often quickly unsettled; that multiple, overlapping contexts exist in even a single, homogenous community of interpreters; and that some sociological description is needed about how all this happens and which groups have more power to settle meanings than others. Hart and his followers, showing little sensitivity to these facts, have allowed the "core meaning" theory to play the role of an old-fashioned referential theory of language. *See* the famous debate between Hart and Lon Fuller for an early challenge to Hart on this score: H. L. A. Hart, "Positivism and the Separation of Law and Morals," *Harvard Law Review* 71 (1958): 593; Lon Fuller, "Positivism and Fidelity to Law—A Response to Professor Hart," *Harvard Law Review* 71 (1958): 630. Moreover, Hart promises a sociological description of how meanings get settled in law, but fails to deliver, as I note in my further critique of Hart in the notes to Chapter 4.

27. Holmes's famous line, "A word is not a crystal ..." comes in Towne v. Eisner, 245 U.S. 418,425 (1918).

28. Corbin's words on the plain meaning rule were tied together from three passages in Arthur L. Corbin, "The Interpretation of Words and the Parole Evidence Rule," *Cornell Law Quarterly* 50 (1965): 161, 164, 171–172.

29. "These ancient laws were invariable texts ..." is from Numa Denis Fustel De Coulanges, *The Ancient City* (1874, reprint, Kitchenet, Canada: Batoche Books, 2001), 160.

30. Shylock's "pound of flesh" speech is in William Shakespeare, *The Merchant of Venice, Act. Four, Scene 1, The Complete Works of William Shakespeare* (London and Glasgow: Collins, 1951).

2. The intrinsic canons of construction are too contradictory and enigmatic to be called rules, and are ignored as often as they are used.

31. By lining up contradictory canons in parallel columns, I have appropriated a device used by legal realist Karl Llewellyn years ago with devastating success. *See* Karl Llewellyn, "Remarks on the Theory of Appellate Decision and the Rules or Canons about How Statutes Are to Be Construed," *Vanderbilt Law Review* 3 (1950): 395. Llewellyn borrowed the list of

contradictions from Driscoll, and put them under columns labeled "Thrust" and "Parry." I've always thought the Llewellyn-Driscoll list could be made more exact, and more directly contradictory. My quotations under the "On The Other Hand" column are typical, not unique. The precise sources for the ones I've used are cited.

32. "Courts are not bound ...": Sparks v. West Point Manufacturing, 145 So. 2d 816, 817 (Alabama, 1962). "Will disregard the punctuation ...": Barrett v. Van Pelt, 268 U.S. 85, 91 (1925).

33. "If the context ..." In re Smith, 88 Cal. App. 464, 468 (1928).

34. "Words in a contract ...": California Civil Code Section 1653 (West 1997).

35. "Words having no meaning ...": Jordan v. Le Blanc & Broussasrd Ford, Inc., 332 So. 2d 534, 538 (La.App. 1976).

36. "Superfluity does not vitiate.": California Civil Code Section 3537 (West 1997).

37. "[T]his rule does not apply ...": Stone v. City of Greenville, 111 S.C. 78, 81 (1918). Moreover, "particular clauses ...": California Civil Code Section 1650 (West 1997). And "it is a cardinal rule ...": Retail Liquor Dealers Protective Ass'n v. Fleck, 93 N.E.2d 443, 446 (Il.App., 1950).

40. But only "if it can be done ...": California Civil Code Section 1643 (West 1997).

41. Or "if the [statutory] language will reasonably permit ...": Carr v. Kingsbury, 111 Cal. App. 165, 171 (1931).

42. This rule "has no application where ...": United States v. McMenamin 58 F. Supp. 478 (1944).

43. "[I]t is only when one statute ...": Crescionnu v. La. State Police Retirement Board, 455 So. 2d 1362 (La. 1984).

44. The expressio maxim "is increasingly considered unreliable ...": National Petroleum Refiners Association v. FTC, 482 F. 2d 672, 676 (D.C. Cir. 1973), *cert. denied*, 415 U.S. 951 (1974).

45. Ejusdem generis "rests on a mere presumption ...": Given v. Hilton, 95 U.S. 591, 598 (1877)."

46. "That a word may be known by the company it keeps ...": Russell Motor Car v. U.S., 261 U.S. 514, 519 (1923).

47. "[T]he rule that uncertain ...": Beverly Hills Oil Company v. Beverly Hills Unified School District, 264 CA 2d 603, 645 (1968).

48. "We do not consider ourselves ...": Teders v. Rothermel, 286 N.W. 353, 354 (Minn. 1939).

49. "Penal laws are not ...": Lott v. State (223 P. 2d 147, 151 (Okla. Crim. App., 1950).

50. "The remedial nature ...": Kalin v. Oliver Iron Mining Co. , 37 N.W. 2d 365, 368 Minn., 1949).

51. Courts "cannot press statutory construction ...": United States v. Locke, 471 U.S. 84, 96 (1985).

Forgetting the canons:

52. "These rules are not the masters of the courts, but merely their servants ...": Benson v. Chicago, St. Paul, Minn. & Omaha Railway, 77 NW 798, 799 (Minn., 1899).

53. Justice Frankfurter's remark reaffirming Holmes's notion that the canons are mere axioms of experience is found in Felix Frankfurter, "Some Reflections on the Reading of Statutes," *Record of the Association of the Bar of the City of New York* 2 (1947): 213, 235.

54. The federal judge who asserts that even as expressions of experience they "are just plain wrong" is Richard Posner, "Statutory Interpretation—In the Classroom and in the Courtroom," *University of Chicago Law Review* 50 (1983): 800, 806.

55. "Almost everybody thinks the canons are bunk" say William N. Eskridge, Jr. & Philip P. Frickey, *Cases and Materials on Legislation* (Minneapolis: West Publishing Co. 1988), 639.

3. Extrinsic evidence of untended purpose cannot constrain interpreters because the evidence is limitless, manipulable, and unordered, and because "intended purpose" is a usually a fiction anyway.

Manipulable evidence:

56. The statute directing the Congressional Record to be a substantial verbatim account of debate is 44 U.S.C. §901 (1982). The Joint House-Senate Committee on Printing issues more detailed rules.

57. About 70% of what appears in the Record is never spoken: "The Record: The More It Changes...," *Congressional Quarterly Weekly Report*, Feb. 11, 1978, p. 348.

58. The unsuccessful suit by disgruntled House members was Gregg v. Barrett, 771 F.2d 539 (1985).

59. The comparison of the dialogs in the Record to "a grade B radio script," was made by U.S. Circuit Judge Abner Mikva (a former congressman), in his "A Reply to Judge Starr's Observations," *Duke Law Journal* 1987: 380, 384.

60. On manipulation of state legislative history materials, see for example, Comment, "Statutory Interpretation in California: Individual Testimony as an Extrinsic Aid," *University of San Francisco Law Review* 15 (1981): 241.

Unordered evidence:

61. Madison disapproved of using his notes or other personal opinions of the framers to interpret the Constitution: See H. Jefferson Powell, "The Original Understanding of Original Intent," *Harvard Law Review* 98 (1985): 885, 935–942.

62. Frankfurter's admission that "no item of evidence has a fixed or even average weight," comes in Felix Frankfurter, "Some Reflections on the Reading; of Statutes," *Record of the Association of the Bar of the City of New York* 2 (1947): 213, 234. He assigned weight to legislative documents, including isolated statements made in the heat of debate, as needed to support his interpretations. See his opinion for the Court in Communist Party of the United States v. Subversive Activities Control Board, 367 U.S. 1 (1961). Among the copious legislative materials to which Frankfurter gives serious weight are bills introduced but never enacted (at 84–85), and a "significant" 36-word statement about Communist front organizations, made in floor debate by Representative Richard M. Nixon (Republican of California) (at 61).

The fiction of intent or purpose:

63. Benjamin Franklin's bequest of his walking stick to Washington is quoted in Robert S. Menchin, *Where There's a Will* (London: Corgi Books, Transworld Publishers, 1981), 138.

64. A good sample of the modernist critique of legislative intent or purpose as fiction can be found in Max Radin, "Statutory Interpretation," *Harvard Law Review* 43 (1930): 863; Reed Dickerson, *The Interpretation and Application of Statutes* (Boston: Little Brown 1975);

Ronald Dworkin, *Law's Empire* (Cambridge, Mass. and London: Belknap Harvard University Press, 1986), 313–337. (Dworkin usefully summarizes the modernist critique of legislative intent, but unfortunately imposes an equally fictitious substitute of his own.)

Levels of intent:

65. There exists considerable scholarship on "the intention" of the 14th Amendment. A good starting place is Richard Kluger, *Simple Justice*, (New York: Vintage Books, 1977), Chapter 24. Various intentions for the 55 mile-per-hour speed limit may be gleaned from its legislative history.

Unforeseen circumstances:

66. The story of the mayor of St. Louis who left $200,000 for relief to emigrants is found in Robert S. Menchin, *Where There's a Will* (London: Corgi Books, Transworld Publishers 1981), 140–141.

Irrelevant intentions:

67. Scalia's scathing dissent is from Edwards v. Aguillard, 482 U.S. 578, 637 (1986). Despite this, Scalia is not sympathetic to legal modernism.

Adding individual intentions together:

68. Writers have offered a wealth of theoretical presumptions to rescue us from the fictional and impossible concept of legislative intent or purpose. To adopt any of these approaches is to abandon the search for legislative intent and to impose upon the statute whatever transcendent value is contained in the presumption: reasonableness, coherence, pragmatism, welfare maximization, limited government, protection of minorities, etc. As I say in the text, these are not interpretive techniques, but rather philosophies of government, some of them good, and should be defended as such. Some influential philosophies of government of this sort, often confused with interpretive techniques for finding legislative intent, are found in: James M. Landis, "A Note on Statutory Interpretation," *Harvard Law Review* 43 (1930): 886; Henry Hart & Albert Sacks, *The Legal Process: Materials in the Making and Application of Law* (tentative draft) (Cambridge, Mass: Harvard Law School, 1958); John Hart Ely, *Democracy and Distrust* (Cambridge, Mass. and London: Harvard University Press, 1980); Ronald Dworkin, *Law's Empire* (Cambridge, Mass. and London: Belknap Harvard University Press, 1986).

Thought Window

69. Dylan Thomas's lines are from his "Fernhill," *The Collected Poems of Dylan Thomas* (New York: New Directions, 1957), 178. Brancusi's "Bird in Space" case is reported in T.D. 43063, *Treasury Decisions* 54 (1929): 428. Rauschenberg's "if I say so" telegram to Iris Clert is mentioned in Carla Gottlieb, *Beyond Modern Art* (New York: Dutton, 1976). On interpretation of The Wizard of Oz *see* Henry M. Littlefield, "The Wizard of Oz: Parable on Populism," in *The American Culture: Approaches to the Study of the United States*, Hennig Cohen, ed., (Boston: Houghton Mifflin, 1968), 370; *The Wizard of Oz*, Michael Patrick Hearn, ed., (New York: Schocken Books, 1983); Michael A. Genovese, "The Wonderful Wizard Lives On," *Los Angeles Times* March 19, 1988, part II, p. 8. The initial controversy over Michelangelo's Sistine Chapel can be traced through Loren Jenkins, "Reclaiming Michelangelo's Masterpiece," *The Washington Post* August 10, 1986, p. GI; "Art Historian James Beck Urges The

Vatican To Clean Up Its Act, Not Michelangelo's Frescoes," *Time* March 30, 1987, p.69; Frederick M. Winship, "Experts Okay Sistine Chapel Ceiling Restoration," *United Press International* April 16, 1987, morning cycle. The quotations on the movie colorization debate are from Penny Pagano, "Colorization Gets a Senate Hearing," *Los Angeles Times* May 13, 1987, part VI, p.1.

4. By making "reasonableness" its ultimate requirement, the old story quietly welcomes subjectivity after all.

70. "The common law is not a brooding omni-presence in the sky," said Holmes in Southern Pacific Co. v. Jensen , 244 U.S. 205, 222 (1916).

71. Aristotle's remark about legislative purpose is from his *Nicomachean Ethics*, Book V, Chapter 10.

72. Heydon's Case, Exchequer, 3 Co. 7a, 76 E.R. 637 (1584).

73. Eyston v. Studd, 2 Plowden 459, 75 E.R. 688 (1574).

74. Riggs v. Palmer, 22 NE 188 (N.Y., 1889).

75. Holy Trinity Church v. U.S., 143 U.S. 457 (1892).

76. Judge Hand rejecting literal meaning in favor purpose: Central Hanover Bank v. Commissioner, 159 F 2d 167, 169 (2d Cir. 1947).

77. Judge Hand following literal meaning: Brooklyn Nat. Corporation v. Commissioner, 157 F 2d 450, 451 (2d Cir. 1946).

78. TVA v. Hill, 437 U.S. 153 (1978).

79. Korematsu v. U.S., 323 U.S. 214 (1944).

Thought Window

80. The coyote scalp story is told by Max Radin, "Statutory Interpretation," *Harvard Law Review* 43 (1930): 863, 879 n. 31. Immigration deadline cases: Lee May and Patrick McDonnell, "Courts Give Some Reprieves on Amnesty Deadline," *Los Angeles Times*, May 5, 1988, part I, p.3. No parking tickets at Christmas: "Some Parking Violations to be Ignored on Holidays," *Los Angeles Times*, December 20, 1986, part I, p.36, col. 5.

There Are No Categorical Rules for Finding the Meaning in the Texts of Judicial Precedents

81. Holmes called Langdell a "legal theologian" in Book Notice, *American Law Review* 14 (1880): 233.

82. On Langdell's methods, *see* Thomas C. Grey, "Langdell's Orthodoxy," *University of Pittsburgh Law Review* 45 (1983): 1. Historian Lawrence Friedman called Langdell's science "a geology without rocks." Lawrence Friedman, *A History of American Law* (New York: Simon and Schuster, 1973), 617.

83. The quotation about the "number of permutations" in Donoghue v. Stevenson is from Julius Stone, *Legal System and Lawyers' Reasonings* (Stanford: Stanford University Press, 1964).

84. *See* William Twining and David Miers, *How To Do Things With Rules* (3d ed., London: Weiderfield and Nicolson, 1991) for a thoughtful, realistic description of how the doctrine of precedent is actually used in the Anglo-American legal system.

85. Cardozo's "figment of excited brains": Benjamin Cardozo, *The Growth of the Law* (New Haven: Yale University Press, 1924), 122.

86. On the number of published and unpublished decisions in the U.S. Courts of Ap-

peal, *see* Administrative Office of the U.S. Courts, *Judicial Business of the United States Courts 2003 Annual Report of the Director*, (Washington, D.C.: 2003), Table S-3.

Reactions to Modernism

87. **Anti-modernists:** Textualism, originalism and strict constuctionism are some current labels that fit various manifestations of ant-modernism. One outspoken anti-modernist is U.S. Supreme Court Justice Antonin Scalia. *See* the description and critique of his approach to statutory interpretation in William N. Eskridge, *Dynamic Statutory Interpretation* (Cambridge, Mass: Harvard University Press, 1994), 226–234.

88. **Open modernists:** For political science literature presenting compelling evidence that judicial behavior is driven by personal values and ideologies, *see*, for example, Jeffrey A. Segal & Harold J. Spaeth, *The Supreme Court And The Attitudinal Model Revisited* (Cambridge: Cambridge University Press, 2002); Robert A. Carp & C.K. Rowland, *Policymaking And Politics In The Federal District Courts* (Knoxville: University of Tennessee Press, 1983); Jon Gottschall, "Carter's Judicial Appointments: The Influence of Affirmative Action And Merit Selection On Voting On The U.S. Courts Of Appeals," *Judicature* 67 (1984): 165, and "Reagan's Appointments To The U.S. Courts of Appeal: The Continuation of A Judicial Revolution," *Judicature* 70 (1986): 48.

89. The academics who accept modernist legal indeterminacy and urge interpreters' discretion be guided by a progressive philosophy include many in the critical legal studies movement, in critical race theory, and in feminist legal theory. Another progressive approach is to appeal to the foundational value of "republicanism" or civic virtue "in which all groups deliberate respectfully for the common good and in which judges need not apologize for playing an affirmative role in advancing this goal." William D. Popkin, *Statutes in Court* (Durham: Duke University Press, 1999), 189. The academics who argue for protecting whatever private parties have agreed to by bargaining are of the law-and-economics or public choice school. They accept that the law is indeterminate, and would guide judicial discretion by their foundational value: a belief that bargaining in markets is the best way to promote the public good. While a modernist view, ironically it has led to textualism. *See* Popkin's book, just cited, at 157 *et seq*. *See also*, Richard A. Posner, *Overcoming Law*, (Cambridge Mass. and London: Harvard University Press, 1995), Chapter 19.

90. **Reluctant modernists:** The professor who wrote that the myth of linguistic certainty and the Santa Claus myth were both culturally important to retain was Frederick Schauer, "Easy Cases," *Southern California Law Review* 58 (1985): 399 439. Schauer subsequently modified his views and became "more agnostic about desirability of Formalism within a legal system, or within judicial decision making," and saw "the relationship of rule-based decision making to legal decision making" to be "conceptually unnecessary and normatively contingent...." Personal letter to the author, January 18, 1991. *See* Schauer's "Formalism," *Yale L.J.* 97 (1988): 509 and *Playing By The Rules* (Oxford: Clarendon Press, 1991). For me, the usefulness of Schauer's work is to show that rules do have an influence in the real world just by being rules, even if they are indeterminate.

91. In "another, large group of reluctant modernists," I have lumped together several schools of thought, each of which has spawned a prolific literature. On the legal process school, *see* William N. Eskridge, *Dynamic Statutory Interpretation*, (Cambridge, Mass.: Harvard University Press, 1994), Chapter 5 and Gary Jan Aichele, *Legal Realism And Twentieth Century American Jurisprudence: the Changing Consensus*, (PhD Dissertation, University of

Virginia, 1983), Chapter 5. "Singing reason" and similar happy phrases extolling the craft of legal methods belong to renowned Legal Realist Karl Llewellyn. *See* Karl Llewellyn, *The Common Law Tradition* (Boston: Little, Brown, 1960). On the academic rush to "practical reason," *see* Daniel A. Farber, "The Inevitability of Practical Reason: Statutes, Formalism, and the Rule of Law" *Vanderbilt Law Review* 45 (1992): 553. "Ordinary judging" is the approach of William D. Popkin, *Statutes in Court*, (Durham: Duke University Press, 1999), Chapter 7 (a modest claim that the practice of ordinary judging is good enough, the job has to be done, and the judiciary is the most competent institution to do it, so we should not worry about its legitimacy). Finally, *see* William N. Eskridge, *Dynamic Statutory Interpretation* (Cambridge, Mass: Harvard University Press, 1994) for the position that it is inevitable that statutes will change with interpreters and over time. Eskridge's deep analysis is openly modernist and even postmodernist (caution: he uses the modernist label differently than used here), except that he announces he is also a "pragmatist" who looks for the interpretation "that most intelligently and creatively 'fits' into the complex web of social and legal practices." (p.201.) That does not sound like much of a real constraint on interpretation, but Eskridge intends it to restrain somehow, so I register him as a (slightly) reluctant modernist.

Chapter 3: The Postmodern Insight

1. The quotation heading the chapter is found in Clifford Geartz, *Local Knowledge*, (New Yorks Basic Books, 1983) 218, 182.

2. *See generally*, Steven Connor, ed., *The Cambridge Companion To Postmodernism*, (Cambridge: Cambridge University Press, 2004). Good, broad essays on cultural postmodernism appear in Todd Gitlin, "Postmodernism: Roots and Politics," *Dissent*, Winter 1989, p.100, and Denis Donoghue, "The Promiscuous Cool of Postmodernism," *The New York Times Book Review*, June 22, 1986, p. 1. On collage as the central insight of postmodernism, *see* Gregory L. Ulmer, "The Object of Post-Criticism," in Hal Foster, ed., *The Anti-Aesthetic: Essays on Postmodern Culture*, (Port Townsend, Washington: Bay Press 1983), 83. For an ambitious synopsis of postmodernism in literature, architecture and film, *see* Linda Hutcheon, *A Poetics of Postmodernism* (New York and London: Routledge 1988). In philosophy, Jean-Francois Lyotard's *The Postmodern Condition: A Report on Knowledge* (Minneapolis: University of Minnesota Press 1984) is a key document. In architecture, Robert Venturi's *Complexity and Contradiction in Architecture* (New York: Museum of Modern Art, 1966) was an early postmodern manifesto (the quotation in the text is from page 16). Charles Jencks is the chronicler of the movement; see his *Postmodernism: The New Classicism in Art and Architecture* (London: Academy Editions, 1987). For samples of postmodern architecture, *see especially* Francesco Dal Co & Kurt Forster, *Frank O. Gehry: The Complete Works* (New York: The Manacelli Press, 1998).

In anthropology, *see* Clifford Geertz, *The Interpretation of Cultures* (New York: Basic Books, 1973), *Local Knowledge* (New York: Basic Books, 1983), *Works and Lives: The Anthropologist as Author* (Stanford: Stanford University Press, 1988). On chaos theory in science, *see* Ilya Prigogine & Isabelle Stengers, *Order Out of Chaos* (Toronto, New York, London, Sydney: Bantam Books, 1984). I have described elsewhere the recent world-wide interest in semiotics (the theory of signs) as another manifestation of postmodernism: Robert W. Benson, "Semiotics, Modernism and the Law," *Semiotica* 73-1/2 (1989): 157.

3. Julio Cortazar, *Hopscotch* (New York: Random House, 1966).

4. Italo Calvino, *If on a Winter's Night a Traveller* (London: Picador, Pan Books, 1981).

5. Georges Perec, *Life: A User's Manual* (Boston: David R. Godin, 1987).

6. Robert Venturi, *Complexity and Contradiction in Architecture* (New York: Museum of Modern Art, 1966), 16.

7. American Historical Association, "Statement on the 2006 Florida Education Bill," January 7, 2007. www.historians.org.

8. Carl Becker, "Every Man His Own Historian," *American Historical Review* vol. 37 (1931): 221.

9. Todd Gitlin, "Postmodernism: Roots and Politics," *Dissent*, Winter 1989: 100.

Thought Window: Hot Engines of Postmodernism

10. Neil Postman, *Amusing Ourselves to Death* (New York: Penguin Books, 1986) is the main source of the point about TV here, and is the critic quoted (his pages 86, 104–105). On the fajita boom, *see* Lorna J. Sass, "Mexican Skirt Steak Has Stampeded to Popularity," *Newsday*, July 27, 1988, Food Section, p. 13; "'Fajita Pita' Boosts Foodmaker Second Quarter Results," *Universal News Services*, April 30, 1987. The Lyotard quotation is taken from page 76 of his book cited above in note 2.

Postmodern Law:

11. *See* Dennis Patterson, ed., *Postmodernism and Law* (New York: New York University Press, 1994).

12. For further analysis of how technology is changing the law, *see* M. Ethan Katsh, *Electronic Media and the Transformation of Law* (New York: Oxford University Press, 1989); Ronald K.L. Collins & David M. Skover, *The Death of Discourse* (North Carolina: Carolina Academic Press, 2d ed., 2006).

13. Frances E. Olsen, ed., *Feminist Legal Theory* (New York: New York University Press, 1995).

14. Richard Delgado & Jean Stefancic, *Critical Race Theory: An Introduction* (New York: New York University Press, 2001).

15. Critical Legal Studies was a loose movement of legal scholars with intellectual roots in Legal Realism, literary criticism, Wittgenstein, the Frankfurt School, Derrida, Foucault, Gramsci, and others. Mainly, however, they seem to be driven by their generation's postmodern experience in power politics and cultural change. "Law is politics," is their slogan. But while the Realists too believed that law was politics, right down to the partisan politics of individual judges, the politics CLS has in mind is the deeper political ideology of liberal individualism, which privileges the individual over community, hierarchy over equality, the private sphere over the public, free will over social-cause explanations. These privileged norms—and the classist, racist, sexist, and domineering arrangements which result from them—are systematically cemented into our culture by legal discourse, they say; law represses departures from the norms because law has been assembled by the politics of the power elite. But it could be disassembled and then reconstructed. CLS literature is now extensive. Some starting points are Mark Kelman, *A Guide to Critical Legal Studies* (Cambridge and London: Harvard University Press, 1987); Richard W. Bauman, *Critical Legal Studies: A Guide To The Literature* (Boulder: Westview Press, 1996); the entire volume 36 of the *Stanford Law Review* (1984); David Kairys, ed., *The Politics of Law* (New York: Pantheon, 1982).

See also my "Peirce and Critical Legal Studies," in Roberta Kevelson, ed., *Peirce and Law* (New York: Peter Lang Publishing, 1991).

16. The "interspace of artifacts" quotation in the text is Duncan Kennedy's, in Peter Gabel & Duncan Kennedy, "Roll Over Beethoven," *Stanford Law Review* 36 (1984): 1, 9.

17. It was the dean of Duke Law School who invited CLS scholars to get out of law teaching Paul Carrington, "Of Law and the River," *Journal of Legal Education* 34 (1984): 222. By the turn of the 21st century, CLS was formally defunct in the United States, but its critique has been absorbed and lives on.

Postmodern Semiotics

18. Many of Stanley Fish's key essays on interpretation appear in his *Is There a Text in This Class?* (Cambridge, Mass: Harvard University Press, 1980) and *Doing What Comes Naturally* (Durham: Duke University Press, 1989). The "interpretive communities" quotation is found in his "Fish v. Fiss," *Stanford Law Review* 36 (1984): 1325, 1336. See his debate in the law journals with Professor Owen Fiss (a reluctant modernist who argues that within the interpretive community of law there are at least some objective constraints in the form of "disciplining rules" of the trade): Owen Fiss, "Objectivity and Interpretation," *Stanford Law Review* 34 (1982): 739; "Conventionalism," *Southern California Law Review* 58 (1985): 177; Stanley Fish, "Fish v. Fiss," *Stanford Law Review* 36 (1984): 1325. *See also* Fish's debate with Professor Ronald Dworkin: Ronald Dworkin, *Law's Empire* (Cambridge, Mass. and London: Belknap, Harvard University Press, 1986), "Law as Interpretation," *Texas Law Review* 60 (1982): 527; "My Reply to Stanley Fish (and Walter Benn Michaels): Please Don't Talk About Objectivity Any More," in W.J.T. Mitchell, ed., *The Politics of Interpretation* (Chicago: University of Chicago Press, 1983) 287; Stanley Fish, "Working on the Chain Gang: Interpretation in Law and Literature," *Texas Law Review* 60 (1982): 551, "Wrong Again," *Texas Law Review* 60 (1983): 229, chapter 16 from *Doing What Comes Naturally* (reviewing Law's Empire).

Fish and Dworkin shadow box a good deal in their exchanges, since the two actually agree and therefore fail to clash on the fundamental point that legal and literary texts get their meanings from the interpretive theories used to read them. But Dworkin insists further (1) that there is such a thing as "the best" interpretation (generally the most coherent), and (2) that in searching for the best interpretation judges are significantly constrained, like authors of a "chain novel." It is these points that Fish effectively refutes. I would add that Dworkin's "best interpretation" claim is a constant in his writings, and usually reduces to an insistence that there is a transcendent norm of coherence. *See* his *Taking Rights Seriously* (Cambridge, Mass: Harvard University Press, 1977) (coherence as "political responsibility"), 77, and *Law's Empire* (Cambridge, Mass. and London: Belknap Harvard University Press, 1986), Chapters 6–7 (coherence as "integrity"). Dworkin admits that the requirement of coherence as "integrity" rises only from "our own political culture." *Law's Empire* at 216. This confession of cultural relativism is refreshing, but it surely weakens his claim that "best" interpretations exist. Moreover, his own best reading of "our own political culture" is a bit chilling in its elitism and sexism. *See* Allan Hutchinson, "Indiana Dworkin and Law's Empire" (Book Review), *Yale Law Journal* 96 (1987): 637. As for Dworkin's "chain novel" constraint, *see* Charles Yablon, "Law and Metaphysics" (Book Review) *Yale Law Journal* 96 (1987): 613 suggesting support for Fish's side of the argument from Wittgenstein and Kripke. For the last, humorous word about Agatha Christie and chain novels, *see* Anthony D'Amato, "Can Any Legal Theory Constrain Any Judicial Decision?" *University of*

Miami Law Review 43 (1989): 513, 528–30.

19. Fish's remark that cultures fill brains is found in his *Is There a Text in This Class?* at 335.

20. Umberto Eeo's "intersubjective meaning": Umberto Eco, *The Limits of Interpretation* (Bloomington: Indiana University Press, 1990), 40.

21. Geertz's happy phrases are from Clifford Geertz, *Local Knowledge* (New York: Basic Books, 1983), 218, 182.

22. One path into the field of semiotics would be through Jack Solomon, *Signs of Our Times* (Los Angeles: J.P. Tarcher, 1988); Robert E. Inns, ed., *Semiotics: An Introductory Anthology* (Bloomington: Indiana University Press, 1985); John Deely, ed., *Frontiers in Semiotics* (Bloomington: Indiana University Press, 1986); Thomas A. Sebeok & Jean Umiker-Sebeok, eds., *The Semiotic Sphere* (New York and London: Plenum Press, 1986); Umberto Eco, *A Theory of Semiotics* (Bloomington: Indiana University Press, 1979) and *Semiotics and the Philosophy of Language* (Bloomington: Indiana University Press, 1984).

23. John Deely ed., *Frontiers in Semiotics* (Bloomington: Indiana University Press 1986), xii.

24. The quotations by Eco explaining semiosis and cultural units are found in Umberto Eco, *A Theory of Semiotics* (Bloomington: Indiana University Press, 1979), 71.

25. *Id.*

Chapter 4: How Judges Fool Themselves

1. The quotation at the head of the chapter is from William O. Douglas, *Stare Decisis* (New York: Association Of The Bar Of The City Of New York, 1949), 31.

2. Harris's comments on Hindu sacred cows are found in Marvin Harris, *Cultural Materialism* (New York: Vintage Books, 1980), 32–33.

3. On the conflict between internal and external perspectives for anthropologists, *see* Clifford Geertz, *The Interpretation of Cultures* (New York: Basic Books, 1973).

4. The judge who denied that law "is but a grab bag of legal rules" is Alvin B. Rubin, "Does Law Matter? A Judge's Response To The Critical Legal Studies Movement," *Journal of Legal Education* 37 (1987): 307–314.

5. *Id.*

6. The District of Columbia Circuit judge who compiled his own statistics is Harry T. Edwards, "Public Misperceptions Concerning The Politics Of Judging: Dispelling Some Myths About The D.C. Circuit." *University of Colorado Law Review* 56 (1985): 619–646.

Two Easy Cases

The age qualification for President is in U.S. Constitution, Article II, Section 1.

Words + context:

7. Contexts are no more self-defining than words. They are simply organizing frames, like genres, topics or thematic projections. *See* Stanley Fish, *Is There A Text In This Class?* (Cambridge, Mass: Harvard University Press, 1980); Umberto Eco, *The Role Of The Reader* (Bloomington: Indiana University Press, 1979); Hans-Georg Gadamer, *Truth And Method* (New York: Crossroad, 1986).

A judge's context:

8. The story of the Japanese mother who drowned her children in Santa Monica Bay

is told in Malek-Mithra Sheybani, "One Person's Culture Is Another's Crime," *Loyola Of Los Angeles International & Comparative Law Journal* 9 (1987): 751.

Other interpreters' views:

9. Lord Atkins' quotation is in Donoghue v. Stevenson, 1932 App. Case 562.

10. The judge talking of the need "to reach decisions that are capable of gaining the acceptance...." was Judge Edwards, cited in note 6 above.

The judge:

11. Political scientists have built a strongly explanatory model based upon extensive statistical evidence showing that what drives the decisions of U.S. Supreme Court justices is their ideology, thus confirming what the Legal Realists had long proclaimed. Jeffrey A. Segal & Harold J. Spaeth, *The Supreme Court And The Attitudinal Model Revisited* (Cambridge: Cambridge University Press, 2002). For examples of political science literature showing strong correlations between liberal or conservative lower-court decisions and political party, appointing president and geography see Robert A. Carp & C.K. Rowland, *Policymaking And Politics In The Federal District Courts* (Knoxville: University of Tennessee Press, 1983); Jon Gottschall, "Carter's Judicial Appointments: The Influence Of Affirmative Action And Merit Selection On Voting On The U.S. Courts Of Appeals," *Judicature* 67 (1984): 165, and "Reagan's Appointments To The U.S. Courts Of Appeal: The Continuation Of A Judicial Revolution," *Judicature* 70 (1986): 48.

12. Harry T. Edwards, cited in note 6 above.

13. A good deal of the judges' unanimity in 83% of the cases mentioned by one study is no doubt rooted in common cultural assumptions. Much of the appellate court docket, for example, consists of pleas from prisoners who have nothing to lose by, and a lot of time to devote to, creative appeals. It is a group with no clout, to put it mildly, and there is unfortunately a broad social and judicial belief, even among liberals, that its appeals are wasteful and should be given short judicial shrift. In this cultural milieu, the judges can even be cavalierly unfair, as were Judge Rubin and his unanimous colleagues in what they apparently thought was the easy case of Archer v. Lynaugh, 821 F.2d 1094 (5th Cir.1987). There, an inmate serving a 45-year sentence under a habitual offender statute, representing himself, took vigorous, reasonable and timely steps to appeal but was impaled by an incoherent technical interpretation of time limits under the Federal Rules of Appellate Procedure that, Judge Rubin conceded, could be misleading even to attorneys.

14. On the ideology of the robe, shared by conservatives and liberals alike, see Thomas W. Church, Jr., "Examining Local Legal Culture," *American Bar Foundation Research Journal* 1985: 449. That law interpreters have "always been a privileged caste," *see* Peter Goodrich, *Legal Discourse* (New York: St. Martin's Press, 1987) and *Reading The Law* (Oxford: Basil Blackwell, 1986). On women and racial minorities becoming judges, *see* Sheldon Goldman, "Reagan's Second Term Judicial Appointments: The Battle At Midway," *Judicature* 70 (1987): 324; Eliot E. Slotnick, "The Paths To The Federal Bench: Gender, Race And Judicial Recruitment Variation," *Judicature* 67 (1984): 370.

15. The rate of unanimous and dissenting opinions is not accepted in political science literature as a good measure of doctrinal consensus. *See* Justin J. Green, "Parameters Of Dissensus On Shifting Small Groups," in Sheldon Goldman & Charles M. Lamb, eds., *Judicial Conflict And Consensus* (Lexington, KY: University Press of Kentucky, 1986); Stephen L. Wasby, "Of Judges, Hobgoblins And Small Minds: Dimensions of Disagreement in the

Ninth Circuit," in the same book.

Conclusion

16. Psychiatrists and shamans genuinely believe in their own methods despite lack of empirical evidence of their effectiveness. *See* Richard Warner, "Deception And Self-Deception In Shamanism And Psychiatry," *International Journal of Social Psychiatry* 26 (1980): 41.

17. Self-deception is a basic mechanism of everyday life for most of us. Herbert Fingarette, *Self-Deception* (London: Routledge & Kegan Paul, 1969).

Chapter 5: How Statutes Get Their Meaning: The Speed Limit Laws

1. The quotation at the head of the chapter is from Felix Frankfurter, "Some Reflections On the Reading Of Statues," *Record Of The Association Of the Bar Of The City Of New York* 2 (1947): 213.

2. The 55 mile-per-hour requirement for federal highway funds was enacted by P.L. 93-643, §114(a), 88 Stat. 2286 (Jan. 4, 1975) and repealed by P.L. 104-59, Title II, §205(d)(1)(B), 109 Stat. 577 (Nov. 28, 1995). *See* Jerry Gray, "Ending Of Federal Speed Limit Wins Congressional Approval," *New York Times*, Nov. 19, 1995, p. A-24. For opposing views of the controversy over the statute and its repeal see the website entries of Advocates for Highway and Auto Safety (http://www.saferoads.org/issues/fs-speed.htm) and Cato Institute ("Speed Doesn't Kill" at http://www.cato.org/dailys/05-28-99a.html).

Chapter 6: How the Constitution Gets Its Meaning: Equality in Brown v. Board of Education

1. The oft-quoted line by Charles Evans Hughes at the head of the chapter came in a speech he made as governor of New York on May 3, 1907 and can be found in *Addresses and Papers of Charles Evans Hughes* (1906–1916), 2d ed., (1916), 185. Hughes served as an Associate Justice of the U.S. Supreme Court from 1910–16 and as Chief Justice from 1930–41.

2. As noted in the text, this chapter draws much of its factual material from Richard Kluger, *Simple Justice* (New York: Alfred A. Knopf, 1975). The quotations of Frankfurter about Vinson and Douglas, and some other details, are taken from an interview of Frankfurter's former clerk and friend, Philip Elman, in "The Solicitor General's Office, Justice Frankfurter, And Civil Rights Litigation, 1946–1960: An Oral History," *Harvard Law Review* 100 (1987): 817.

3. Kluger published a second edition in 2004 with a new final chapter evaluating black progress, and lack of it, in America since the *Brown* case was decided. Some progressive African-American scholars view *Brown* ultimately as a failure because it has served as a cover for racism and 50 years later the equality it promised still has not been realized. *See, e.g.*, Derrick Bell, *Silent Covenants: Brown v. Board Of Education And The Unfulfilled Hopes for Racial Reform* (New York: Oxford University Press, 2004); Charles J. Ogletree, Jr., *All Deliberate Speed: Reflections On the First Half Century Of Brown v. Board Of Education* (New York: W.W. Norton, 2004).

4. In 2007, the U.S. Supreme Court undermined the *Brown* precedent in Parents Involved in Community Schools v. Seattle School District (No. 05-908, June 28, 2007).

5. The New York Times quoted former lawyers for the *Brown* plaintiffs to the effect that the new decision had badly misinterpreted *Brown*. Adam Liptak, "The Same Words, but Differing Views," *New York Times*, June 29, 2007.

Chapter 7: How Case Precedents Get Their Meaning: Palsgraf v. Long Island Railroad

1. This chapter was inspired by John Noonan's essay "The Passengers of Palsgraf," in his book *Persons And Masks Of The Law* (Berkeley: University of California Press, 2d ed., 2002).

2. The quotation by Cardozo at the top of the chapter is in his *The Nature of the Judicial Process* (New Haven: Yale University Press, 1921), 64.

3. Quoting Cardozo: "There is in each of us a stream of tendency ..." from *The Nature of the Judicial Process*, 12.

4. "What is it that I do when I decide a case? ..." from the same book, 10–11.

5. For Cardozo's work with the American Law Institute to bring "certainty" out of the "wilderness" of precedent, *see* Noonan's book cited above, 146 *et seq*.

6. References in the rest of this chapter are from the *Palsgraf* decision itself, the majority opinion of which is reprinted in the Appendix.

Index